JOHN JAY

COLONIAL LAWYER

BeardBooks

JOHN JAY

COLONIAL LAWYER

Herbert A. Johnson

Originally published by Garland Publishing, Inc.
Reprint 2006 by Beard Books, Washington, D.C.

ISBN 13: 978-1-58798-270-6
ISBN 10: 1-58798-270-6

In Memory of
Harry O. Johnson
1895-1966

TABLE OF CONTENTS

PREFACE TO THE BEARD BOOKS EDITION

It was an unexpected pleasure to learn that Beard Books was interested in publishing a new edition of my doctoral dissertation, submitted at Columbia University in 1965 and republished from a camera-ready manuscript by Garland Publishing, Inc., in 1989.[1] The current text substantially follows that of the 1989 Garland edition. The original preface to the dissertation is included to provide renewed thanks to those who guided and were otherwise helpful in the process of research and writing over forty years ago.

Although this monograph continues to be the only book devoted exclusively to John Jay's law practice, in the years since its publication there have been some major developments in the study of Jay's career. Richard B. Morris before his death edited and published two substantial volumes of Jay's unpublished papers,[2] and that editorial project now continues at Columbia University under the direction of Elizabeth Nuxoll. We are also indebted to Professor Morris for a thoughtful series of essays on Jay and the Supreme Court, and new work on the pre-Marshall Court has done much to illuminate John Jay's contributions as the first Chief Justice of the United States Supreme Court.[3] International lawyer Walter Stahr recently completed

---

[1]*John Jay: Colonial Lawyer,* in Garland Series, Outstanding Studies in Early American History, John Murrin, ed.,(New York: Garland Publishing, Inc., 1989).

[2]*John Jay: The Making of a Revolutionary: Unpublished Papers, 1745-1780* (New York: Harper & Row, 1975), and *John Jay: The Winning of the Peace: Unpublished Papers, 1780-1784* (New York: Harper & Row, 1980).

[3]On the 200th anniversary of Jay's birth I contributed a paper on his U.S. Supreme Court career, published as "John Jay and the Supreme Court," *New York History*, LXXI (2000), 59-90. The most useful materials on Jay and his career on the Court can be found in *Seriatum: The Supreme Court Before John Marshall*, Scott D. Gerber, ed. (New York: New York University Press, 1998).

the first full length biography of Jay published since 1935.[4] Despite this gratifying revival of Jay studies, the conclusions in *John Jay: Colonial Lawyer* have stood the test of time. Given these considerations it has seemed inappropriate for me to alter the original dissertation in this edition; rather I have made corrections of obvious typographical errors, and clarified passages where the meaning was not clear. Accuracy has dissuaded me from attempting to bring up-to-date the footnote citations to materials that have been relocated to new archival locations or different manuscript collections. Instead the bibliography has been expanded to include cross-references to new locations, most of which are in the New York State Archives in Albany.

The dissertation served as a spring board for my broader study of colonial New York legal history. A modest revision of chapter six of this dissertation was published in the *American Journal for Legal History* in 1967. With the transfer of the Prerogative Court records to Queens College's Historical Documents Collection in the early 1970s, and the restoration of that valuable archive to a usable condition, it became possible to describe the work of that court from its inception in 1686 to 1776. A manuscript discovered in the rich collections of the New York Historical Society cast

---

The most useful materials on Jay and his career on the Court can be found in *Seriatum: The Supreme Court Before John Marshall*, Scott D. Gerber, ed. (New York: New York University Press, 1998).

[4]Walter Stahr, *John Jay: Founding Father* (New York: Hambledon and London, 2005) substantially supplants Frank Monaghan, *John Jay: Defender of Liberty against Kings and Peoples* (New York: Bobbs-Merrill Co., 1935), although Monaghan did have access to some materials no longer available to Stahr. Of course Stahr was the beneficiary of secondary materials published in the past seven decades, as well as the work of the Papers of John Jay staff in collecting widely dispersed unpublished documents.

new light on the important case of Forsey v.Cunningham, and the Bicentennial of the American Revolution spurred a reconsideration of John Jay's legal career in a summary of the dissertation.[5] These more recent publications draw upon the dissertation and supplement its findings; they by no means exhaust the field.

Beyond New York colonial history, we have witnessed a growing scholarly interest in the law practices of future statesmen. Almost simultaneously with the submission of *John Jay: Colonial Lawyer* in dissertation form, the three volume edition of John Adams' legal papers was published to provide us with an exhaustive study of the second president's practice. The wealth of Adams' office files provides the tantalizing speculation of how much more we might know about John Jay had not his early records been lost during the British invasion of New York City in 1776. Yet from what remains of Jay's legal files we can safely surmise that his was a much more modest professional practice than that enjoyed by John Adams. Possibly the relatively small and less diversified character of colonial New York's economy may be partially responsible for the narrower scope of Jay's practice. But certainly the shorter duration of Jay's time at the colonial bar also

---

[5] "The Prerogative Court of New York, 1685-1776," *American Journal of Legal History*, XVII (1973), 95-114; "George Harison's Protest: New Light on Forsey v. Cunningham," *New York History*, L (1969), 61-82; and "John Jay: Lawyer in a Time of Transition, 1764-1775," *University of Pennsylvania Law Review*, CXXIV (1976), 1260-1292. These articles along with a version of dissertation chapter six ("Civil Practice in John Jay's New York," *American Journal of Legal History*, XI (1967), 69-80, were reprinted in *Essays on New York Colonial Legal History* (Westport: Greenwood Press, 1981).

played a major part in limiting his success. It also meant that Jay began his public career with less exposure than Adams to the more theoretical areas of Anglo-American law and constitutional history.[6]

A notable contrast to Jay's practice is provided by the later professional careers of Alexander Hamilton in New York and John Marshall of Virginia. Each was admitted to practice after military service in the American Revolution. Hamilton rapidly rose to professional success and public office in New York City's diverse society and rapidly developing economy. His circumstances were far more favorable than Jay's situation. A substantial portion of the New York bar was loyalist in political leanings and left the new state with the British evacuation of New York City. The war itself had limited the number of young men who could train by clerkship, leaving Hamilton and his contemporaries particularly rich prospects in post-war New York. John Marshall during a lull in military service attended law lectures by George Wythe, was admitted to county court practice and moved to Richmond in 1783 to launch a highly successful central court and appellate practice. Both Hamilton and Marshall benefitted from economic and legal imbalances connected with the American Revolution. Hamilton defended loyalists against retributive legislation in the New York's Trespass Acts, and Marshall fought the collection of British mercantile debts in both Virginia state courts and the newly instituted U.S. Circuit Court for Virginia.[7] These contrasts between Jay, Hamilton and Marshall suggest that John Jay began his practice too late to reach leadership of the colonial bar, and that he was already too deeply involved in public service to resume practice when peace-

---

[6]*Legal Papers of John Adams*, L. Kinvin Wroth and Hiller B. Zobel, eds., 3 vols. (Cambridge: Harvard University Press, 1965).

[7]*The Law Practice of Alexander Hamilton,* Julius Goebel, Jr. and Joseph H. Smith, eds., 5 vols. (New York: Columbia University Press, 1964-1981); *The Papers of John Marshall*, Charles F. Hobson, ed., V [Selected Law Cases, 1784-1800], (Chapel Hill: University of North Carolina Press, 1987).

time conditions became optimum for professional success.

In the preface to the Garland edition, I mentioned a challenge to this dissertation by a faculty examiner, "Is this a *real* contribution to knowledge, or just a good research report?" Obviously my receipt of the Ph.D. degree would indicate that the reply was adequate to support the award of the degree. On the other hand, does this type of narrowly focused study serve a useful purpose, either for the writer or the reader? Quite clearly it is valuable to be able to follow the early professional life of a major statesman like John Jay, for we learn a great deal that explains future success and behavioral patterns. This particular dissertation, written despite the disappearance of Jay's office files, illustrates the inherent value of court records to document not only a lawyer's career, but also to cast light upon a multitude of other economic and social issues that may present themselves for historical research.

The forty years that have intervened after this dissertation was submitted have seen the emergence of a "law and society phase" of American legal history, which until recently tended to ignore the mechanics of law practice and the careful use of court records. Fortunately, younger scholars have done much to combine an institutional approach, by which *John Jay: Colonial Lawyer* was shaped, with the broader "law and society" historiography that promises to bring legal history and research in court records back into the main stream of American historical scholarship. The republication of this dissertation may serve to preserve what may eventually be the most valuable residuum of institutional studies–careful analysis of court records and attorney's file papers to highlight the processes by which the courts and the profession conducted their business. Indeed, responsible use of legal records demands an understanding of these administrative details, lest the historian be led into substantive statistical error and misinterpretation. Al-

---

F. Hobson, ed., V [Selected Law Cases, 1784-1800], (Chapel Hill: University of North Carolina Press, 1987).

though this dissertation falls far short of being a guide to research in American colonial legal history, it does provide a rough outline of the steps that were followed by the bench and bar in presenting and deciding cases, and it gives future students of legal history some help in resolving difficulties in using colonial court archives.

Another function this dissertation may serve is to provide assistance to archivists and record managers charged with the heavy responsibility of deciding which historical court records can be destroyed and which must be preserved for future study. It shows that writ books, registers on the return of process, attorney fee records, and even the endorsements on file papers are critical to the documentation and evaluation of a law practice. It is important that the interdependence of record groups be well understood before destruction is authorized. At the same time, economy of storage facilities requires that record managers be alert to the legal profession's penchant for retaining duplicate copies of the same documents; while duplication may not justify the destruction of a class of documents, it certainly should lead record managers to be alert to the need to retain the most complete copy of a document. Some classes of records serve a valuable indexing function–for historians as well as for those who prepared them. These less obvious and more routine books and lists also must be preserved to guide researchers to file papers or minute book entries that otherwise could be overlooked. For all of the foregoing reasons it is a pleasure to know that this dissertation will again be available to interested readers.

No historical research can succeed without a group of dedicated professionals and encouraging friends who helped the author along the way. The original Preface identifies those who assisted with the dissertation, and the Garland edition preface brings that process forward to 1988. In this Preface it is appropriate that Dan Zafren of Beard Books be recognized and thanked for support, patience, and encouragement in preparing this edition for publication

Franklin, North Carolina
April 18th, 2006

Herbert A. Johnson

A BIBLIOGRAPHIC NOTE TO READERS

When this dissertation was prepared in the period 1962-65, the court records of colonial New York were scattered throughout the State. The Supreme Court of Judicature records, a portion of the High Court of Chancery records, and the local court records for New York County back to the days of Dutch occupation, were located in the Records Division, Office of the New York County Clerk, then located in the Hall of Records. in Manhattan. The Prerogative Court records were filed in the Office of the Surrogate's Court of New York County. Additional Chancery Court records were in the Office of the Clerk of the Court of Appeals in Albany. Local county records for Dutchess, Westchester, and Queens Counties, were filed in the County Clerk's Offices of those counties. The Vice-Admiralty Court records for the Province of New York were deposited in the National Archives in Washington.

Readers interested in locating these various records should be aware that a substantial consolidation of early New York court records has resulted in the transfer of many of these records to the New York State Archives in the early 1980s. The transferred records include most of the Supreme Court of Judicature, High Court of Chancery, and Prerogative Court records. Since the author has not re-examined these records in their new location, the footnotes reflect the 1965 location of the records, which may facilitate locating the documents in their new resting place. To assist readers the Bibliography has been annotated to reflect the location of various archival materials, both in the New York State Archives and in other locations, as of August 1988 when the Garland edition went to press.

H. A. J.

PREFACE TO THE GARLAND EDITION

Writing a preface to a doctoral dissertation submitted twenty-three years ago is not a simple matter, it is best to avoid nostalgia and the insertion of irrelevant autobiographical detail. It is perhaps sufficient to say that time has resulted in many changes—individuals mentioned in the original preface have died, records have moved to other depositories, mentors have retired, if the author has not improved in scholarly ability judgment over the last quarter century, his stagnation not due to a lack of self-improvement opportunities.

Reviewing the dissertation I have been impressed the tenacity and care of my early research efforts, and times rather embarrassed at the stylistic dullness of prose. I am more understanding of one faculty examiner who asked, "Is this a real contribution to knowledge, or just a good research report?" I believe now as I did then, that the dissertation stands as a genuine, although modest, contribution to our knowledge of colonial legal history. When submitted it was one of the first studies of a colonial lawyer's practice, and none of the legal papers volumes covering the colonial period had appeared. Subsequently, the Legal Papers of John Adams appeared in ttaee volumes,[1] providing a rich sample of the extensive colonial law office files of the second President. Shortly before this dissertation was completed, Professor Julius Goebel published the first volume of the law papers of Alexander Hamilton, and this has been followed by four others edited by him and Joseph H. Smith.[2] The superb collection of legal papers of Daniel Webster that appeared recently, gives a detailed picture of the varied and exciting career of one lawyer vto attained national stature.[3]

---

[1]L. Kinvin Wroth and Hiller B. Zobel, eds., *The Legal papers of John Adams*. 3 vols. (Cambridge: Harvard University Press, 1965).

[2]*The Law Practice of Alexander Hamilton: Documents and Commentary*, 5 vols. (New York: Columbia University Press, 1964-81).

[3]Alfred S. Konefsky and Andrew J. King, eds., *The Papers of Daniel Webster; Legal Papers. Volume 1: The New Hampshire Practice: Volume 2, The Boston Practice*. 2 vols. to date (Hanover: The University Press of New

More modest in scope and available manuscript sources The Papers of John Marshall; Law Practice, Vol. 5,[4] and forthcoming one volume collection of Andrew Jackson's legal papers.[5] The past three decades have provided monographic coverage of legal education and the legal profession in the colonial and early national period. Against this much richer background of recent scholarship,! this dissertation raises some new and interesting qjestions that did not present themselves in 1965. For example, comparison to John Adams1 practice suggests that Jay was relatively less successful than his Massachusetts ccntenporary, due in part to his youth, but also attributable to the modest place of New York in colonial economic development. Jay worked hard to build his practice, but financial success and professional stature remained goals yet to be achieved rather than achievements earned. This marked him as a young lawyer who might listen to the blandishments of the British secret service and then enlist as an informant or agent against the leadership of the American Involution. The temptation to do so was stronger than suggested in my dissertation, for Jay had not yet arrived at the pinnacle of professional success.

John Jay's legal career has been documented, with thorough annotation, in John Jay; The Making of a Revolutionary, Unpublished Papers, 1745-1780, Richard B. Morris, editor,[6] providing materials on the law practice not previously printed in the editions of Jay's papers prepared by William Jay and Henry P. Johnston. One interesting letter, not noted in my dissertation, is that of May 6, 1774, in which Jay's new bride, Sarah Livingston Jay, tells her mother about his combining a honeymoon trip with

---

England, 1982-).

[4]Charles F. Hobson, ed., *The Papers of John Marshall: Volume 5: Selected Law Cases, 1784-1800*, (Chapel Hill: University of North Carolina Press, 1987).

[5]Jackson's legal papers have been edited by Professor James W. Ely, Jr., of Vanderbilt University School of Law.

[6](New York: Harper & Row, 1975).

Spring circuit duties in Westchester, Dutchess and Ulster Counties.[7] Since 1965 Jay Papers editors have located a fee book for the Mayor's Court of New York, covering the missing years 1770-1776. Long in private hands this record indicates that Jay appeared in over three hundred cases in that court during a period of less than six years.[8] It therefore confirms Jay's penchant for hard work, and his growing caseloa. Legal historians look forward to the publication of Jay's law papers in a supplementary volume also to be edited by Professor Morris.[9]

These interesting but modest additions to our knowledge of Jay's legal career do not justify altering the original dissertation and I have refrained from doing so in regard to the text and its footnotes. Also retained intact are the original preface, appendices, and the bibliography of Jay's law library. However the substantial change that has taken place in archival administration in New York State demands that some alteration to be made in the bibliographic sections. Most radical has been the creation of a New York State Archives in 1982 and the transfer of substantial portions of the colonial depository in Albany. The original wills and other papers of the Prerogative Court of New York were in deplorable state and thorough examination was not possible in the early 1960s. Fortunately they were transferred to the Historical Documents Collection at Queens College where renovation and preservative methods facilitated renewed scholarly use.[10] Having spent countless hours tracking down the Prerogative Court records, I am painfully aware of the fact that, presented in its original form, this

---

[7]*Ibid.*, 124-125.

[8]*Ibid.*, 8.

[9]*Ibidem.*

[10]I have tried to remedy the dissertation's deficiencies in this regard through the publication of "The Prerogative Court of New York, 1686-1776," *American Journal of Legal History*, XVII (1973), 95-144, also printed in my *Essays on New York Colonial Legal History* (Westport: Greenwood Press, 1981), at pp. 55-104.

dissertation may mislead many a scholar to the wrong depository in the wrong city. To prevent this I have added in italics after the bibliographic entries concerning court records, the location of those records as of August 1988. The reader is cautioned to consult the bibliography for current information concerning manuscript court records.

Preparation of this Garland Publishing, Inc., edition of my dissertation would not have been possible without the assistance of Doris Cooper and Nancy Shealy, who retyped the original dissertation into camera-ready copy. Dr. James Folts of the New York State Archives and Dr. Leo Hershkowitz of Queens College helped to resolve bibliographic problems. To them and to Garland Publishing, Inc., I am grateful for their efforts in helping to bring this material into more general use by legal historians.

The University of South Carolina
Columbia, South Carolina
August 1988

HERBERT A. JOHNSON

PREFACE TO THE ORIGINAL DISSERTATION

John Jay was but one of the numerous group of lawyers who led the American people into revolution against the Crown and Parliament of Great Britain. With the rise of the new nation, Jay attained high governmental positions that could never have been his under the old colonial system. To a certain degree, he was a fairly typical example of the "young man" of the Revolution who matured into a statesman as the movement for independence progressed.

On the other hand, it was as an established attorney wiith an enviable reputation at the New York Bar, that Jay viewed the approach of the war for independence. Despite his youth he had acquired professional stature under the old government, and had much to lose by an insurrection against royal authority. Doubtless part of his reluctance to advocate rebellion in 1774 and 1775 can be attributed to this situation.

From his pre-Revolutionary career in the law, John Jay carried into his public life certain abilities and capacities, as well as some of the narrow professionalism, of the practicing attorney. Close analysis of his practice and training provides some new perspectives from which to study his later public career.

Jay's legal career has been given rather cursory treatment by his past biographers. Frank Monaghan devoted a total of eighteen pages to Jay's life, both professional and social, during this period.[11] George Pellew spends seven inaccurate pages on the subject, and concludes, "The practice of a country lawyer today could scarcely be less interesting."[12] After such a conclusion drawn by a descendant of John Jay, it is not surprising that the study of Jay's law career has been left untouched through the years! Added to the dire predictions of Pellew concerning the dullness of Jay's years as a lawyer, is the deterring factor of scattered materials that demand patience, and no small degree of luck, before they provide a coherent picture. While one can hardly blame Jay's biographers for failing to expend this effort, it seems to me that Pellew

---

[11]Frank Monaghan, *John Jay, Defender of Liberty* (New York: Bobbs-Merrill, 1935), pp. 32-50.

[12]*John Jay* (Boston: Houghton, Mifflin & Co., 1890), pp. 14-22; quotation at p.18.

is unjustified in concluding that Jay's law practice was uninteresting.

I have approached this study with two purposes, both of which I feel have been achieved. First, it seemed necessary that the first twelve years of Jay's adult be studied in depth, so that future students of his career in public life would have some information concerning his pre-Revolutionary activities. Secondly, the analysis of a colonial lawyer's practice in the decade preceding American Revolution promised to reveal the legal system of the Province of New York in greater detail, and from practitioner's viewpoint. Quite properly the second objective has been subordinated to the first, for there are many other New York lawyers whose papers and practices would be much more useful in achieving the second objective.[13]

Needless to say, this study would have been impossible without the ready access I have had to the manuscript collections and photocopy collections at Columbia University. For the opportunity to use the manuscripts, I owe thanks to Mr. Roland Baughman, Head of the Special Collections Library; for the great assistance available through the use of photographic copies assembled in the John Jay| Papers Project, I owe thanks to Professor Richard B Morris, the Director of that publication project.

In my travels in search of Jay materials I have met a large number of librarians and public officials who have extended invaluable assistance to me. My friends in the Records Division of the New York County Clerk's Office, supervised by Mr. George Feinstein, have been most patient and permitted me to "rummage" at will through the papers deposited with them. They have been most tolerant of my impositions upon their time, and very gracious in handling the many requests I have made of them. At the New York Historical Society, I was welcomed and assisted by Mr. Wilmer Leech and Mr. Arthur Brerton of the Manuscript Division, and I have done most of my newspaper research in the Society's excellent collection of eighteenth century papers.

Outside of the city of New York, I have been fortunate in contacting the county clerks in Albany, Westchester, Dutchess and Queens Counties;

---

[13]The Papers of James Alexander and John Tabor Kempe, both at the New York Historical Society, New York City, would be much more productive in this regard.

in each case, I have met ready assistance in regard to what must have seemed unusual requisitions for records. In particular, I must mention the great assistance extended by Mr. Frederic A. Smith, the County Clerk of Dutchess County. His interest in the colonial documents under his control has resulted in an index that was most useful in my work. Without his aid I could not have completed my research at Poughkeepsie within the limited time I had available; both he and his staff made possible an accurate study of Jay's practice in the inferior courts of justice.

At Albany I met with the kind and valuable assistance of Miss Juliette Wolohon at the State library, and Mr. James Gary in the office of the Clerk of the Court of Appeals.

The Ulster County records were made available to me by Dr. Leo Hershkowitz of Queens College. To Hershkowitz' research in the Hall of Records, I owe discovery of the writ book upon which I based my discussion of Jay's practice in the New York City Mayor's Court. The staff at the Columbia Law Library permitted me to conduct a physical examination of the Jay Collection in the Treasure Room, and in addition, have been of recurring assistance to me in my search for unusual materials in the field of law. I gained access to the library of the pesociation of the Bar of the City of New York through the intercession of my friend, Abraham S. Robinson, Esq., of New York City. My introduction to the mysteries of the "Round Room" at the Public Record Office in London, was made easier by my friend Mr. David Syrett. Miss Helen F. Beach of the National Archives, Washington, D.C., was most helpful in regard to my research of Jay's work in Vice-Admiralty cases.

The entire manuscript has received the careful perusal of Professor Joseph H. Smith of Columbia Law School. His contents have been of great value to me, and his assistance and encouragement has sustained me upon several occasions in the four years I have known him. Those errors that remain in the manuscript should be considered an infinitesimal fraction of the many I have made, but which have been prevented by the sharp eye of one of the best legal historians of the day.

Finally I must mention my obligation to Professor Richard B. Morris, who in the course of nearly five years, has helped me along my way as a graduate student. He has been an inspiring teacher, an abundant source of ideas and information in seminar discussions and elsewhere, and the most congenial "boss" one could ever have wanted while a research assistant on the John Jay Papers Project. He too, has read this manuscript, and saved me from error on numerous occasions. Above all else, he has been a sure guide in the rather crooked path that I have taken through graduate school.

Wives are always mentioned with gratitude in prefaces and I too am deeply grateful to my wife for her unselfish encouragement to me. From the time she walked with me "Out of the College Yard" on a cold winter's day in January of 1962, she has been living with this dissertation. She has borne the task of editing my prose with patience forbearance. Her criticism has corrected many a sentence that might have proven utterly incomprehensible. That her comments were made at the risk of domestic conflict elevates her contribution to the level of the heroic, and she has earned the gratitude of every one of my readers.

HERBERT A. JOHNSON

March 1965
Bronx, New York

I. OUT OF THE COLLEGE YARD
MAY 22, 1764

John Jay awoke on his Commencement Day to find the sky overcast and the wind blowing sharply from the southeast. When the Trustees fixed the 22nd of May as graduation day they could hardly have counted upon the fickleness of the prevailing southwesterly winds that cool the City of New York during Springtime. In the earlier part of the week the dry and cool wind from the northwest brought to the students at the College Hall the faint odor of Harrison's Brewery, about a mile to the northwest at Greenwich Village. However as the 22nd dawned, a breeze from the southeast brought warmer air, laden with moisture that would threaten the scholarly procession with a disrespectful drenching.[1]

With the end of the academic year Jay's room was in considerable disarray, for it was necessary to pack the accumulated belongings of two

---

[1]Meteorological data is from the Notebook of Egbert Benson of the Class of 1765, King's College, Benson Papers, Box 1, New York Historical Society. For location of Harrison's Brewery see John Montressor, *Plan of the City York and Its Environs* (1766), Map Division, New York Public Library.

[2]On June 1st Jay was to commence his law clerkship with Benjamin Kissam, and he had arranged for quarters close to Kissam's office, Peter Jay to John Jay, Feb. 28, 1764, Columbia University Libraries, Special Collections. He had moved to the College Hall in 1762, Frank Monaghan, *John Jay* (New York: Bobbs-Merrill Co., 1935), pp. 27, 31 (hereafter cited Monaghan, *Jay*); see also Peter Jay to John Jay, n.d. [1762], Columbia University Libraries, Special Collections.

[3]According to Jay's son, William Jay, it had already become a practice for Jay to place compositions on a table at the side of his bed to facilitate changes that might to him during the night, *The Life of John Jay* (2 vols., New York: J & J Harper, 1833), I, 13 (hereafter cited Wm. Jay, *Life*). It is likely that he would have followed such a procedure with an important document such as the text of his Commencement speech.

years residence preparatory to moving to new quarters by June 1st.[2] Nevertheless Jay had carefully placed his Commencement speech on the writing desk he habitually kept at the side of his bed.[3] Normally an extremely orderly person, Jay was not a little bothered by the trunks cluttering up the large living room of his suite. Yet the disarray so altered the familiar surroundings as to dispel the inevitable sense of nostalgia at leaving King's College Hall. For here in these simple rooms he had enjoyed many an evening in earnest discussion with his friends. Ahead lay the adventure of legal clerkship and a career at the Bar, yet on this day he left behind the pleasant, studious, and somewhat monastic life within College Yard.

Just a few weeks before Jay's graduation had been anything but certain, and only the sympathetic of understanding of President Myles Cooper, normally a strict disciplinarian saved young Jay from the humiliation of remaining another year at the College. After what seemed an interminable time of speculation, President Cooper decided to take what for him was an extraordinary step--he departed from a rule of his own making, reversed a decision of expulsion against Jay, and permitted the grateful eighteen year old to return to his studies and graduate.

Of course it was not inferior academic work that jeopardized Jay's graduation in 1764. Well grounded to Latin by his mother and his tutor, George Murray, drilled in mathematics and French by the Reverend Peter Stouppe, Jay had found but little difficulty in meeting the academic requirements of the College.[4] In fact he had already begun his readings in law,[5] and found time to indulge in some

---

[4]Wm. Jay, *Life*, I, 11-12; Monaghan, *Jay*, pp. 23, 24, 26; a French copybook is in the Columbia University Libraries, Special Collections; a mathematics copybook is in the possession of Mr. Frederick Jay Wells of New York City; a Latin copybook, seen by Monaghan, has not been located.

[5]Hugo Grotius, *Law of War and Peace* and Puffendorf's *Law of Nations* were in the fourth year curriculum, *Columbia University. Early Minutes of the Trustees. Volume I, 1755-1770* (New York: 1932), March 1, 1763 (hereafter cited *Early Trustees Minutes*). Jay's father had protested the expense of a law dictionary purchased by John in 1763, Monaghan, *Jay*, p.29.

lighter reading in contemporary literature.[6] The threat to Jay's graduation was in the form of a disciplinary lapse which pitted him against the authority of the newly appointed President of the College just a few weeks before Jay was to graduate. As William Jay recounts the family tradition, Jay was present in the College Hall when some fellow student decided to break a table to spite the College Steward. Cooper arrived on the scene unexpectedly and questioned all of the students concerning the identity the culprit. While John denied that he had committed vandalism, he refused to reveal the name of the malefactor or to state that he did not know the culprit's identity. Brought before a board of the faculty, Jay was "rusticated" for a few weeks until Cooper, no doubt influenced by his exemplary academic and disciplinary record, relented and permitted him to return to his studies and graduate with class.[7] Other than this oral tradition passed on by William Jay, there is no record of John's clash with the College authorities, yet the fact that he recalled it so vividly nearly half a century after the occurrence testifies to the deep impression the incident made upon John Jay.

Waiting to greet the candidate for graduation, was his very close friend, Robert R. Livingston, Jr., the tall, graceful and high-spirited son of Judge

---

[6]Jay was so impressed with James MacPherson's "Ossian's Address to the Sun," a Scottish primitive poem later reprinted in *The Poems of Ossian* that he copied it into his notebook, Monaghan *Jay*, p. 28; although seen by Monaghan this notebook has not been located. It is also quite possible that Jay joined his friend Livingston in reading the racy novel by Laurence Sterne entitled *Tristram Shandy*, see Walter DuBois, Jr. to R.R. Livingston, Jr., Dec. 6, 1763, in Robert R. Livingston Papers, Box 1, New York Historical Society (hereafter cited as Livingston papers, Box _).

[7]Wm. Jay, *Life*, I, 14-15; Monaghan, *Jay*, pp. 29-30. Since Jay would have taken his Bachelor's examination during the first two weeks in April, it is likely that the incident took place during the latter part of April.

Robert R. Livingston of Clermont.[8] "Bob" Livingston was a member the Class of 1765 and one year Jay's junior. Despite his youth, Livingston was a charming companion to the ladies and known to his associates as "... a very Proteus in Love ..."; in this respect he was quite the opposite of John Jay who, coming from a deeply religious and quiet home in Rye, found it difficult to overcome his awkwardness in presence of the opposite sex. Concerning Jay's prowess with the ladies, Walter DuBois, Jr., was known to comment, "... Every One who has the Happiness of his Acquaintance, must know him to be more ignorant [about the ladies] than in any other Art whatsoever."[9] The two young men nevertheless seem to have been strongly attracted to each other, and were known to be close associates. At the commencement of Jay's third year at the College, DuBois wrote to Livingston,

> I suppose you spent the Evening at College, if you did, I'm sure it prov'd a satisfactory One; for Me, I can safely say that I never reap such real Pleasure in Any Company, as I do in the Conversation of the few select Ones, who visit Jay's Room; which might very justly be call'd a Receptacle of agreeable young Fellows.[10]

It would seem that Jay and Livingston served as a moderating influence upon each other, for DuBois noted that Livingston, always variable and romantically inclined, had suddenly, "... Commenced methodical; ...".[11] Perhaps the stabilizing influence of the serious minded and industrious John Jay had something to do with the transformation.

---

[8]George Dangerfield, *Chancellor Robert R. Livingston of New York 1746-1813* (New York, Harcourt, Brace & Co., 1960), p. 45 (hereafter cited as Dangerfield, *Livingston*).

[9]Walter DuBois, Jr. to Livingston, Jan. 6, 1764, Livingston Papers, Box 1, New York Historical Society.

[10]DuBois to Livingston, Sep. 7, 1763, *ibid.*

[11] *Ibid.*, Feb. 19, 1763.

Upon the termination of a meeting of the Trustees the procession began to form in the College Library with Jay taking his place alongside his fellow graduate, Richard Harison. After the Faculty and Trustees joined the procession, the entire group began to move slowly into the College Yard and up the gentle slope toward the East Gate. Once out of the Yard, the academic procession followed Robinson Street uphill to Broadway.[13] From his place in the procession Jay could look south along the tree lined thoroughfare toward Fort George, and see the coach that was carrying General Thomas Gage from his residence on Broad Street to the Commencement at St. George's Chapel.[14] Jutting high into the grey sky was the graceful spire of Trinity Church, topped by a lightning rod, newly invented by Benjamin Franklin, that just a few weeks before had saved the Church from destruction.[15]

After crossing Broadway the procession wound its way across the

---

[12]*Early Trustee's Minutes*, May 22, 1764. *A History of Columbian University 1754-1904* (New York: 1904), p. 38.

[13]Robinson Street, now Park Place, was directly opposite to the East Gate of the Yard; the slope of the land is no more than 10E.

[14]Gage and the members of the Governor's Council were present at the Commencement, Milton Halsey Thomas, "King's College Commencements in the Newspapers", *Columbia University Quarterly*, XXII, 224-247, at p.231. The Lieutenant Governor, Cadwallader Golden, was out of town. Original account is at New York *Gazette* or *Weekly Post Boy*, May 31, 1764. See also John R. Alden, *General Gage in America* (Baton Rouge: Louisiana State University Press, 1948) pp. 65, 67.

[15]David Colden to Sir William Johnson, May 7, 1764, "Letters and Papers of Cadwallader Colden: Volume VI, 1761-64", New York Historical Society, *Collections*. LV, 310-13. John Jay's family had, for three generations, worshipped at Trinity Church, and young John had upheld the tradition while residing at King's College. One half of pew number seven was purchased by Augustus Jay in 1726, MS Vestry Minutes, Trinity Church, New York, I, 156. See letter of Peter Jay to Nicholas William Stuyvesant, September 21, 1763 in Jay Papers, New York Historical Society.

Common, which was bounded on the north by the Poor House and the Powder House. Triangular in shape, the Common's apex was at Vesey Street and its broad base rested at the northern edge of the City. On the West it was bounded by Broadway, and on the East by the High Road to Boston that ran away toward the northeast, past the tanning yards and the burial grounds for Blacks and Jews.[16] Looking in that direction Jay could see a windmill on the opposite shore of the Collect Pond, and another windmill further west on Mount Pleasant. At this point the scholars would have reached the midpoint of their half mile walk St. George's Chapel.[17]

Once across the High Road to Boston the procession entered Deckman Street and started downhill toward the East River.[18] Completed in 1752 as the "First Chapel of Ease" in Trinity Parish, St. George's boasted a lofty 172 feet steeple, readily visible over the rooftops of the houses on Deckman Street. Built in a crowded, ill constructed portion of Montgomerie Ward known as "The Swamp", the Chapel was a graceful structure designed by Robert Crommelin, the architect of King's College Hall.[19] The scholars moved a little more rapidly on the down hill slope, and Jay had but a short time to glance down Gold Street toward Golden Hill, upon which was situated the law office of Benjamin Kissam. Four months previously he had signed his clerkship agreement with Kissam, and Peter Jay rejoiced that he had been able to provide a good legal training for his son without the necessity of exposing him to the heady social atmosphere

---

[16]See map of John Montressor, *op. cit.*, nt.l.

[17]According to the Montressor map, the distance is about 5/12 of a mile. One can walk the distance at a leisurely pace in about 13 minutes.

[18]Deckman Street is the present day Beekman Street; the slope of the hill toward the East River is about 15E.

[19]The Chapel was 92 feet in length, 72 feet in breadth, and stood at the corner of Beekman and Cliff Streets, on the site presently occupied in 1965 by the Keystone Iron and Wire Works (88 Beekman St.). It was destroyed by fire in 1814. Morgan Dix, ed., *A History of the Parish of Trinity Church in the City of New York* (New York: G.P. Putnam's Sons, 1898), pp. 246, 247, 259, 261.

of the English Inns of Court.[20]

John Jay had determined to pursue a legal career in 1762 despite the wish of his father that he enter the ministry.[21] By February of 1763 Peter Jay was reconciled to his son's choice of a profession but was deeply troubled over the difficulties involved in obtaining the necessary training. In 1756 the attorneys of New York agreed to restrict Bar admissions by refusing to accept clerks for the next fourteen years,[22] thereby denying the young men the opportunity to prepare themselves in a New York law office.

After writing to John's brother, Sir James Jay, in London, and his commercial correspondent and cousin, David Peloquin, in Bristol, Peter Jay concluded that legal training in England would be quite an expensive proposition. He also confided to Peloquin that,

> ... though I have hitherto no Reason to doubt of his behaving Well, as he is a youth remarkably sedate, and is well disposed, but nevertheless it's prudent to gard [sic.], as much as possible, against the danger of bad Company he would be exposed to in London...[23]

---

[20]The expenses of maintaining a "gentleman's way of life", and the inadequacies of the education received at the Inns deterred most colonial parents from sending their sons to London, see Paul M. Hamlin, *Legal Education in New York* (New York: New York University Law Quarterly Review, 1939), pp. 16, 19-20, 22, 29. The Inns were actually legal societies that bestowed the title of counsellor-at-law after compliance with the barest of formalities, *ibid.*, p. 14, 16.

[21]This is the assertion of Jay's biographer, Monaghan, *Jay*, p. 29.

[22]Hamlin, *Legal Education*, p. 160-61.

[23]Peter Jay to James Jay, February 15th and April 14th, 1763, Peter Jay Letterbook #3, Columbia University Libraries, Special Collections. The passage quoted is from a letter to David Peloquin dated April 14, 1763 in the same Letterbook.

Peloquin could give the worried father little encouragement, and admitted that he was not well acquainted with the members of the Bar at Bristol who were "... so thick set in the city that most people wonder in what manner many of them get their bread."[24] The search for a suitable placement continued throughout 1763 until January of 1764, when a change in the policy of the New York Bar again made available the opportunity of clerking with New York attorneys.[25] Within eleven days Peter Jay had made preliminary arrangements with Benjamin Kissam, whom he described as a "Gentleman eminent in the Profession",[26] and wrote to John instructing him to sign the clerkship agreement with Kissam.[27] The law clerk-to-be looked forward eagerly to June 1, 1764 when he would commence his duties with Kissam, and probably felt it appropriate that he had to pass so close to Kissam's office on his way to the Commencement ceremonies. Just as he had walked out of the College Yard into the bustling life of the

---

[24]Monaghan, *Jay*, p. 29. David Peloquin to Peter Jay, July 26, 1763, MS letter in possession of Mr. John Jay of Williamstown, Mass.

[25]Hamlin, *Legal Education*, p. 161-62.

[26]In a letter of Peter Jay to David Peloquin dated May 15, 1764, in which Jay informed Peloquin of the change in plans; located in Peter Jay Letterbook #3, Columbia University Libraries, Special Collections.

[27]Henry P. Johnston, ed., *The Correspondence and Public Papers of John Jay* (4 vols., New York: G.P. Putnam's Sons 1890-94), I (1890), 2 (hereafter cited Johnston, *Corres.*). In his instructions Peter Jay requested John to arrive at the best possible arrangement regarding the fee and the term of service. He also wished a condition that should either Kissam or John die before the end of the clerkship, the contract would be void. As the agreement does not survive, we cannot tell how successful Peter Jay was in this regard, but the fact that he approached Kissam so soon after the Bar Agreement was signed probably indicated an eagerness to contract that would have prevented him from getting any concessions.

City, in like manner he would very soon leave the tranquility of classical studies for the hurried scholarship and turbulent activity of a busy lawyer's office.

Arriving at St. George's the academic procession entered the Chapel and the students took their assigned places. While no list of the spectators survives we know that only two members of Jay's immediate family could have been present. His younger brother Frederick might have been among the spectators if he was able to obtain a few hours leave from his duties as a clerk to James DePeyster, a well-to-do New York merchant related to the Jay family.[28] John's eldest brother Augustus, who earned his way in New York City by managing the affairs of Peter Jay also might have attended the commencement. Sir James Jay, John's physician brother, had returned to England in 1762, much to the regret of their father, and sister Eve Jay was still convalescing at Rye from a dangerous illness that had nearly caused her death the previous year. With Eve sickly and John's mother, Mary Van Cortlandt Jay, severely crippled with rheumatism, Peter Jay did not make the trip from Rye to see his son's graduation.[29]

Once all were seated and an invocation was said, President Myles Cooper rose to comment upon the past year's achievements and to commend the young graduates. In a little more than a year as President, Cooper had earned the affection of his students; even his strict discipline was tempered with mercy, as young John Jay was well aware.[30]

To demonstrate their academic abilities, the two candidates for the Bachelor of Arts degree were to give speeches and then engage in a formal debate. Jay gave a dissertation in English on the subject, "The Happiness

---

[28]Peter Jay to James Jay, April 14, 1763, Letterbook #3, Columbia University Libraries, Special Collections.

[29]Peter Jay to David Peloquin, May 6, 1762; Apr. 14, June 1, 1763; Nov. 15, 1763, *ibid.*

[30]For sketch of Cooper see Clarence Hayden Vance, "Myles Cooper", *Columbia University Quarterly*, XXII, 261-86.

and Advantages arising from a State of Peace",[31] a most appropriate topic in the first year of peace that the North American colonies had enjoyed since 1754. Jay's speech was delivered immediately after the salutatory address by his classmate, Richard Harison.[32] The two graduates then disputed on the topic of "National Poverty versus National Riches", to the satisfaction of the entire audience.[33] At the conclusion of this debate they were both awarded their degrees by President Cooper.

After the valedictory address in Latin by the foremost candidate for the degree of Master of Arts, and the awarding of Master's degrees, the Commencement closed with benedicticion. The academic procession reformed for the return to the College Hall. Now an alumnus of the College, John Jay could look forward to joining with the Trustees, Faculty in the annual Commencement Day banquet. A regal repast was in preparation back at the College Hall, far superior to the usual frugal fare provided with deadly monotony by the College steward[34] While the menu of Jay's Commencement Day banquet does not survive, there is a detailed bill submitted by the caterer for the banquet held in May of 1763, from which we can obtain some concept of the festive nature of the occasion. Fifty-nine diners were served; they managed to consume 56 bottles of Madeira wine, 11 bottles of claret wine, 14 bottles of "Sider", and nearly £ 13 worth of "Punch".

---

[31]Milton Halsey Thomas, *Columbia University Quarterly,* XXII, 232; New York *Gazette and Weekly Post Boy,* May 31, 1764.

[32]*Ibid.*, p. 231; in his assertion that John Jay delivered the salutatory address in Latin, William Jay is no doubt taking unjustifiable pride in his father's academic standing, see *Life,* I, 15; cf. New York *Gazette and Weekly Post Boy*, May 31, 1764, that the only Latin address delivered that day was the valedictory address by Henry Holland, who received his M.A. degree.

[33]Thomas, *Columbia University Quarterly*, XXII, 232.

[34]The daily bill of fare was frugal, monotonous and cost 13 shillings per week. For the menu, which did not vary from week to week, see College Papers, Box "To 1763", Columbia University Libraries, Special Collections.

Glass Breakage totaled seven shillings.[35] After such a meal and heated with the warmth of good wine, John Jay returned to his suite in the College Hall well content with himself and with the world that soon was to lie at his feet.

---

[35] *Ibidem.*; when dealing with the traditions of Columbia University I have found it safest to follow the rebuttable presumption that once instituted, a tradition will not change. Thus the strong likelihood is that the wine flowed as freely in 1764 as it had in 1763.

II. DEEDS, DECLARATIONS AND DRUDGERY

On the first day in June of 1764 John Jay began his duties as a clerk in the busy law office of Benjamin Kissam.[1] During the four years and five months that elapsed before he was admitted as an attorney at law, he was to learn much about his chosen profession. As a clerk he would master the technicalities of draftsmanship, pleading, and legal research. In his social life he would progress from the awkwardness of adolescence to the polished manners of a young aristocrat about town. And perhaps most important in terms of his life's work in the public service, he was to be given his first direct contact with the political situation that was beginning to undermine the foundations of the British Empire in North America.

When John first decided upon a career at the Bar, his father advised him, "... as its your inclination to be of that Profession, I hope you'll closely attend to it with a firm resolution that no difficulties in prosecuting that Study shall discourage you from applying very close to it, and if possible, from taking a delight in it."[2] Perhaps Peter Jay's reference to the "difficulties" of clerkship tempered John's natural enthusiasm, for past events confirmed his father's cautious admonition that he would have to "attend to it ... very closely."

At about the time of John Jay's birth, William Livingston had rebelled in a most public fashion against the dreary life of a law clerk. Having commenced his clerkship with James Alexander in 1741, young Livingston had been raised since childhood in the home of an indulgent grandmother, to whose liberality has been attributed the boy's impatience and irritability.[3] In 1744 it appeared that Livingston was progressing with the clerkship as well as might be expected, des-

---

[1]Monaghan, *Jay*, p. 32.

[2]Peter Jay to JJ, Aug. 23, 1763, Jonnston, *Corres.*, I, 1.

[3]Theodore Sedgwick, Jr., *Memoir of the Life of William Livingston* (New York: J. & J. Harper 1832), pp. 48, 52.

spite the fact that some reports reached his father that he was neglecting his studies and staying out late at night.[4] Nearly a year later there appeared the first of two anonymous essays in which Livingston protested against the drudgery of a law clerk's life and the inattention of the attorneys to whom they were apprenticed. When the second essay appeared in March of 1746, James Alexander discovered the identity of the author, and after the resultant breach William Livingston was apprenticed to William Smith, Sr., for the completion of his studies.[5]

The conditions under which law clerks were trained had been somewhat improved in the intervening two decades, for the variety of printed forms reduced transcription tasks to a minimum. Nevertheless there still remained lengthy pleas in Chancery, bulky legal briefs of counsel, wills and non-routine contracts, all of which required preparation in the handwriting of law clerks.[6] While the formal nature of Supreme Court litigation would appear to readily lend itself to use of printed forms, it would seem that the etiquette of the profession required that such papers be handwritten. While recourse was had to professional scriveners, the likelihood is that much of

---

[4]This charge was denied by Livingston who claimed he studied late into the night, and that his late returns to quarters were due to Alexander's nocturnal instructions in mathematics and surveying, *ibid.*, p. 56.

[5]*Ibid.*, p. 57.

[6]Hamlin, *Legal Education*, p. 41. I have located a codicil to the will of Abraham DePeyster, drawn up in John Jay's hand in 1767, to which he was a subscribing witness, Original Wills, 1767-1768, Surrogate's Court of New York County, Hall of Records, N.Y.C.; the will and codicil are printed in "Abstracts of Wills ...: Vol. VII, June 6, 1766-November 29, 1771...", New York Historical Society, *Collections* XXXI, 104. However, there are also wills on printed forms, e.g., Will of George Christy, Dec. 16, 1763. Orig. Wills 1763-64, Surrogate's Court of New York County, Hall of Records, N.Y.C..

this work was performed by law clerks.[7] In addition to this transcription, the senior clerks were doubtless expected to manage the business affairs of the law office by keeping an accurate register of costs and disbursements, preparing bills to clients for services rendered, and drafting routine correspondence. Briefly, the colonial law clerk performed all those duties which today are assigned to a legal stenographer coupled with the functions of a managing clerk and a legal researcher.

While the utilization of clerks as scriveners was less frequent than it had been during Livingston's clerkship, the attention which an active attorney could devote to the education of his clerks was no greater in 1764 than it had been in 1745. In their own studies and conducting research for their masters, clerks would often find themselves confronted with a vast array of inadequately indexed sources that might, with a large expenditure of time and effort yield the answers to their questions. The sense of frustration which this evoked may be found in the statement of Peter Van Schaack, one of Jay's close friends,

> For my part, how many hours have I hunted, how many books turned up for what three minutes of explanation from any tolerable lawyer would have made evident to me! It is vain to put a law book into the hands of a lad without explaining difficulties to him as he goes along.[8]

A sole practitioner's time was largely occupied with attendance at courts, meetings with clients and partaking in those public activities fitting to his position

---

[7]Mayor's Court Papers, Benjamin Salzer Collection, Columbia University, Special Collections Library, Box 2, (1775). The declaration appears to be drawn by a scrivener; blanks are left for the details peculiar to the case, and these details are supplied in another hand.

[8]Henry C. Van Schaack, *Life of Peter Van Schaack* (New York: D. Appleton & Co. 1842), p.9. Van Schaack later had the opportunity to explain the law to young men, for he founded a law school at Kinderehook, New York, after the Revolution, see Hamlin, *Legal Education*, p. 42.

in society. It is not all surprising that Van Schaack could state that no more than one or two attorneys in New York did tolerable justice to the tasks of educating their clerks.[9] That the members of the Bar were well aware of the problem is evidenced by the curriculum for law study suggested by William Smith, Jr.,[10] but the mere suggestion of useful books could not substitute for the personal supervision of a trained lawyer.

Jay's transition from collegiate study to the more pedestrian study of the law was completed on that balmy first day of June when he entered Kissam's office on Golden Hill. Previously he had followed the carefully planned curriculum of King's College; now he was to pursue the makeshift system of learning which for centuries had been characteristic of the English Bar. The young law clerk could learn as much or as little as his inclination dictated, but only assiduous attention to the conduct of his master's business and careful application to his own studies, would earn him the approbation necessary for admission to practice. From the meager evidence that survives, it appears that John Jay accepted the challenge with vigor, and irnnediately applied himself to the study of law in a manner that met with the wholehearted approval of his father.[11]

Kissam was a well known and extremely busy attorney, and we may be certain that his active office provided as many advantages for the study of law as any other in New City. A member of an old Long Island family,

---

[9]Van Schaack, *Life of Peter Van Schaack*, p. 9.

[10]Hamlin, *Legal Education*, p. 62; Milton M. KLein asserts that Hamlin is incorrect and that this plan of study was drawn up in about 1747 by William Smith, Sr., "Rise of the New York Bar: The Legal Career of William Livingston", *William and Mary Quarterly*, 3rd ser., XV, 334-58 at p. 337.

[11]David Peloquin to Peter Jay, Sep. 24, 1764, MS Letter in collection of John Jay at Williamstown, Mass. (referring to a missing letter of Peter Jay).

Kissam was about thirty-four years of age when Jay began his clerkship.[12] The Kissam family was prominent in the Bar that practiced before the Court of Common Pleas at Jamaica; they could also boast one of their number as a Judge of that Court.[13] It would seem that Benjamin Kissam rarely travelled to Long Island to present his cases, but that such litigation was referred to one of his relatives.[14] Doubtless Kissam's preference for New York City practice was increased by his marriage to Catharine Rutgers in 1755 which resulted in his obtaining possession, by right of curtesy, of her large estate called Rutgers Farm.[15]

Unfortunately there is very little information available concerning Jay's patron, but one of his descendants relates that Kissam was a man of deep piety who admonished his children to be dutiful to God, guarded in their actions and upright in their intentions.[16] When Jay learned of Kissam's death at New York City in October of 1782, he wrote to Robert R. Livingston, "I have lately heard of Mr. Kissam's death. It affected me much. He was a virtuous and agreeable man, and I owed him many obligations."[17] He spoke of Kissam as one of the best men he ever knew, one of the best friends he ever had; this despite Benjamin

---

[12]Edward Kissam, *The Kissam Family in America from 1644 to 1825* (New York: Dempsey & Carroll's Art Press, 1892), pp. 20, 21.

[13]Daniel Kissam (1726-1782) and Daniel Kissam (1739-1812) were both judges of this court, *ibid.*, pp. 18, 23.

[14]Minutes of the Court of General Sessions and the Court of Common Pleas, 1722-1787, County Clerk of Queens County, Jamaica, New York, *passim.* A case in which Benjamin Kissam did appear came before the Court of Common Pleas on Sept. 19, 1764 (Cornell v. Smith); presumably the Supreme Court of Judicature was on circuit, and Kissam could spare the time to travel to Jamaica.

[15]Kissam, *Kissam Family*, p. 20.

[16]*Ibidem*

[17]July 19, 1783, Wm. Jay, *Life*. I, 179.

Kissam's loyalty to the Crown throughout the American Revolution.[18]

More directly concerned with Jay's introduction the law, was Kissam's senior clerk, Lindley Murray, who had been apprenticed to Kissam in 1763 presumably in spite of the lawyer's agreement against the acceptance of clerks before 1770. After a year's training in Kissam's office, the young son of a Quaker merchant was in a position to make Jay's first days less perplexing than they might otherwise have been. While Lindley Murray was approximately the same age as John Jay, Murray's preparatory studies had been with a private tutor rather than at King's College. After he completed his training in the classics, he sought the assistance of Benjamin Kissam, his father's attorney, in the hope of convincing his merchant father that he should be permitted to study the law. Gradually the two prevailed against the Quaker conscience of John Murray, who feared that the practice of law was less compatible with the Quaker ethic than the business of a mercant could be.[19] Many years later during his self-imposed exile in England and after gaining considerable fame as a grammarian, Lindley Murray wrote of his clerkship days,

> I cannot, however, say that I always found the study of the law to be pleasant. It contains many barren and uninviting tracts, and extensive fields of laborious employment. It abounds with discordant views, with intricate and perplexing discussions, and requires deep and patient investigation. But I was not discouraged with my occupation. It was the profession of my own choice; it was a respectable business; and it promised to afford me competent support.[20]

---

[18]*Ibid..* I, 16.

[19]Elizabeth Frank, ed., *Memoirs of the Life and Writings of Lindley Murray* (New York: Samuel Wood & Sons, 1827), pp. 3, 32, 33.

[20]*Ibid..* pp. 33-34.

It would seem that Murray's patience and scholarship would make a favorable impression upon his junior in Kissam's office, and that both young men were fully attuned to the pious approach to life for which their mentor is remembered.

Although John Jay entered Kissam's employ during the three month Spring recess of the Supreme Court, there was nevertheless a great deal of work to be done in preparation for the July-August term.[21] The first Saturday of that term was motion day, and Kissam was making procedural motions in eight cases commenced by the arrest of the defendants under a *capias ad respondendum*. The necessary motion papers had to be drawn up in readiness for the returns of the county Sheriffs. A declaration in ejectment had to be drawn up, replete with its strange fictitious pleas. In three other cases Kissam planned to make motions for judgment for the plaintiff's failure to file a declaration, and in one case he expected to file a notice of appearance for a defendant.[22] The cases of Angevine v. Russel, Everson v. Brown and Everson v. Brown Jr., had gone to judgment at the April term of the Court, but the judgment rolls had to be prepared for signature and filing.[23]

While the Supreme Court of Judicature was recessed, the Mayor's Court of the City of New York continued to hear cases as a Court of Common Pleas. The docket was extremely long, and Benjamin Kissam had fifty-one cases awaiting trial as of June 26, 1764.[24] Of these, one was scheduled for presentation on

---

[21]On April 28, 1764 the court recessed until the last Tuesday in July, Minute Book of the Supreme Court of Judicature, Oct. 19, 1762-Apr. 28, 1764, N.Y. Co. Clerk, Hall of Records, N.Y.C. p. 451 (hereafter referred to as Min. S. Ct. Jud., ([Dates], p._).

[22]Min. S. Ct. Jud. July 31, 1964. Aug. 2, 1766, pp. 29-30.

[23]Parchments 159-E-4, 86-C-10, 135-L-5, N.Y. Co. Clerk, Hall of Records, N.Y.C.; Min. S. Ct. Jud., Oct. 19, 1762-Apr. 28, 1764, p. 451.

[24]Rough Minutes, Mayor's Court of New York City, I Jan. 25, 1763-Oct. 29, 1765, N.Y. Co. Clerk, Hall of Records, N.Y.C. pp. 201-09. The engrossed minutes omit the name of the attorney.

July 24th, one case was to be discontinued upon motion of the parties, and one case was to be reported to be at issue.[25] Each step required preparation of papers and supporting documents.

With such a work load, we can be certain that John had little time to ponder over Kissam's law books; the hard-pressed Lindley Murray had more than enough to do in maintaining Kissam's registers, billing clients and preparing trial in the Mayor's Court. To the new clerk were assigned the onerous, but essential, tasks of copying the necessary papers. While none of the motion papers survive, all three of the judgment rolls in the Supreme Court cases mentioned above were written by John Jay. From the seventeen judgment rolls which survive concerning Kissam's Supreme Court practice between June of 1764 and November 1765, we can gain some idea of the assignment of duties in the law office. Sixteen of those seventeen judgment rolls are in the handwriting of John Jay; only one roll, filed in October 1765 is in Murray's handwriting.[26] Apparently only when there was a particular rush in business, as there was immediately

---

[25]Bennett v. Anthony, *ibid.*, p. 215. When Kissam appeared for trial one juror was absent and the case was marked off; Kissam and opposing counsel then stipulated to abide by the decision of arbitrators who would fix the boundary of the real property in question, *ibid.*, pp. 219, 220. Case marked at issue was McClaine v. Robinson, *ibid.*, p. 214; discontinued--Rooms v. Livingston, *ibid.*.p 217.

[26]In New York County Clerk's Office under the following Parchment file numbers:
Angevine v. Russel 159-E-4
Butler & Franklin v. Everet 182-D-6
Clement v. Hallett 32-G-6
Craig v. Thompson 37-L-7
Everson v. Brown 86-C-10
Everson v. Brown. Jr. 135-L-5
Henderson v. Simons 58-C-7
Jay v. Kinne 130-C-4
Leverage v. Alner 159-J-9

before the Stamp Act became effective on November 1, 1765, did the senior clerk act as scribe. In addition to the sixteen judgment rolls, Jay's handwriting appears on the endorsement of a writ of *fieri facias* on two writs of inquisition.[27] Since the endorsement on all of the judgment rolls is in Jay's hand, we must conclude that part of the junior clerk's duties was to carry the completed judgment rolls to the judge, usually Daniel Horsmanden, for signature, and thence to the Supreme Court clerk for filing.

Kissam's Supreme Court practice during the first twenty months of Jay's clerkship consisted primarily of commercial matters.[28] Only one action was based upon an assault and battery.[29] Among the commercial cases based upon writings obligatory were disposed of in the shortest period of time, while debts not evidenced by such documentary proof were collected more slowly. The latter type of litigation, based on allegations in assumpsit, required that a jury be assembled

---

Murray v. Haldan 155-D-6
Murray v. Sackett 71-A-10
Murray v. Strang 139-C-8
Randall v. Bunster 68-D-8
Smart v. Wallace 123-C-8
Smith v. E. Boyd 54-J-9
Smith v. J. Bovd 135-F-10
(Following roll in Murray's hand: Franklin v. Storm 18-C-5)

[27]*Fieri facias* endorsement in Butler v. Everet, Parchment 182-D-6; writs of inquisition in Jay's hand in Randall v. Punster, PL 1754-1837, R631 and Leversage v. Alner, PL 1754-1837, L1224, all in N.Y. County Clerk's Office, Hall of Records, N.Y.C.

[28]Eleven cases are on writings or bills obligatory, the eighteenth century equivalent of the present day bond; five cases are in assumpsit. Of the assumpsit cases, three are for goods had and received, one for the loan of money, and one for labor.

[29]Leversacfe v. Alerna.

after entry of a default judgment to assess the plaintiff damages. Hence the delay in obtaining a jury could substantially detain the plaintiff's attorney in his attempt to reduce the case to a final judgment. In one of Kissam's assumpsit cases, judgment was delayed for over a year, doubtless for this reason.[30]

The lack of file papers or judgment rolls in Mayor's Court cases makes it impossible to present a similar cross section of Kissam's practice that Court; however, as mentioned above, he did have fifty-one cases on the docket of the Court when Jay began his law clerkship. From this fact, and the predominance of suits for the recovery of debts in the Supreme Court, we may conclude that Benjamin Kissam's practice was largely in the field of commercial transactions.

In the conduct of his practice before both Courts, Kissam seems to have accorded priority to the causes involving larger sums of money. Since the amount of litigation to collect a small debt is equal to that required in the case of a large debt, the wise attorney is one who expedites the larger case and collects the proportionately greater fee. This was evidently Kissam's approach; for every one of his cases where the recovery was £200 or over, Kissam reduced the matter to judgment in three months or less. In smaller cases the period from instituting suit until judgment extended from three months to a year.

As the scion of a mercantile family, John Jay required but slight instruction in these economic aspects of the legal profession. His business acumen had already progressed to the point that he was frequently charged with family business that had to be completed at New York City. Kissam's shrewd business management would seem to have merely reenforced the existing capacity of John Jay to arrange his affairs in such a manner that his work would yield the maximum profit.

As might be anticipated, Jay's mind occasionally wandered from his painstaking task of copying judgment rolls. One of the young clerk's lapses is preserved for posterity in the New York County Clerk's Office. In the judgment roll

---

[30]Randall v. Bunster.

of Randall v. Bunster,[31] a long and involved case because of the time in litigation, there occur four insertions in Jay's hand, presumably indicating editorial corrections on re-reading. At one point Jay was so benumbed by the boring task that he omitted the critical word "promised" from the passage "then and there faithfully promised to pay.[32]

The judgment rolls of Jay despite the above lapse are remarkably free from errors and are examples of flawless handwriting. While the same meticulous care in the preparation of written documents prevailed throughout Jay's lifetime, his handwriting was in time to degenerate in clarity. A flawless legal instrument was the mark of a careful clerk and a respectable lawyer. There can be little doubt that both Kissam and John Jay would heartily endorse the sentiments expressed by Peter Van Schaack who wrote a fellow member of the Bar,

> .. .the deed drawn in your office was rather slovenly copied, and by its many alterations afterward looked rather out of the way ... Excuse the freedom of these hints; but we cannot be too attentive to matters of this kind. A lawyer's reputation, like a woman's, is often lost by one error.[33]

One of the most interesting manuscripts that has survived concerning this early period of John Jay's clerkship is a legal memorandum drawn up in Jay's neat hand on March 5, 1765.[34] Signed by Benjamin Kissam, the

---

[31]Parchment 68-D-8.

[32]*Ibid.* Pleas in assumpsit were relatively infrequent, and it is very likely that this was the first judgment roll prepared by Jay in regard to such a case. The delay mentioned is caused by the issuance and unproductive return of "writs of inquiry". These writs were for the purpose of assembling a jury to assess damages.

[33]Van Schaack, Life of Peter Van Schaack. p.14.

[34]Miscellaneous Manuscripts, Hamilton, New York Historical Society, New York.

paper deals with the construction to be placed upon the will and codicil of Elizabeth Hamilton, deceased. This lady had devised and bequethed two-sevenths of her residuary estate to Abraham DePeyster. In her codicil, for some unexplained reason, dated the same day as her will, she indicated that DePeyster was intitled to take the entailed estate that would descend to him, and no more, provided that upon a valuation of her entailed realty as a fee simple it would equal two-sevenths of her residuary estate, and no more. Subsequent to the execution of the will and codicil, the testatrix instituted the necessary legal procedure to remove the entail from the real estate. She was successful in "docking" the entail and the entailed estate was converted into a fee simple estate. Thus at the time of her death there was no entailed estate which could descend to DePeyster.

The question that was presented to Kissam was whether the testatrix intended that DePeyster be entitled of her residuary estate, and merely wished to indicate that his portion was to consist of the entailed realty, or whether testatrix intended that DePeyster receive only the realty subject to the entail, which she believed to be equivalent to the value of two-sevenths of her estate. In the latter case it was possible to construe the devise to mean that since there was no realty subject to entail upon Elizabeth Hamilton's death, the devise to DePeyster would adeem and he would receive nothing. In words, was the devise to Abraham DePeyster a specific devise of entailed property, that might be revoked or to subject to ademption upon the docking of the entail, or was it a devise of two-sevenths of the residuary estate, to be paid out in the form of the realty which had once been entailed?

Kissam's opinion, later concurred in by David Ogden, was that the codicil and will should be construed together as one instrument, and that when the entail was eliminated prior to the death of Elizabeth Hamilton, the condition that DePeyster's portion of the residuary consist of the entailed realty was also eliminated. Testatrix' intent was to bestow upon DePeyster the two-sevenths of her residuary estate, and his taking was not conditioned upon the existence of entailed realty.

Although the legal issue thus presented was probably resolved by Benjamin Kissam and Lindley Murray, and only the copying was assigned to the neophyte, John Jay, it was in the writing of such well reasoned opinions that the law clerk's progress in the law was furthered. In a day before New York cases were regulary reported, and but few English decisions received wide circulation, a lawyer's opinion was probably the closest a colonial law student could come to a "recent decision on the law."

In addition to serving his master in the copying legal opinions and litigation forms, John Jay began to prepare his own "Commonplace Book".[35] Into such a volume it was customary to copy the necessary forms of practice, such legal precedents which might prove useful, and such legislative materials that bore directly upon the conduct of a law practice. In comparison to the "Commonplace Books" of other New York attorneys, that of John Jay is surprisingly brief, containing out!ines for only extraordinary procedures not likely to be used in every day practice. Nevertheless the outline of steps to be taken in each of these three procedures is completed in considerable detail, buttressed by citation to English authorities. Jay singled out for this particular attention proceedings to recover possession under the act against forcible entry and detainer, not unlike summary proceedings available against a hold-over tenant today. Also included were proceedings under the Attachment Act, which provided a method for seizing the property of an absconding debtor before obtaining judgment against him, and finally, proceedings on the Act for the Preventing of Trespasses, a procedure somewhat in the nature of an injunction to be used to delay lumbering until title to the realty could be ascertained.

Interspersed with these dreary copying tasks, were occasional opportunities for Jay to study the law. Yet even as he began this career which for him would last for the next decade, events began to point toward that political revolution which would forever alter his way of life and project him onto the public scene. As a young law clerk Jay was in the very vortex of these controversies, for the legal profession in New York City had already become the rallying point of colonial resistance. The strong likelihood is that Jay was in the Supreme Court

---

[35]Located in the New York State Library, Albany, New York. For more extensive manuscript commonplace books see the bound volume in the New York Historical Society entitled "Legal Notes of James Alexander"; other commonplace books are in the Columbia Law Library (Joseph Murray and John Chambers).

of Judicature on that 24th day of October 1764 when the jury was sworn in the famous case of Forsey v. Cunningham.[36] Within a short time that case was to dramatically demonstrate the strength and unity of the New York Bar, and to rally public support in opposition to Lieutenant Governor Cadwallader Colden.

There can be no doubt of John Jay's attitude toward Cadwallader Colden, whose insistence upon Judge's commissions being issued "at pleasure" rather than "during good behavior" caused considerable resentment in the Bar at large, and in the Jay family in particular. When Colden finally prevailed upon most of the Justices of the Supreme Court to accept "pleasure" commissions, Jay's uncle and god-father, John Chambers, placed principle office, and resigned his post as Associate Justice of the Court. The old man had died just a few months before Jay began his clerkship, deprived of his high office but sincerely admired by all. John Jay's brother, Frederick, resided with John and Anne Chambers during 1763, the year after Chambers' resignation; John was a frequent visitor in their home and sympathized with Chambers' position.[37]

After a short term out of office the perennial acting governor was again in charge of the Province of New York when, in November of 1764, Cunningham appealed to the Governor in Council for relief from a jury verdict of £ 1500 against him. Colden's Council strongly advised him against entertaining such an irregular appeal, but the elderly man persisted, eventually forwarding a petition

---

[36]Jay's liberty to attended Court was part of his agreement with Kissam, Peter Jay to David Peloquin, May 15, 1764, Peter Jay Letterbook #3, special Collections Library, Colombia University. On October 24, 1764 Kissam participated in a trial of Low v. Prendergast which immediately preceded Forsey v. Cunningham, Min. Bk. S. Ct. Jud., July 31, 1764-Aug. 2, 1766, pp. 68, 69.

[37]Peter Jay to Sir James Jay, April 14, 1763, Letterbook #3, *ibid.*; Milton M. KLeiri, "Prelude to Revolution in New York: Jury Trials and Judicial Tenure," *William and Mary Quarterly*, 3rd ser., XVII 439-462, particularly p. 453.

of Cunningham to the Board of Trade in London. By this time all of the lawyers in New York refused to assist Cunningham in continuing his case, and informed public opinion was strongly against Colden. Even the Attorney-General informed the Lieutenant Governor that he was in error concerning the law: there was simply no appeal from the verdict of a common law jury. Ten days before the effective date of the Stamp Act, the Supreme Court of Judicature found a procedural reason to prevent Cunningham from taking his appeal, despite the fact that the Privy Council appeared to uphold the position of Colden and instructed that an appeal be permitted.[38] This delay coupled with the closing of the Courts during the Stamp Act crisis, resulted in an end to this matter until the Privy Council, after receiving the advice of the principal law officers of the Crown, reversed itself in late December 1764 and denied Cunrangham's right of appeal.[39]

Not only those in the legal profession, such as John Jay, knew of the case of Forsey v. Cunningham; by the middle of October 1764 the issue was clearly before the public. Cadwallader Colden, the oppressor of Judges was now abridging the right to trial by jury! From the columns of John Holt's New York *Weekly Post Boy* the people of New York studied all of the details of the controversy, applauding Chief Justice Horsmanden's strong denial of Cunningham's right to appeal, and

---

[38]Min. S. Ct. Jud., July 31, 1764-Aug. 2, 1766, pp. 327-334.

[39]See Sedgwick, *Livingston*, p. 121-125; Edward P. Alexander, *A Revolutionary Conservative; James Duane of New York* (New York: Columbia University Press, 1938);, pp. 26, 27; Dangerfield, *Livingston* p. 30; Alice Mapelsden' Keys, *Cadwallader Colden: A Representative Eighteenth Century Official* (New York: The Macmillan Co. 1906); pp. 300-302; for the most recent treatment see Klein, *William and Mary Quarterly*, 3rd Ser., XVII, 439-462; for a detailed description of the case, from violent inception to constitutional ramifications, see Joseph H. Smith, *Appeals to the Privy Council From the American Plantations* (New York: Columbia University Press, 1950) pp. 390-416.

muttering against the tyranny of Colden.[40] It is not at all unlikely, as Klein implies,[41] that the resentment over Forsey v. Cunningham, rather than the effort to collect the Stamp Tax, was the cause of the riot that broke out on the evening of November 1, 1765. The Lieutenant Governor's coach house was broken into, his carriage drawn through the streets occupied by an effigy of Colden, and then while the effigy was hung and burned, the carriage was destroyed. Whether the riot was caused by the Stamp Act or by the temporary victory of Colden in the Cunningham case, it gave a clear indication to John Jay of the powerful influence exercised by the lawyers in the Province of New York, for in both instances the Bar was foremost in leading the opposition to these alterations in the colonial constitution.

More directly related to the legal training of Jay was the "Lawyer's Strike" which occurred on the effective date the of the Stamp Act, November 1, 1765. The Act required that all legal instruments and litigation papers bear a stamp before they would be valid; the members of the Bench and Bar therefor decided to suspend litigation until the Act should be repealed. This not only provided a token compliance with the law, but also forcefully demonstrated the unity of the lawyers in opposing the tax. While the more radical elements of the population would have preferred continued operation of the Courts in defiance of Parliament the judges and most of the attorneys favored passive resistance. Consequently only criminal cases, which did not require the use of the hated stamps, were tried in New York between November 1, 1765 and April of 1766, when news of the

---

[40]Sedgwick, *Livingston*, p. 121-125. The constitutional arguments of all of the judges and many prominent members of the Bar, all against Colden's assertions, were reprinted in *The Report of an action of Assault and Battery Tried in the Supreme Court of Judicature for the Province of New York in the Term of October 1764 Between Thomas Forsey and Waddel Cunningham* (New York: John Holt, 1764).

[41]*op cit.*, n.37.

repeal of the Stamp Act was received.[42] We have already noted the flurry of activity in the last days of October 1765, which was responsible for Lindley Murray's being pressed into service as a scrivener to help John Jay. When midnight of October 31st arrived the holographic race with the clock was over; the clerks laid down their pens, massaged their aching hands, and along with their master, temporarily withdrew from the practice of law. As the other lawyers in the Province followed the same procedure the merchants were heard to complain to their correspondents who demanded that debts be collected from recalcitrant debtors, "... we cannot call [them] to an Account by Law, as at present we have no law, ...".[43]

The political friction developing within the British Empire thus accorded to our young law clerk a merciful reprieve from his drudgery among the parchments. Although no evidence of his political opinions survives there is little doubt that he concurred in the universal opposition to Colden and the Stamp Act. Now that Colden and the English seemed to prevail, he was content to leave the solution of the political crisis to his elders, and prepared for what he doubtless considered a well earned vacation.

---

[42]Carl L. Becker, *The History of Political Parties in the Province of New York 1760-1776* (Madison, Wis.: University of Wisconsin Press, 1909), p. 45; Edmund S. Morgan and Helen M. Morgan, *The Stamp Act Crisis: Prologue to Revolution* (Chapel Hill, N.C.: University of North Carolina Press, 1953); p.175.

[43]Anton-Hermann Chroust, "The Lawyers of New Jersey and the Stamp Act," *American Journal of Legal History*, VI, 297, uses the strike terminology. John Watts to Moses Franks, Dec. 22, 1765, "Letter Book of John Watts", New York Historical Society *Collections*, LXI, 406. The reaction of the Bar in the New England colonies paralleled that in New York. For a consideration of the underlying reasons for opposition see Richard B. Morris, "Legalism versus Revolutionary Doctrine in New England," *New England Quarterly*. IV, 195-215.

III. FREE FROM THE DRUDGERY OF BUSINESS

A grave sense of foreboding prevailed in the Province of New York as the effective date of the Stamp Act approached. Not only were there constitutional issues involving Parliamentary taxation, but there also existed a tension throughout the North American colonies that could easily erupt into a violent outburst against the authority of the Parliament and the Crown. In New York City, heavily garrisoned by regular troops, a hasty move on the part of the royal authorities or the colonial leaders could result in bloodshed and misery. As John Jay's father wrote to cousin in Bristol, "God only known what will be the Issue of the general discontent that now prevails, I do indeed dread its consequences . . ."[1]

The crisis came more quickly than even Peter Jay anticipated, for he and John's mother were appalled to find themselves in New York City on November 1, 1765 when violence had already broken out. As the elder Jay later confided to Peloquin, they "... thought it most prudent to withdraw to ... [their] more peaceable Habitation in the Country,"[2] Their son, John, was less disturbed by the events of that day. After all the city had gone into mourning over the death of Liberty on the preceding day, and the gambling tables at the Coffee House had been draped in black crepe.[3] Riots among the lower classes were not uncommon in the city; this was apparent from the burning of a Royal Navy captain's sideboat by an irate mob in July of 1764.[4] Furthermore John and his friend Robert R. Livingston, Jr. were planning an excursion to New England, and the young law clerk, now released from his

---

[1]To David Peloquin, Sep. 19, 1765, Peter Jay Letterbook #3, Columbia University Libraries, Special Collections.

[2]Nov. 25, 1765, *ibid.*

[3]"The Montressor Journals," New York Historial Society *Collections*. XIV 336.

[4]The incident was caused by the impressment of four seamen by the vessel commanded by the unfortunate captain, New York *Gazette or Weekly Post Boy*, July 12, 1764.

onerous task as scrivener, looked forward with anticipation to the projected "frolick".[5] Familiarity with the mood of the city mob, coupled with a certain boyish indifference to the dangerous character of the crisis, were probably the factors that induced John to remain in the city when parents made their precipitous retreat.

Without any record from the pen of John Jay it is difficult to determine what were his thoughts concerning the riot of November first, but the violent outburst of popular resentment could not have failed to make a strong impression upon the young law clerk. On the evening of October 31st, the multitude roaming the streets had divided itself into three squads and broke lampposts and windows while crying "Liberty."[6] The evening of the first of November brought more ambitious activities to the attention of the "Mob". About two thousand participants were actively involved in the proceedings, during which Lieutenant Governor Colden's coach house was emptied of its vehicles, which were drawn through the streets to be destroyed in flames while occupied by effigies of Colden. Discouraged in their attempt to storm the walls of Fort George, the crowd contented themselves with plundering the home of a supercilious British Major who had earned their enmity. Obtaining permission to ring all of the church bells except those of the Church of England, the rioters kept the city awake until the following morning with the dissonant din of bells.[7]

Judge Robert R. Livingston, the father of Jay's friend "Bob," was among the individuals particularly esteemed by the mob because of his leading role in the Stamp Act Congress. In its boisterous passage through the city streets, one group paused before the Livingston house to give a raucous salute to the Judge. At the time they happened to be carrying an effigy of Lord Mansfield hanging from a gallows. The sight of a hanging effigy in judicial robes led "Bob" Livingston's

---

[5]JJ to Robert R. Livingston, Jr., Oct. 31, 1765, Historical Society of Pennsylvania, Gratz Collection, Case 1, Box 7.

[6]New York Historical Society *Collections*. XIV, 336.

[7]*Ibid.*. p. 337; Keys, *Cadwallader Colden*. pp. 320-21; Dangerfield, *Livingston*, p. 36.

younger sister to fear that the crowd had come to hang her father.[8] Fortunately for the Livingston family the rioters were appreciative of the Judge's efforts on behalf of the colonies and selective in their choice of victims for plundering. As the evening progressed however, the actions of the crowd became less and less governed by political considerations. After devastating the home of Major Thomas James they turned to sacking some bawdy houses despite the fact that the profession of the inhabitants was one of the few not affected by the provisions of the Stamp Act.[9]

Prudent merchants, the following day, began to remove their account books from the city to avoid the danger of destruction.[10] General Gage commented upon the dangerously high pitch of emotion exhibited by the rioters, which in his eyes nearly approached rebellion, and would, had matters gone much further, have produced dreadful consequences.[11] In far off Johnstown, Sir William Johnson was shocked at the reported violence of the demonstration and the "...audacious Insult on ... [the] Officers of the Crown...".[12] Yet despite the cautious sentiments expressed by these popular royal officials, the disorders were to continue.

What was particularly striking about the mob action in the months that followed, was the manner in which it reflected the sentiments of the New York

---

[8]For the role of Livingston in the Stamp Act Congress see *Authentic Account of the Proceedings of the Congress Held at New York in MDCCLKXV on the Subject of the American Stamp Act* (Annapolis, Md.: 1767), pp. 3,8; and Dangerfield, *Livingston*, p. 27.

[9]*Ibid.*, p. 36.

[10]Editorial Note, *The Papers of Sir William Johnson* (13 vols. to date, Albany: The University of the State of New York, 1921-__), IV, 872 (hereafter *Johnson Papers*).

[11]To the Common Council of New York City, Nov. 14, 1765, Boston *Evening Post*, Nov. 25, 1765.

[12]To Cadwallader Colden, Nov. 15, 1765, *Johnson Papers*, IV, 869.

Bar. In his journal Captain John Montressor pointed to the lawyers as being "... at the bottom of this disloyal Insurrection and seconded by many people of property...".[13] Even more revealing is Montressor's later notation concerning Sons of Liberty placards suggesting that the citizens of New York "... hunt as with Hounds John Cogshill Knapp, a lawyer interloped amongst them."[14]

The unhappy tale of John Cogshill Khapp, a member of the Inner Temple who tried to break the monopoly of the New York City lawyers was a story known throughout the city. John Jay doubtless followed its details in the weekly press. In June and July of 1764 Knapp and Charles Morse, a member of Clement's Inn, arrived in New York and opened offices as scriveners and registers of deeds. Morse shortly thereafter suspended operations, but Knapp persisted and expanded the scope of his employments to include placing of mortgage money and acting as a broker for the sale of slaves.[15] It was his attempt, completely unsuccessful, to practice law without applying for admission in accordance with New York procedures, that raised the ire of the legal fraternity. In July of 1764 the sign in front of his office was torn down and the persecuted barrister condemned the incident in the newspaper, claiming that since he was admitted to practice in England he should be permitted to practice in the courts of New York.[16] By August of the same year he inserted an advertisement in the papers advising his clients that "... notwithstanding the many undeserving private Insults Mr. Knapp has been shown ... he is fully determined to persevere in this his undertaking ...".[17] When a month later he moved his office to Rotten-Row, the members of the profession may

---

[13]New York Historical Society *Collections*. XIV, 339.

[14]*Ibid*. p. 342.

[15]New York *Gazette or Weekly Post Boy*, June 14, July 5, 12, 1764.

[16]*Ibid*., July 26, 1764.

[17]*Ibid*., Aug. 2, 1764.

have indulged themselves in a few choice comments concerning Knapp's new address.[18]

Vindication for the New York lawyers seemed in sight when they were able to acquaint the public with the fact that Knapp had been convicted of theft in England, and subsequently transported to the colonies. According to the information sent by an anonymous subscriber to the New York *Gazette* or *Weekly Post Boy*, over one hundred persons had appeared at his trial to testify against him.[19] After this notice Knapp's weekly ad was suspended until the twenty-fifth of April, by which time he apparently found that he could profitably continue in business despite the unfavorable publicity.[20] Having failed to discourage Knapp by revealing his background, the New York lawyers must have viewed with satisfaction the call of the Sons of Liberty for the use of more forceful techniques to rid the province of his presence. Whether the members of the Bar were directly responsible for the attitude of the Sons of Liberty is of course a matter of conjecture; nevertheless their unity of opinion with the rioters concerning Knapp seem to give considerable weight to Montressor's opinion that the lawyers had a role in the direction of the Stamp Act rioting. Of one thing we can be certain--the members of this closely knit professional group must have been gratified to see their interests would be protected by the Stamp Act mob.

As November passed into December matters in the Province of New York began to get out of control and civil authority became ineffective. The appearance of the first stamped paper from Quebec on December sixteenth caused a major disturbance the following evening.[21] On the twenty-of December imprisoned debtors broke out of the jais, having despaired of release because of

---

[18]*Ibid.*. Sept. 13, 1764.

[19]*Ibid.*, Mar. 7, 1765.

[20]New York *Gazette or Weekly Post Boy*, Apr. 25, 1765.

[21]Boston *Evening Post*, Dec. 23, 30, 1765, New York Historical Society *Collections*, XIV, 342, 343.

the suspension of legal processes.[22] A snow fall on the eighteenth of December, coupled with the preoccupation with making new effigies for burning, created a temporary lull in the disorders.[23] With the New Year there came new rioting in New York City, and Montressor noted: "Children nightly trampooze the Streets with lanterns upon Poles and hallowing, but allowed of, the Magistracy either approve of it, or do not dare suppress it, though children."[24] By this time the disorders had moved into the countryside. In early January a belated New Year's celebration of an Albany volunteer fire department resulted in a disturbance modelled after the New York City violence of November 1, 1765. The leading citizens of Albany, encouraged by the reports of the delegates to the General Assembly and gaining additional courage from alcoholic refreshments, decided to stage their own Stamp Act riot and selected postmaster Henry Van Schaack as their victim.[25] With this spread of disturbances throughout the Province even Peter Jay's "peaceable" retreat at Rye must have seemed relatively unsafe by February of 1766.

When John Jay left New York City to spend the spring months at Rye, he bade a reluctant farewell to his friend, Robert R. Livingston, Jr., who accompanied his family to their estate at Clermont.[26] In the three years since the

---

[22]Boston *Evening Post*, Jan. 6, 1766.

[23]New York Historical Society Collections XIV, 343.

[24]Captain John Montressor, *ibidem.*

[25]*Ibid.*, p. 345; John Glen, Jr. to Sir William Johnson, Jan. 7, 1766, *Johnson Papers*, V, 5; Boston *Evening Post*, Feb. 3, 1766; for an interesting analysis of the Albany riot, and Van Schaack's reaction, see Beverly McAnear, "The Albany Stamp Act Riots," *William and Mary Quarterly*. 3rd ser., IV, 486-498.

[26]On March 4, 1766 Jay was at Rye and Livingston was at Clermont, see letter of that date, JJ to Livingston, Livingston Papers, Box 1; Jay was still at Rye on April 25, 1766, Benjamin Kissam to JJ, Johnston, *Corres.*, I, 3.

young men had become acquainted at King's College, their association had grown quite close, and their parting by the Stamp Act crisis must have been distateful to both. It was in March of 1765 that the two young men, after due consideration to their mutual professional interests and similar social positions, decided that they should enter into an agreement to admonish each other for defects of character.[27] The friendship thus perfected was one formed by the stabilizing effects of unlike temperaments rather than by the compatibility of similar personalities; Jay was the first to admit his lack of social graces while Livingston seems to have taken to heart the admonitions of his somewhat somber friend.[28]

While it is most unlikely that Jay and Livingston comtemplated a professional partnership as early as March of 1765,[29] their contrasting but complementary personalities made such an arrangement most suitable. Jay's difficulty in oral recitations while at College, while at College, was overcome by perseverance; he became a powerful and persuasive speaker by 1778, but in youth he suffered from this limitation.[30] Livingston on the other hand excited favorable comments concerning the delivery of his commencement speech in 1765.[31] Jay was scholarly and methodical while Livingston was urbane and impetuous. Although law partnerships were nearly unheard of in colonial New York, these two young men were

---

[27]JJ to Livingston, Apr. 2, 1765; Livingston Papers, Box 1; Apr. 19, 1765, Chalconer Papers, Duke University Libraries, Durham, N.C.

[28]Monaghan, *Jay*, p. 37.

[29]This is the assertion of Dangerfield at *Livingston*, p.44.

[30]Monaghan, *Jay*, pp. 27, 28, characterizes Jay's style as "quiet and limpid," but Conrad Gerard asserted his persuasive speeches caused his opponents to elect Jay to the Presidency of Continental Congress to eliminate him from debate, John J. Meng, ed., *Despatches and Instructions of of Conrad Alexandre Gerard, 1778-1780* (Baltimore: Johns Hopkins Press, 1939) pp. 424-425.

[31]Dangerfield, *Livingston*, p. 47.

the most likely to benefit from such a professional alliance.[32] In the years to come their friendship, formed to cure defects of character, was to become the basis upon which both would build a strong foundation for success in the practice of law. Jay's affiliation with Livingston was therefore far more significant than he, in 1765, could have believed or imagined.

The two friends, after their New England "frolick" in the winter of 1765, parted in the early months of 1766. At his family's home John could indulge his penchant for riding which earlier had induced him to obtain permission to keep a horse at New York City. According to the family tradition Peter Jay was reluctant to grant the request, but was won over when his son pointed out that keeping an animal would facilitate frequent visits to Rye. This reasoning prevailed over his father's conviction that horses were poor companions for young men, and John had his mount.[33] In addition to his own horse, Jay also had charge of a lamed horse of Benjamin Kissam, which was being pastured at Rye during the spring of 1766.[34]

Because Lindley Murray's term of service with Kissam was drawing to a close, Jay spent a considerable part of his time at Rye in a careful application to law studies. In addition he was engaged in reading Plato, Montesquieu, Shakespeare, the *Spectator Papers* and Thomas Sheridan's *Lectures on Elocution*.[35] The knowledge acquired from these works would doubtless have been of assistance to Jay in the preparation of his commencement address in 1767 at which time he would receive his Master of Arts degree from King's College.

Jay, already a veteran at the writing desk of a law clerk, was appalled at the manner in which his friend Livingston had spent the months of freedom. As

---

[32]For comment upon the infrequence of law partnerships see Alexander, *A Revolutionary Conservative*, p. 35.

[33]Wm. Jay, *Life*. I, 21; George Pellew, *John Jay* (Boston: Houghton, Mifflin & Co., 1890), p. 17.

[34]Kissam to JJ, Apr. 25, 1766, Johnston, *Corres*., I, 3.]

[35]Mongahan, *Jay*, p. 38.

As early as March of 1766 he called his friend to account, admonishing him,

> You have been highly entertained of late and by your Account of the matter have obtained every Qualification necessary to form a Buck and entitle you to the appellation of a Man of Pleasure... Recollect for a Moment what time has elapsed since we have been free from the Drudgery of Business--that such an Opportunity will probably not again offer, and therefore that it was by no means to be neglected.[36]

Each had spent his vacation in a manner suited to his own personality, and Jay was perhaps too harsh in his censure Livingston. Their time of leisure would last another two months, and it was not until late summer that the Supreme Court of Judicature would be in full operation again. In the intervening period the Livingston family was to experience some very unpleasant incidents, and Jay's mentor, Benjamin Kissam, was to gain new stature in the eyes of his young clerk.

When April of 1766 arrived the New York lawyers, deprived of fees for the past five months were eager for news of the repeal of the Stamp Act. Packetboat after packetboat arrived without bringing definite reports concerning the passage of the repealing bill through Parliament. Viewing their account books with sinking hearts, the attorneys experienced joy and dismay as reports of repeal were quickly countermanded by later information.[37] As William Livingston was later to note dismally in his records "The small am[oun]t of this years profit [is] owing to the Stamp Act."[38] Added to their discomfort was the continued pressure from the Sons of Liberty demanding that the courts be reopened and that business go on as

---

[36]Mar. 4, 1766, Livingston Papers, Box 1.

[37]Robert R. Livingston to Robert Livingston, Mar. 18, April 12, 1766, Livingston Papers, Box 1.

[38]Quoted by Milton M. KLein, at *William and Mary Quarterly* 3rd ser., XV, 354.

usual, but without the use of stamped paper.[39]

On the twenty-fifth of April Benjamin Kissam wrote to Jay at Rye, requesting that his horse be sent to New York City since he was planning to accompany the Rev. Mr. Charles Inglis, an Anglican missionary, on a jaunt to Philadelphia. If news of the repeal should arrive in his absence, Jay was to cone down to New York iirmediately, because absence, Jay was to come down to New York immediately, because

> ... upon the Repeal of the Stamp Act, we shall doubtless have a luxuriant Harvest of Law, I would not willingly, after the long Famine we have had, miss reaping my part of the crop. ... as soon as [the news] reaches you, I beg you'll come down and be ready to secure all business that offers.[40]

In the early morning hours of the day after this letter was written, Kissam's sleep was interrupted by the ringing of bells, announcing the arrival of news that the hated Act had been repealed. Kissam did not notice the dissonance of the bells, as did the British Army Captain, John Montressor, for good news no matter how received is pleasing to the ear.[41] Unfortunately Kissam's sleep was disturbed in vain, for again the news proved to be inaccurate. Since notice of royal approval of the repealing bill did not reach New York City until the twentieth of May, the Suprene Court of Judicature term at the end of April dealt with only criminal cases.[42]

---

[39]Becker, *History Political Parties*, p.40.

[40]Johnston, *Corres*, I, 3.

[41]Kissam to JJ, Apr. 26, 1766, Columbia University Libraries, Special Collections; Montressor complained that "... the Bells of this place ... having no peal made a most hideous Din." New York Historical Society *Collections*, IXV, 362.

[42]*Ibid.*, p. 367; Peter Hasenclever to Sir William Johnson, *Johnson*

Repeal for many residents of New York was far from a joyous occasion, for once it occurred the relentless processes of debt collection were again free to operate.[43] Among the most debt-ridden residents of the Province were the tenants of the Hudson River manorial lords, kept landless by the realty engrossing practices of their landlords and oppressed by the high rate of perpetual rents exacted from them. As repeal became more likely in the spring of 1766, the tenant farmers of the Hudson River valley took courage from the tenderness shown by the authorities toward the New York City mobs, and scattered uprisings began to take place.[44] By late April New York City was alarmed by the march of several hundred tenants of Van Cortlandt manor, who appeared at the outskirts of the city and threatened to burn the townhouse of their landlord if he would not execute deeds to convey to them full title to their farms.[45] The first of May found five hundred tenants sullenly encamped at Kingsbridge while to the north riots broke out in Westchester and Dutchess counties.[46] On the seventeenth of May the unrest spread to Livingston Manor where "... hundreds of Tenants ... turned levellers."[47] The 28th Regiment of Regulars sent up river to quell the "insurrection"

Papers. V, 202-203; Min. S. Ct. Jud., July 31, 1764-Aug. 2, 1766, p. 383.

[43]Morgan, *Stamp Act Crisis*, pp. 169, 172; Irving Mark, *Agrarian Conflicts in Colonial New York* (New York: Columbia University Press, 1940); p. 135. See also testimony in Irving Mark and Oscar Handlin's article, "Land Cases in Colonial New York, 1765-1767-*The King v. William Prendergast,*" *New York University Law Quarterly Review*, XIX (1942), 164-194.

[44]Mark, *Agrarian Conflicts*, p. 139; Sir Henry Moore to Secretary Henry Conway, Apr. 30, 1766, Edmund B. O'Callaghan, *Documents Relative to the Colonial History of the State of New York* (15 vols., Albany: Weed, Parsons & Co., 1853-1887), VII, 825 (hereafter *Doc. Rel. Col. Hist.*).

[45]Apr. 29, 1766, New York Historical Society, *Collections*, XXV, 363.

[46]Mark, *Agrarian Conflicts*, p. 139; New York Historical Society *Collections*, XIV, 363.

[47]*Ibid*., p. 366.

after the rioters had been proclaimed traitors, succeeded in restoring peace to the area, but not before seven militia men had been killed in an affray with the tenants.[48] Reporting to London on the success of the 28th Regiment, Governor Sir Henry Moore informed the home government that the leaders would be tried by a Court of Oyer and Terminer within eight or ten days.[49] This was truly speedy justice.

This was the sorry state of Provincial affairs when John Jay arrived at New York City to resume his duties as a law clerk. By the twenty-seventh of May his friend Livingston was back at his desk in the office of William Livingston,[50] and Jay had probably returned to the City even earlier due to the urgings of Kissam to "secure all business." As law offices began to reopen throughout New York City, the Governor and Council were faced with the task of restoring orderly civil government in New York; their first consideration was the trial of the agrarian "traitors" scheduled for late July.

The Court which sat in judgment on the tenant farmers was not the Supreme Court of Judicature, as asserted by Irving Mark and Oscar Handlin, but rather a Court of Oyer and Terminer raised with some difficulty from among the lawyers and prominent men of the Province.[51] William Smith, Jr. recognizing the imponderable political duplications of such service, was most reluctant to accept

---

[48]Mark, *Agrarian Conflicts* p. 142; Cadwallader Colden to Secretary Henry Conway, June 24, 1766, *Doc. Rel. Col. Hist.*, VII, 833 (contrasting treatment of Sons of Liberty and tenant rioters).

[49]*Ibid.*. VII, 845.

[50]Indenture of that date, William Livingston Papers 1695-1774, Massachusetts Historical Society.

[51]Mark and Handlin, at *New York University Law Quarterly Review*, XIX, 167. But see William H.W. Sabine, ed., *Historical Memoirs from 16 March 1763 to 9 July 1776 of William Smith* ... (New York: Colburn & Tegg, 1956), p. 34; also see Sir Henry Moore to Lords of Trade, Aug. 12, 1766, *Doc. Rel. Col. Hist.*. VII, 849.

the Governor's commission to sit upon the Court, but finally he consented so.[52] Chief Justice Daniel Horsmanden presided over the deliberations of the Court of Oyer and Terminer which included Whitehead Hicks, Thomas Jones and John Morin Scott,[53] It was to this tribunal that Prendergast issued his challenge that if opposition to government was rebellion, no member of the Court was entitled to sit in his case.[54] James Duane, son-in-law to the Lord of Livingston Manor, welcomed the opportunity to serve with Attorney General John Tabor Kempe as counsel for the Crown.[55]

To that Court of Oyer and Terminer rode Benjamin Kissam, entrusting his newly found cases before the Supreme Court to his clerks and his court appearances to John Woods,[56] Upon himself he had taken the burdensome and unpopular task of defending Prendergast, the leader of the farmer rebels. While it is possible that Kissam was assigned to the defense of the accused in accordance with established English practice in treason trials, it is equally possible that he volunteered his services because of his sympathy for their plight. To John Jay at New York Kissam wrote,

> Here we are, and are likely to be so, I am afraid, these ten days. There are no less than forty-seven persons charged, all upon three several indictments, with the murder of those persons who lost their lives in the affray with the sheriff. Four or five of them are in jail, and will be tried

---

[52]Sabine, ed., *Smith Memoirs*, p. 34.

[53]For members of Court see Mark and Handlin, "Land Cases ...", *New York University Law Quarterly Review*. XIX, 384.

[54]The remark, on hearsay evidence no doubt, is recounted in Montressor's journal, New York Historical Society *Collections*, XIV, 384. ,

[55]Alexander, *A Revolutionary Conservative*, p. 45.

[56]Min. S. Ct. Jud., July 31, 1764-Aug. 2, 1766 p. 387.

> this day; what their fate will be, God only knows; it is terrible to think that so many lives should be at stake upon the principles of constructive murder; for I suppose that the immediate agency of but a very few of the party can be proved.[57]

The references to constructive murder would indicate Kissam was alluding to the trials of Prendergast's followers which began on August 14, 1766.[58] While there was cross examination of the witnesses for the Crown, there is no direct evidence that Kissam took part in those cases although it seems quite likely that he did so.

We do know that Kissam appeared on behalf William Prendergast and advanced strong legal arguments for his acquittal of high treason. Citing English precedents, Kissam argued that Prendergast and his associates were asserting their private rights rather than attempting to right a public grievance or attempt to alter the law.[59] In short they had private grievances which, under English law, could be the subject of riots without subjecting the participants to the penalties of high treason.[60] While this plea must have been quite persuasive with

---

[57]Aug. 25, 1766, Wm. Jay, *Life*. I, 21.

[58]Notes on July 1766 Assizes in Dutchess County, New York Historical Society, New York City. (King v. McArthur et al.).

[59]The citations are given by Mark and Handlin, at *New York University Law Quarterly Review*, XIV, 194. The citation to Sir Michael Foster, *A Report of Some Proceedinqs on the Commission of Oyer and Terminer* ... (Oxford: At the Clarendon Press, 1762) [copy at Columbia Law Library], p. 118, is incorrect, due to an error by the writer of the manuscript notes.

[60]Citing *ibid*., p. 211; Sir John Kelyng, *A Report of Diverse Cases in Pleas of the Crown* ... (London: Isaac Cleave, 1708); [Association of the Bar of the City of New York Library], p. 75; Sir John Popham, *Reports and Cases* (London: Thomas Roycroft, 1656) [Columbia Law Library], p. 122; and William Hawkins, *A Treatise of the Pleas of the Crown* (2d ed. rev., London: E & R Nutt & R. Gosling, 1724-1726 [Coumbia Law Library], I, 34, 37.

the Court, the very magnitude of the uprising cast strong doubts upon the private objectives of the participants. In addition the rioters had interfered with the administration of justice, and were alleged to have set up their own courts. All in all, the court found grounds to distinguish the precedents cited by Kissam from the case presented to the Court.

The other argument Kissam advanced in favor of the acquittal of Prendergast was less susceptible of distinction by the Court. It was simply the assertion that, under the law of England, there were no accessories to the crime of treason. All were to be considered principals.[61] Since all of the rioters were not indictable for high treason, then Prendergast was also not indictable. In the absence of the Court's opinion we do not know why this argument was rejected. On the record of the case it would seem that this point was the strongest legal issue to be raised in favor of the acquittal of Prendergast.

If an argument could be made on the law concerning Prendergast's innocence of high treason, there was little that could be said on the facts that would help the unfortunate man. The Crown's attorneys had assembled a large number of witnesses; from an appearance bond that survives it seems clear that at least some of these "witnesses" had participated in the riots and had been promised immunity from prosecution if they would testify against Prendergast and his more active followers.[62] Based on the evidence of these men and officials harassed by Prendergast, the Court found Prendergast guilty of high treason against the King. Then followed the ancient sentence, which evoked a horrified disbelief in William Hawkins over forty years earlier; as Hawkins relates the traditional sentence it is as follows:

> he shall be ... hanged by the Neck, and cut down alive, and that his Entrails

---

[61]Foster, *ibid.*, p. 213; Kelyng, *ibid.*, p. 19.

[62]Appearance Bond dated Aug. 1, 1766, Miscellaneous Manusripts, Dutchess County, New York Historical Society, New York City, in which most of the men on the recognizance are yeomen from the southern precinct of Dutchess County.

> be taken out and burnt before his Face, and his Head cut off, and his Body divided into four Quarters, and his Head and Quarters disposed of at the King's pleasure.[63]

Concluded Hawkins in scholarly disbelief, "And I find little or no Variation in Substance from this Judgment, ... ".[64] Fortunately the difficulty of finding an executioner, coupled with a stay of execution from the Governor and a royal pardon, saved Prendergast from this barbaric punishment.[65]

John Jay's attitudes concerning Kissam's defense of Prendergast does not survive to enlighten the curiosity of historians. Yet Kissam's letter to Jay concerning the trials reveals a compassion and humanity that is noteworthy. His deprecation of guilt by association evidences a deep respect for what we would today term "due process of law, " but which in those more pedestrian times would have been considered a rule of evidence in criminal causes. The passage reveals a warm-hearted man, shocked by the violence of the agrarian revolt, but nevertheless reluctant to permit a wholesale execution of the participants to satiate the thirst for revenge that permeated the propertied classes. Can it not be assumed that John Jay, in spite of his mother's Van Cortlandt relatives and his friendship for the Livingstons, would have been impressed by the professional responsibility demonstrated by Kissam in the Prendergast case?

The years 1765 and 1766 were packed with events of immense importance for the Province of New York, happenings which deepened Jay's understanding of the political realities of his day. During those years he had found a dearly beloved friend in Robert R. Livingston, Jr. , and had achieved the confidence and respect of his teacher, Benjamin Kissam. These were but the first of many trying times that would shape his life; having passed through this

---

[63]*Pleas of the Crown*, II, 443.

[64]*Ibid.*

[65]Staughton Lynd, *Antifederalism in Dutchess County*, (Chicago: Loyola University Press, 1962) pp. 50,51.

period of civil disturbance, and having seen its effect upon the lives and emotions of men, he would thereafter treasure stable government and society.

IV. FROM CLERK TO COUNSELLOR: 1766-1768

One of the remarkable aspects of John Jay's legal clerkship was the spirit of comraderie and mutual respect which prevailed between Jay and Benjamin Kissam. So unusual was such a cooperative attitude between lawyer and clerk that Paul Hamlin cites it as one of the few examples of pleasurable legal education in the Province of New York.[1]

At a very early stage in Jay's clerkship his father Peter Jay wrote of his satisfaction at the fondness Kissam displayed for John and the care which Kissam took in instructing the toung in the intricacies of the law.[2] As the years passed and Jay's usefulness to his master increased, their relationship began to approach that of partners in the practice of law rather than the unequal relationship of lawyer and clerk. The mere fact that such a situation was permitted to exist is a tribute not only to Kissam's self-confidence, but also to Jay's discretion and good judgment in not mistaking friendship for a license to engage in undue familiarity or public insubordination.

One of the most sparkling letters ever written by Jay is a witty reply to an inquiry by Kissam, revealing not only the sharp wit of the clerk, but also the easy relationship between the two. While he was attending the Court of Oyer and Terminer in August of 1766, Kissam wrote to Jay to discover the state of his practice in New York City. To this Jay replied,

> You desire me to 'give you some account of the business of the office'; whether my apprehension is more dull than common, or whether I have slept too late this morning and the drowsy god is still hovering over my sense I know not; but I really do not understand what you have me do.[3]

Did Kissam wish to know the names of the new clients, or what was doubt-

---

[1]*Legal Education*, pp. 43, 44.

[2]To David Peloquin, Oct. 9, 1764, Peter Jay Letterbook #3, Columbia University Libraries, Special collections.

[3]Wm. Jay, *Life*. I, 17-19.

less more important, the amount of their fees, or did he wish to know how often his clerks went into the office? Concerning the last interrogatory John pleaded that a man's evidence is not to be admitted in his own cause, and then continued,

> If I should tell you that I am all day in the office, and as attentive to your interest as I would be to my own, I suspect you would think it such an impeachment of my modesty as would not operate very powerfully in favour of my veracity.[4]

Remembering his status as a clerk, Jay added that he would be more straight-laced, but he felt that Kissam would understand that no disrespect was intended. To this Kissam replied that he had been delighted to receive Jay's letter, and would be most offended if Jay did not feel free to write in such a vein in the future. He wished only to know whether the office business had decreased during his absence, and granted Jay a "*nolls prosequi* for the heinous crime of writing a free and familiar letter...".[5] The lawyer's reply is clear evidence of the value he attached to what he called his "... high and inestimable privilege of friendship" with his young clerk.[6]

It was fortunate that such a pleasant atmosphere prevailed in Kissam's office, for the years of clerkship ahead were not to be significantly easier than the drudgery of Jay's first two years. Lindley Murray's clerkship during the latter months of 1766, and Jay was left alone to handle the endless tasks of copying judgment rolls and preparing papers for litigation.[7] This work, coupled with the more important duties of scheduling court appearances and

---

[4]*Ibidem.*

[5]*Ibid.*, I, 19-21.

[6]*Ibidem.*

[7]The only source from which I have been able to find the date of termination of Murray's clerkship is Frank, ed., *Memoirs of Lindley Murray*, p. 35. The court minute shows he was admitted on Oct. 20, 1769, Min. S. Ct. Jud., Apr. 18, 1769-May 2, 1772, N.Y. Co. Clerk, Hall of Records, N.Y.C.

maintaining the law registers, became too much for Jay,[8] and Kissam had frequent recourse to the various scriveners who prepared forms for the use of attorneys.[9] Of the judgment rolls that survive from the last two years of Jay's clerkship, thirteen are written entirely in his hand; the remaining twenty-one bear his handwriting on the endorsement and in the amount awarded in judgment.

When not engaged in one of the above tasks, Jay would have been

---

[8]Judgment rolls in Jay's hand are as follows:

Barnes v. Forman, 162 G-10	Jauncy v. Hicks. 119 B-3
Barnes v. Woolsey, 119 K-4	Runedet v. Mapes, 99 A-5
Corsa & Bull v. Barnard, 157 K-1	Swansea v. Corsine Extrs., 26 C-3
Corsa & Bull v. Van Rensselaer, 105 H-9	Titus & Willets v. Seaman et al. 153 A-8
Hunter & Birdsell v. Smith, 158 K-l	Weaver v. J. Boyd, 155 K-7
Jackson ex dem Van Rensselaer v. Lansingh, 118 K-3	Willis v. Brown, 53 E-5
	Wright v. Burn, 109 K-4

All Parchments, N.Y. Co. Clerk, Hall of Records, N.Y.C.

[9]Those not in Jay's hand, but originating in Kissam's office are:

Barnes v. Noble, 178 H-10	Halsted v. Sands, 168 A-2
Barnes v. Noble, 9 F-8	Hyatt v. Fowler, 67 F-3
Birdsall v. Birdsall, 121 F-6	Kissam v. Van Rensselaer, 4 F-6
Birdsall v. Knapp, 40 K-7	Lawrence v. Willet, 36 F-9
Bloodgood v. Bloodgood, 20 E-5	Murray v. Davis, 101 F-5
Bull v. Boyd & Boyd, 90 C-8	Pell v. Wright, 97 G-7
Bull v. Boyd & Boyd, 197 D-9	Shearwood v. Case, 129 D-7
Cairns v. Van Rensselaer, 131 B-l	Townshend v. Carpenter, 78 K-6
Grenell v. Rapalie, 11 E-5	Van Geisen v. Ogden, 13 E-5
Hallet v. Totten, 11 E-5	Watson & Murray v. Frost, 113 E-5
	Weaver v. E. Boyd, 141 B-9

All Parchments, N.Y. Co. Clerk, Hall of Records, N.Y.C.

involved in any one of the numerous non-professional tasks that arise in the operation of a law office. For example in March of 1767, he prepared a bill for services rendered by Kissam in regard to an involuntary assignment for the benefit of creditors.[10] While few examples of law clerk's work have survived from the colonial period, there is no reason to believe that the routine correspondence of the office and the financial management of client's accounts were not entrusted to experienced law clerks. Looking back to the time of his clerkship with John Jay, Lindley Murray remarked that as a clerk John was "... remarkable for strong reasoning powers, comprehensive views, indefatigable application, and uncommon firmness of mind."[11] From the catalogue of tasks assigned to clerks, it would seem that the cardinal virtue of John Jay was his "indefatigable application" which sustained him through many pressing and onerous duties.

During the two and a half years following the repeal of the Stamp Act, Kissam's practice in the Supreme Court of Judicature seems to have become more diversified. Jay thus benefited from opportunities to handle an action in ejectment,[12] an assignment for the benefit of creditors,[13] and an action on a protested bill of exchange.[14] One case that must have attracted Jay's attention as he drew up the judgment roll was that of Wright v. Burn.[15] Young Nicholas Wright had

---

[10]Mar. 29, 1767, Bill to Florus Bancker, et al. Trustees of James Duthrie, New York Historical Society, New York Miscellaneous Manuscripts, ix, 22.

[11]Frank, ed., *Memoirs of Lindley Murray*, p. 34.

[12]Jackson ex dem Van Rensselaer v. Lansingh, Parchment 118 K-3, Min. S. Ct. Jud., Oct. 21, 1766-Jan. 21, 1769, pp. 457, 481, N.Y. Co. Clerk, Hall of Records, N.Y.C.

[13]Trustees for Creditors of Dods v. Robinson, Parchment 10 K-10, *ibid.*, see advertisement in New York *Mercury*, 16, 1767.

[14]Mirray v. Davis, Parchment 101 F-5, *ibid.*

[15]Parchment 109 K-4, *ibid.*

been apprenticed to a joiner named Andrew Burn. The indenture was for a two year period and the apprentice was to receive a stipulated salary during the period service. After the two years were completed and Wright had secured his release, he brought suit against his former master for the non-payment of his salary. The former apprentice recovered £ 88 12s. 11d. from Burn. Jay could hardly have failed to compare this short term apprenticeship with a salary, to his own apprenticeship agreement with Kissam for a five year term with a premium payable to Kissam and to the disadvantage of his own situation.[16]

Events subsequent to the commencement of Jay's clerkship rendered obsolete the agreement he had made with Kissam in January of 1764. By a 1767 rule of the Supreme Court of Judicature, the term of service required of college graduates was reduced to three instead of five years.[17] In addition the period of suspension of law practice by the Stamp Act introduced doubt concerning when Jay's clerkship should terminate. What seems to have occurred in Jay's case was that he and Kissam agreed to make an allowance for the six month's suspension of practice by the Stamp Act, and then decided that their mutual interest would best be served by Jay's applying for admission to the Bar about a year earlier than provided in the original agreement. Another factor which might have influenced this decision was the fact that Robert R. Livingston, Jr., who was a year junior to Jay at King's College, was to complete his clerkship in 1768 and would apply for admission in October of 1768. Jay was probably one of the few lawyers in colonial New York who were trained during the course of a four year clerkship; from the evidence that survives it seems that he would have preferred a shorter clerkship, but did not blame Kissam for holding him to serve beyond the three year period fixed in 1767.

In addition to practice in the Supreme Court of Judicature, Kissam also represented the claimants in a salvage case before the Court of Vice Admiralty of the Province of New York. John Jay drew up the libel in May of 1768, bringing to the attention of Judge Richard Morris the sad tale of the sinking of the brigantine

---

[16]The fee paid to Kissam was probably £200; see discussion at p. 9, above.

[17]Hamlin, *Legal Education*, pp. 37, 39.

The Nancy.[18] Heavily laden with textiles, hats, buttons and hardware, the brigantine had sprung a leak and her crew had worked themselves to the point of exhaustion at the bilge pumps. Nevertheless she continued to settle further into the Atlantic, and the crew were at the point of desperation when the snow *Amelia*, on her westward voyage from London to New York, came upon the helpless vessel. Just a short time after the cargo and crew were transferred to the decks of *Amelia*, the ill-starred *Nancy* sank out of sight.

This dramatic rescue, related in the libel drawn by Jay, formed the basis for the salvage claim on the part of the owners and crew of the Amelia. The goods had been badly water-soaked and a prompt sale was imperative lest the cargo become completely useless and unmarketable. Just eight days after the libel was filed, Robert Murray as owner of the Amelia was given custody of the cargo of the Nancy, and the goods, after the necessary preservative measures were taken, were sold at public auction.[19]

Unlike the Supreme Court of Judicature, the Vice Admiralty Court because of its small docket and civil law antecedents, received evidence in the form of depositions in answer to written interrogatories. For this reason we can obtain a very good reconstruction of the facts of the case. In regard to the case of Sinclair v. Goods of the Nancy, we can see that the libellants, represented by Kissam, had a very good claim that was supported by a number of

---

[18]Robert Sinclair (Snow Amelia) v. Goods from the Brigantine Nancy, decision reported at Charles M. Hough, *Reports of Cases in the Vice Admiralty of the Province of New York ...* (New Haven: Yale University Press, 1925), pp. 225-227.

[19]Libel drawn by Jay, filed May 4, 1768, affidavit of Robert Sinclair dated May 9, 1768, inventory of goods May 11, 1768, account of sale at auction dated August 23, 1768, Vice Admiralty Court, Province of New York, File Papers, Salvage Papers A-Z, National Archives, Washington, D.C. (hereafter, Vice Admiralty Papers, Salvage A-Z).

corroborating witnesses.[20] Unfortunately a few of the passengers of the *Amelia* felt that they too should share in the salvage rights since they had assisted crew of the Amelia in removing the cargo from the Nancy.[21] It was not until January of 1769 that Judge Morris came to a decision concerning the proceeds on the sale of the salvaged goods. He awarded one-half of the value of the goods to the owners, crew and passengers of the Amelia, and the other half to the original owners of the goods. He refused to make any apportionment of the proceeds between the crew and passengers of the Amelia, but did declare the owners of the Amelia were in any event entitled to one-quarter of the proceeds, the other one-quarter to be divided between the crew and passengers.[22] Presumably the crew members and passengers were left to apply to one of the common law courts to determine their respective shares in the salvage.

Admiralty cases were by no means a regular part of Kissam's practice, but John Jay was fortunate during his four years with Kissam to have the opportunity to work on two causes in admiralty. During the first four months off his clerkship he assisted Kissam on the case of Apthorpe v. Gregg (The Prince of Wales),[23] The *Prince of Wales* was bound for St. Eusatius and was laden with European goods; she was seized by customs collector Lambert Moore for failing to file a statement of cargo and destination as required by law. Kissam successfully opposed the libel by the customs officers by showing that the captain had made a timely attempt to file the required papers, but that the naval and customs

---

[20]Interrogatory dated May 13, 1768, depositions dated May 14, 17, 1768, all in *ibid.*

[21]Claiins dated Sept. 6, 1768, Jan. 16, 1769, in *ibid.*

[22]Hough, *Vice Admiralty Cases*, pp. 225-227; the original decree is at Vice Admiralty Papers, Salvage A-Z, and except for minor variations in capitalization is as reproduced by Hough.

[23]Hough, *Vice Admiralty Cases*, pp. 220-222.

offices were closed.[24] Despite John Tabor Kempe's assertion on the part of the customs officials that the claimant's answer was "uncertain, untrue and insufficient to be replied to ...",[25] the Court held for the claimant and ordered the customs officers to release the goods to the captain.[26] While a notice of appeal to the High Court of Admiralty was filed, Hough states that the appeal was not perfected.[27] Throughout the file papers the neat handwriting of John Jay attests his contribution to Kissam's successful defense; he engrossed the claimant's answer to the libel, and drew up the stipulation of facts between the parties.[28]

While this training in admiralty law was of little practical value to John Jay as a lawyer, since he never appeared in the Vice Admiralty Court as either proctor or advocate, it did provide him with a working knowledge of admiralty procedures which was to be of considerable use to him in his career during and after the American Revolution.[29] As a diplomat and Secretary for Foreign Affairs, Jay would be presented with several questions involving admiralty law. His introduction to these subjects while a law clerk was later to serve him very well.

Admiralty law was not the only aspect of English civilian law that prevailed in the province of New York, and Jay as a law clerk came into contact with still another civil law court. This was the Prerogative Court which, under the authority of the Governor, exercised jurisdiction in the area of admitting wills to

---

[24]State of Facts Stipulated by Parties, Aug. 9, 1764, Vice Admiralty Papers, Customs Cases M-Z, National Archives, Washington, D.C.

[25]Replication, July 16, 1764, *ibid.*

[26]Hough, *Vice Admiralty Cases*, p. 222.

[27]*Ibid*, p. 219.

[28]Both in Vice Admiralty Papers, Customs M-Z, under dates July 3, 1764 and Aug. 9, 1764.

[29]For lack of practice by Jay in vice admiralty see Vice Admiralty Minutes, 1758-1774, Vol. III, National Archives, Washington, D.C., *passim.*

probate and granting administration over estates. As if to emphasize the ecclesiastical origin of its powers, the New York Prerogative Court utilized a seal with a bishop's mitre as its principal device.

Upon the death of Abraham DePeyster in September of 1767 John Jay was called to testify concerning the execution of DePeyster's will and codicil.[30] Not only had Jay drawn up the codicil in his own handwriting, but he also was a subscribing witness to both the will and the codicil.[31] The young law clerk appeared before notary public John French on October 6, 1767, about two weeks after DePeyster's funeral, to make the necessary affirmations concerning the formal execution of the will and the codicil. As DePeyster died while in office as Treasurer of the Province of New York, there were numerous claims against his estate, and the administration was an extended one. Since Jay was a witness to both of the documents which constituted DePeyster's last will and testament, it seems quite probable that Kissam's office was involved in this administration, although no evidence to that effect has survived. If the estate was administered through Kissam's office, the experience gained by John Jay would have proved of great value during his years of practice.

With the varied and voluminous practice of Kissam's office, Jay would have had but little time for "extracurricular activities." However, the energy and enthusiasm of youth sustained him after his long days at the writing desk, and he found the time to engage in recreational activities. At first glance one might imagine that his membership in the Debating Club was merely a supplement to his law clerkship because advocacy is one of the necessary abilities of a lawyer. As we have already noted, Jay's public speaking did leave something

---

[30]Details concerning the funeral attended by Governor, Council and most of the prominent men of the province on Sept. 19, 1767, are at New York *Mercury*, Sept. 21, 1767.

[31]Will and codicil printed at New York Historical Society *Collections*. XXXI, 104. Original documents at Original Wills 1767-1768, Surrogate's Court, N.Y. Co., Hall of Records, N.Y.C., with affidavits of witnesses attached.

to be desired, and to that extent the Club was of professional value. However, Jay must have enjoyed these meetings, not only because of the opportunity to expound one's moral and political judgments, because the group was composed of so many close friends.[32]

The Debating Club met every Thursday evening at six, and meetings continued until ten. Members were fined six pence for tardiness and two shillings for an absence.[33] Arguments were submitted in writing to the President for that meeting, and oral debate was held according to the written plan. The procedure was not unlike the argument of points of law before a court. Of the numerous debates which were held, we have available the written arguments in only two, both of which show the extent of Jay's participation in the debate.[34]

In January of 1768 the Club debated the question, "Whether in an Absolute Monarchy it is better that the Crown should be elective than hereditary?" Jay and his associate[35] contended that elective monarchy was preferable because if the son of a King was entitled to rule his father's interest would secure him the election. If on the other hand the election was contested between members of the nobility, the elective process would guarantee a contest between men of the greatest merit, for the nobility have an equal interest with the people in the government of the state. Finally, if a man were elected king in a constitutional way

---

[32]Membership included Lindley Murray, former clerk of Kissam, Egbert Benson and Peter Van Schaack, friends from King's College, and James DeLancey, second cousin to Jay; Monaghan, *Jay*, p. 39, lists the members.

[33]Manuscripts of the Debating Society, Rules, in BV Sec (Moot), New York Historical Society, New York City (hereafter Debating Society Mss.).

[34]Debating Society Mss, *ibid.*

[35]It is not clear whether this was Benjamin Kissam or Samuel Kissam; Monaghan contends it was Samuel Kissam, see *Jay* p. 39, but the deference shown to the "Mr. Kissam" in debate procedure leads me to question the assurance of Monaghan's contention.

from among candidates of equal merit, the people would submit. To quote from the written argument by Jay, "People won't risque by Rebellion their Lives Property to get rid of a good King."[36] The striking parallel between the terminology of this sentence and the last lines of the Declaration of Independence only emphasizes the contrast between the sentiments toward revolution expressed in the two passages.

Later in 1768 the Debating Club considered the question whether Virginius was morally justified in putting his daughter to death to save her from the lust of the tyrant Appius. Kissam opened the argument with the observation that according to the law of Rome, children were subject to their parents; Lindley Murray countered with the assertion that this fact did not justify murder. Jay supported Kissam by urging that Virginius had no sinister motive in killing his daughter, but rather wished to defend the honor of his family. Furthermore this death served a good purpose in raising a constitutional opposition to the tyranny of Appius who held the power of life and death over Rome. Jay further contended that the moral sense of a people is best determined by reference to their laws, for the laws are "... generally composed by the wisest persons in the State." This, of course, was not to deny that a higher law existed, for "... Men at the Day of Judgment are to be judged according to the Law Written in their Hearts."[37] Despite this last concession to a moral law superior to the laws of men, it seems fairly obvious that Jay and Kissam were advancing the position that the municipal law of Rome was to be the ultimate arbiter of the moral dispute. They thereby avoided the moral issue by contending that the matter was determinable by legal reasoning. When carried to an extreme, such a position gives rise to the generally unfounded comment that lawyers tend to seek moral rules between the covers of books of law. Jay's advancement of such an argument indicates the extent to which his legal training had begun to direct his patterns of thought.

---

[36] *Ibid.*

[37] *Ibid.*

While in debate young lawyers could advance the moral position of man-made law, their hearts and minds were often sorely vexed over the harshness of the criminal law of colonial New York. We have already referred to the macabre death sentence meted out to William Prendergast.[38] In regard to lesser crimes, sentences were also remarkable for their severity. Jay's friend, Robert R. Livingston, Jr. in November of 1768 wrote a piece for publication pointed to the pitiable plight of a young woman given a temporary stay of execution from a death sentence so that she might give birth to an unfortunate child that would be left motherless by her execution a few days after its birth.[39] A few months earlier Peter Van Schaack writing about a similar case, observed,

> How unhappy is the Condition of Mankind, that their frailties expose them to such unhappy Ends, and yet the Altar of Justice requires such Sacrifices-to preserve human Society Individuals must bleed; to secure a reverence for the Laws that connect that Society the Violators must suffer-...[40]

Yet even Van Schaack's justification for the severe penal code must have been shaken by reports in the daily newspapers concerning criminal incidents at the scenes of public executions. For example, on February 16, 1767, four criminals were hung near the Fresh Water Pond; notwithstanding this example, a man in the crowd "... had his Pocket Book stole."[41] In the hearts of these young men there was a vague impression that the criminal law was too harsh; they chose to justify its existence, as did Van Schaack, or condemn it, as did Livingston, the fact

---

[38]See p. 47, above.

[39]Nov. 3, 1768, Livingston Papers, Box 1.

[40]To Peter Silverster, Aug. 1, 1768, Van Schaack Papers, Columbia University Libraries, Special Collections.

[41]New York *Mercury*. Feb. 16, 1767.

is that serious thought was being given to the problem.

In addition to working diligently for Benjamin Kissam and enjoying the political and social atmosphere of colonial New York City, John Jay had managed to continue his classical studies, at least as far as was necessary to qualify him for the Master of Arts degree at King's College. The large percentage of college graduates who qualified for the Master of Arts degree within three years of their commencement as Bachelors of Arts would indicate that amount of addition preparation required for the higher degree was rather small. Nevertheless possession of the degree conferred an additional honor upon the recipient, and nearly every graduate of King's College appeared for his second diploma. John Jay was no exception to the rule.

Commencement in 1767 was held at the newly completed St. Paul's Chapel on Broadway, rather than St. George's Chapel in Montgomerie Ward. Again Jay and his college classmate, Richard Harison, engaged in an English debate for the entertainment of the assembled dignitaries. The topic assigned to them was "Whether A Man ought to engage in War without being persuaded of the Justness of his Cause?" Jay's subsequent address upon the usefulness of passions was praised for its judicious reasoning and elegance of style. He and Harison were then presented with their diplomas, carefully inscribed in Latin phrases drawn up by President Myles Cooper himself. The two then retired with the academic procession presumably to enjoy a repast at the College Hall similar to that of 1764.[42] Now a well trained "gentleman of the law," Jay probably looked back upon his college days with a certain nostalgia and detachment. He had learned a great deal since he received his Bachelor of Arts degree, and now he held the highest degree awarded by King's College.

With the approach of the fall of 1768, John had reached a point in his legal training when Kissam could recommend him for admission to the Bar. With Kissam's approval and endorsement Jay's name was presented for examination.

---

[42]New York *Mercury*, Nov. 3, 1766, June 1, 1767; see diploma draft, in Cooper's hand, King's College Papers, 1763-1776, Columbia University Libraries, Special Collections. Jay's engrossed diploma is also in the Special Collections Library at Columbia.

Such a notice of examination was required by the bar agreement of 1764,[43] but these examinations appear to have occurred only upon rare occasions. Where the attorneys in New York City were convinced of the abilities of the applicant, it may have been entirely eliminated. Hamlin notes one instance in which a committee of attorneys were ordered to examine an applicant in the presence of judges of the Supreme Court, but his failure to find instances of bar examinations would seem to indicate that the rule concerning examinations was one to be applied only if the Bar could not agree upon the qualifications of the applicant for admission.[44]

On October 26, 1768 Governor Sir Henry Moore, "... being well assured of the Ability and Learning of John Jay, Gentlemen ..." appointed him an attorney at law and authorized him to appear in all of the Provincial courts of record in accordance with the laws of New York and England.[45] Five days later Jay appeared in the Supreme Court of Judicature accompanied by his friend Robert R. Livingston, Jr., and each produced his license from the Governor. David Jones, the justice presiding on that day, examined their licenses, and then administered the prescribed oath and declaration.[46] On the same day Jay signed the roll of attorneys, thereby completing the requirements for admission to practice.[47] Now a fully qualified attorney at law he stood at the threshold of his career in the law, a profession he believed was to be his life's work.

---

[43]Hamlin, *Legal Education*, p. 38.

[44]*Ibid.*, p. 50, Peter Van Schaack to Peter Silvester, Aug. 1, 1768, Van Schaack Papers, Columbia University Libraries, Special Collections.

[45]JJ, License to Practice Law, Columbia University Libraries, Special Collections.

[46]Min. S. Ct. Jud., Oct. 21, 1766--Jan. 21, 1769, p. 567 N.Y. Co. Clerk, Hall of Records, N.Y.C.

[47]Roll of Attorneys, Oct. 26, 1754-June 3, 1847, Ledger J, Parchment Roll #1, N.Y. Co. Clerk, Hall of Records, N.Y.C.

V. A JUNIOR MEMBER AT THE BAR

When Jay had begun his law clerkship in 1764 the attorneys admitted to practice in all of the courts of record of New York were a relatively small group, closely interrelated by blood or marriage, and united by a community of interest with the large landowners and prosperous merchants of the Province. Furthermore, the shared experience of long clerkships and interminable hours at a scrivener's desk strengthened the bonds of professional cohesion, and gave to the practitioners of the law a comradery and *esprit de crops* that made an impress not only upon the litigation of the colony, but also substantially influenced the political life of New York.

Into this elite group, John Jay was readily accepted, not merely because of his admission to practice, but also by virtue of his connections with the leading landowning and mercantile families of New York. Through his paternal grandmother John was related to the Bayards, his mother was a member of the Van Cortlandt family, and his cousins included DePeysters, DeLanceys and Stuyvesants. While a long and onerous clerkship was the principal means to secure admission to the Bar, the social status and family relationships of the newly admitted attorney determined his acceptability among his fellow counsellors and his opportunities to gain wealthy clients.

One of the remarkable aspects of the Supreme Court Bar in 1765 was its small size and interrelationships. During the period from 1762 to 1765 the attorneys regularly appearing before the Court numbered no more than thirty-six;[1] from their ranks were drawn the judges of the Supreme Court of Judicature[2] as well as other royal officials.[3] Of these thirty-six lawyers, sixteen had

---

[1]See list in Appendix A.

[2]William Smith on Apr. 19, 1763, David Jones on Apr. 21, 1763, George Duncan Ludlow on Dec. 14, 1769, Thomas Jones on Sept. 29, 1773 and Whitehead Hicks on Feb. 14, 1776.

[3]Lambert Moore was Collector of Customs for the Port of New York, James Duane served as attorney general *pro temp* in 1767 in the absence of John Tabor Kempe, the regular incumbent of that post, Thomas Jones before elevation to the Supreme court had served as Recorder of the City of New York from 1769

received degrees Yale, the College of New Jersey (Princeton) , or King's College. In 1765 the average age of these practitioners was about thirty-eight, the youngest being Edward Antill at twenty-three, and the oldest being the senior William Smith at sixty eight.[4]

With the Bench and Bar in such close and constant contact, professional gossip was inevitable. Chief Justice Daniel Horsmanden, known to the Bar as "Daddy Horsmanden" or Old Horsey,"[5] married a maiden lady several years his junior, and Judge Robert R. Livingston reported to his father,

> Mr. Horsmanden has set all the Town a laughing at his intended marriage with Miss Jevan which is to be concluded in a Day or two. It is said that the Courtship was intend[ed] for Mrs. Haines, and after he had made her a couple of visits he told her that He believe she could not be at a Loss to gess [sic] the Intention of his coming to see her, this she took in high derogation but he put it off by telling her he would call the next Day and accordingly he came and finding her in a Humour more likely to insult him than to receive him with civility, he came off by telling her that he meant no more than ask her consent to pay his Addresses to her sister, this she readily gave, and the Old Maid will get her Husband. Many are the Jests this Occasions, it has made even the Dull witty, but they are such as fit not for my

---

to 1773, and as attorney for King's College from 1758 to 1776.

[4]See Appendix A.

[5]*Smith Memoirs*, p. 54, 58.

Pen.[6]

Judge Livingston himself was to fall victim of the gossip of Judge Thomas Jones who reported for posterity that, "... [Livingston] was excessively timid, and when he found Great Britain in earnest [in 1775], he put an end to life by the use of a halter."[7] With all of the unity existed among the lawyers in regard to professional concerns, there persisted a certain pettiness and covetousness for judicial position that is inherent in the above remarks. What is significant is not that these base emotions of sarcasm and jealousy existed, but rather the close contact between members of the legal profession which was necessary to secure such personal information.

Even before Jay had been admitted to the Bar in 1768, the monopoly of the law began to give way, although efforts to restrict entry to the profession had been in part successful. The clerkship rules of 1756 blocked entrance to the legal profession for eight years and after 1764 the requisite clerkship was a deterrent to all but those in a financial position to serve an extended period of time without compensation.[8] Thus the number of attorneys below thirty years of age was extremely small, and the practice of law promised to be most lucrative for a young man who could look forward to a gradual reduction in the number of attorneys with an extensive clientele. For these reasons Jay may well have begun his clerkship convinced that his professional services would be in strong demand by 1769.

With the institution of new clerkship regulations in 1767 the situation was substantially altered, and three year clerkships for college graduates became the rule. Thereafter the number of admissions per year rose rapidly. In 1765 only Edward Antill had been admitted, in 1766 John Dutton Crimsheir was admitted, in 1767 the number of admissions rose to three and decreased to two in the

---

[6]July 6, 1763, to Robert Livingston, Livingston Papers, Box 1, New York Historical Society, N.Y.C.

[7]Thomas Jones, *History of New York During the Revolutionary War*, Edward Floyd Delancy, ed. (2 vols., New York: Printed for the New York Historical Society, 1879), I, 233. Jones of course was a Loyalist; I have found no evidence for his statement, nor does he give a source.

[8]See discussion *supra* at pp. 8, 9, 54, 55.

following year. During 1769 six attorneys were admitted to practice, while in 1770 the admissions numbered twelve. From 1765 to 1770 twenty-four lawyers were added to the small group of seasoned practitioners discussed above.[9] Although the preparation of these young men varied from the five years of Edward Antill and the four year clerkship of John Jay, to the three year clerkships of the others, all were in competition for the legal business of the colony, a large proportion of which would tend to remain in the hands of the older attorneys with established reputations.

At the same time that the number of attorneys practicing before the Supreme Court was on the increase, the economic life of the Province settled into a lethargy caused by the impact of the Townshend Acts and the chronic lack of a circulating medium.[10] While the processes of debt collection provided ample opportunity for the employment of legal services, the decline in prosperity doubtless meant either a decline in professional fees or a delay in receiving payment for services rendered. In either case the newly admitted lawyer would be sorely pressed to make his expenses. It is not surprising that of the twenty-four men admitted to practice between 1765 and 1770, only eleven continued in active practice before the Supreme Court. John Jay and Robert R. Livingston, Jr., are numbered among this fortunate eleven.[11]

From the surviving evidence we cannot tell whether Jay contemplated a partnership with Livingston before the date of their admission to the Bar, nor can we be certain that the change in admission rules and the economic depression led the young men to seek safety in the merger of their interests. Very possibly the two had realized the valuable complementary relationship that existed between their

---

[9]Min. S. Ct. Jud., Oct. 21, 1766-Jan. 21, 1769, pp. 28, 29, 50, 247, 567, 606-607; Min. S. Ct. Jud., Apr. 18, 1769-May 2, 1772, pp. 15, 107, 113, 186 (an Irish barrister), 188, 194, 243, 288, 319.

[10]Becker, *History Political Parties*, p. 79. That the rise of bar was due to economic prosperity, see Milton Klein, at *William and Mary Quarterly*, 3rd ser., XV 335.

[11]The others are Edward Antill, John Crimsheir, Rudolphus Ritzema, Peter W. Yates, Robert Yates, George Clinton, Peter Van, Schaack, Egbert Benson and Richard Harison.

talents for the practice of law, and this recognition ripened into serious consideration as the situation described above became apparent to them. Because of the large number of admissions and the economic situation, it is difficult to give credence to William Jay's assertion that his father "almost immediately" gained an extensive and lucrative practice.[12] Even with the combined clientele of the Jay and Livingston families, the Jay-Livingston partnership got off to a precarious start. In January of 1769 business was so slow that Jay was able to handle matters alone while Livingston travelled to Clermont.[13] At the April 1769 term only four of their cases were on the motion calendar, and of those only two are clearly identifiable as originating among Jay's relatives.[14] Clearly had the two begun practice without family backing and a unification of their prospective cases, both would doubtless have been forced out of business within a very short period of time. Dangerfield's conclusion concerning the partnership, that it was never very active, seems to be substantially correct.[15]

Despite the limited amount of cases carried by the Jay-Livingston partnership, the relationship was permitted to continue until October of 1771, at which time Jay's cases were ruled off in the joint law register maintained for Supreme Court cases.[16] Thereafter Livingston's cases continue in the register, and some even indicate that Jay is opposing counsel. The dissolution of the partnership was begun gradually, the two appearing in court separately after January of 1771, but it was not until October of 1771 that the firm name of Jay and Livingston no longer

---

[12]Wm. Jay, *Life*, I, 2.

[13][?] January 1769, JJ to Livingston, Livingston Papers, Box 1, New York Historical Society, N.Y.C.

[14]Min. S. Ct. Jud., Apr. 18, 1769-May 2, 1772, p. 53. The two cases attributed to Jay concern the estate of John Chambers, his uncle.

[15]*Livingston*, p. 48.

[16]See Law Register of John Jay and Robert R. Livingston, Jr., BV Sec., New York Historical Society, N.Y.C., *passim*. (hereafter Law Reg. J&L).

appeared on motion days in the Supreme Court.[17] It is perhaps some indication of the relative size of the partnership practice that Jay individually paid as much in clerk's fees to the Supreme Court clerk in 1771 as the partnership of Jay and Livingston had paid to the same official in the two and a half years of its existence.[18]

One of the advantages of partnership practice is the amount of freedom it permits the partners; freed from the need to personally attend every aspect of a client's business, the partner can rely upon his associate to appear in court whenever such an appearance would be inconvenient for him. As noted above, Livingston during the winter of 1769 took a trip to Clermont while Jay remained in New York City. Both young men acted as business agents for their families and John rapidly replaced his elder brother Augustus as the New York City representative for the Jay interests.[19] Even more important in terms of his own growth as a lawyer, Jay spent the summer and early fall of 1769 as Clerk to the Commissioners appointed to determine the location of the disputed New York-New Jersey Boundary.

Jay's appointment to serve as Clerk to the Boundary Commission was very likely the result of the influence of his former teacher, Benjamin Kissam, who had been selected by the Province of New York to act as one of the agents pleading its case before the Commission. The Commission had had been

---

[17]Account Book of George Clark, Clerk of the New York Supreme Court, *sub, nom*. John Jay and Jay and Livingston, New York Historical Society, N.Y.C. Jay appears separately at Jan. 1771 term, and again at the April 1771 term, Min. Ct. Jud., Apr. 18, 1769-May 2, 1772, pp, 336, 384, 385.

[18]Account Book, *ibid.*

[19]The preference for Jay's services began while he was still a clerk, see advertisements to rent property appearing in New York *Mercury*, Jan. 19, 1767, Jan. 25, 1768, New York *Gazette and Weekly Post Boy*, Feb. 8, 1768. John's brother, Frederick, a merchant at Curacao, kept him posted on speculative opportunities, see letter June 5, 1769, Columbia University Libraries; Special Collections.

appointed on October 7, 1767, and the royal warrant named thirteen royal officials in the colonies, or any five of them, to sit as commissioners to fix the boundary that had been in dispute since the establishment of New Jersey as a separate colony in 1664.[20] By the time the members named had been served with notice of appointment, and then made arrangements to travel to New York City, it was the 18th of July 1769. Not until the 20th of July was a quorum of five members present, and at that time Jay was appointed Clerk of the Commission, with George Derbage to serve as Assistant Clerk.[21]

The clerks to the Commission were required to keep a thorough account of the proceedings, recording them in a minute book, along with filing the written interrogatories and answers, which constituted the evidence introduced before the Commission.[22] Since appeals were permitted to the Privy Council and a close review of the proceedings would be made by the officers of the Crown, the procedure followed by the Commission was civilian in nature and bore little or no resemblance to the procedure in a common law court. Jay's experience as a law clerk with Vice Admiralty Court pleading and proof doubtless served him well in his work for the Commission, and the transcript made by him and his assistant gives a detailed picture of the issues presented to the Commission.

On the first day of the hearings both New York and New Jersey presented their claim to the Commissioners. While the critical issue was the location of the boundary terminal point on the Delaware River, the proper situs for the eastern terminal point was not at all certain. The New York agents pointed out the

---

[20]New York and New Jersey Boundary Papers, Vol. III, Commission of 1769, at p. 1 (hereinafter Boundary Papers, III, _). This is a contemporary copy used in preference to original which is in delicate condition. Both at New York Historical Society, New York City.

[21]*Ibid.*, 1, 3.

[22]The original interrogatories are at John Jay Papers, Box 7, Boundary Papers, 2, New York Historical Society, N.Y.C., but are transcribed in Boundary Papers, III, *passim.*, and I have used the certified transcript.

effect upon Crown revenues of extending the New Jersey titles to the detriment of the province of New York, for in East Jersey quit rents were payable to the proprietors. At the same time they urged the paramount rights of New York, pointing out that its boundaries had been traditionally considered to encompass all lands not clearly within the grants to New Jersey and Pennsylvania on the west and south.[23] The position taken by the New Jersey agents was to rely upon the 1719 survey which placed the western terminus of the boundary line at the intersection of the Fish Kill and Delaware Rivers; the eastern point they were willing to concede to be at 41° on the western shore of the Hudson River.[24] They pointed out this line, from 41E on the Hudson to 41E40' on the Delaware had not been contested by New York since 1719; the disagreement arose only after title to the Minisink patent became an issue between the two colonies in 1755.[25] The extent of the divergence of the claims can be seen by tracing the line of the 1719 survey as the ultimate position of New Jersey, and the line from New York City to Easton, Pennsylvania as the ultimate claim of New York.[26]

From July 20th, 1769 until the end of the month, the Commission received documentary evidence concerning the claims of both provinces. Jay's fellow attorney, Rudolphus Ritzema, translated the early Dutch land grants into English at the request of the agents for New Jersey. The Commission agreed to accept certified copies of these and other documents of record, rather than incurring the expense of insisting upon exemplified copies of the grants.[27] Through the last day of July and the first three days of August, the Commission received docu-

---

[23]Boundary Papers, III, 8-16, See Beverly W. Bond, Jr., *The Quit Rent System in the American Colonies* (New Haven: Yale University Press, 1919), pp. 99-107.

[24]*Ibidem*., 24, 34, 38.

[25]*Ibidem*., 34.

[26]See "General Map...", reproduced in Appendix B.

[27]Boundary Papers, III, 46, 48.

ments in evidence, and after a brief rest, began hearing testimony on August 5th.[28] The burdensome task of copying these land grants and marking evidence for future identification fell to Jay and his assistant. Once the testimony began, the interrogatories were taken in writing; the writing invariably appears to be that of John Jay.[29] While the minutes indicate that the witnesses were sworn before the commission, and their testimony received, the form of the interrogatories, as well as the neatness of the handwriting, precludes any possibility that Jay was making a *verbatim* transcript of the proceedings. It is far more likely that the written interrogatories were introduced, as were the cross interrogatories, additional interrogatories and answers; after the bulk of the testimony was thus reduced to writing, the witnesses may have appeared briefly for a short examination by the Commissioners. However, the testimony was received, the work for the Clerk of the Commission was considerable, and Jay must have been hard pressed to perform the copying tasks assigned to him.

The testimony on the part of New Jersey was introduced primarily to strengthen that province's contention that the 1719 line should be accepted.[30] No further testimony was elicited, and New York was then permitted to proceed with documentary evidence.[31] When this work was completed after nearly a week of sessions, the commission recessed until August 23rd; its clerks probably remained at their desks to bring their copying up to date.[32]

When the Commission met according to adjournment, New Jersey introduced a small number of additional documents, and the Commission then proceeded to receive additional documents or hear testimony from the agents

---

[28]*Ibid.*, 55-312.

[29]The original interrogatories and answers are at John Jay Papers, Box 7, Boundary Papers 2, New York Historical Society; the text is in Jay's hand.

[30]'Boundary Papers, III, 314-330. See also map in Appendix B.

[31]*Ibid.*, 330-516. 3

[32]*Ibid.*, 516, 517.

of New York.[33] At this point the agents for New York departed from the established pattern by calling witnesses for the purpose of proving New York settlement and sovereignty in the area of Ramapo and the Pompton River. The testimony adduced also served to cast doubt upon the place of the eastern terminus boundary line since certain aged residents of Tappan recalled the boundaries of their county to have extended several miles south of the line run by James Clinton in accordance with the instructions of the Commissioners.[34] Caught off balance by this tactic of the New York agents the New Jersey attorneys obtained a witness to contradict the testimony given on the part of the province of New York, only to have their witness admit that the authority of New York had been recognized at Ramapo.[35] Another witness for New Jersey had his testimony impeached to some degree when the New York agents pointed to the fact that he was financially interested in the settlement of the boundary.[36] As the New Jersey agents attempted to stay the flow of testimony against their Province, one of their number, James Parker, wrote for assistance. Complaining bitterly that the one attorney acting of counsel for the New Jersey agents cold not carry the burden of refuting this new evidence, he sharply reminded his absent colleagues:

> Upon the whole Gentlemen I must tell you that I think you have deserted our Cause & the Cause of the Province at a time when your Assistance is most wanted... I should not do my duty not to mention this matter & to declare that I shall look upon you accountable for any Loss that may be

---

[33] *Ibid.*, 518-536.

[34] *Ibid.*, 537-566. The New York tactic seems to have been designed to obtain a boundary line along the azimuth of 278E rather than the boundary as finally fixed at the 309E azimuth line from the 73E 55' meridian of west longitude.

[35] Testimony, Isaac Van Deusen, at *ibid.*, 572, 573.

[36] Testimony John Zabrieski, at *ibid.*, 584-586.

> sustained by your withdrawing yourselves from the court at this Critical time & shall when called upon by my Constituents think it my duty to say where the Fault lies.[37]

If Parker's delinquent associates returned immediately they may have been of some assistance, for the testimony continued until September 22nd, when the Commission adjourned to permit the agents for both Provinces adequate time to prepare their arguments in summation.[38]

On September 30th, the surveyors' reports fixing the eastern terminus at a rock on the western bank of the Hudson at 41E0'0", and the western terminus at the intersection of the Mackhakamuck and Delaware Rivers at 42E21'37", were read and filed by the Commissioners.[39] After reading the written arguments of the agents of both colonies, the Commission took five days to deliberate over its decision. The decision announced was based upon the surveyors' findings, and two Commissioners dissented on the ground that the new position of the boundary would be a grave injustice to the people settled in the area near Tappan.[40] The Court refused to receive the appeals that were submitted by the agents for both Provinces, having determined that a period of two months should elapse before appeals should be filed. The Commission adjourned for two months to meet again at Hartford to receive appeals, but neither a quorum of Commissioners, nor any of the agents were at Hartford at the time set for the next meeting.[4]

---

[37]To David Ogden, Richard Stockton and C[ornelius] Skinner, Sept. 3, 1769. Misc. Mss. Parker, New Yorker Historical Society, N.Y.C.

[38]Boundary Papers III, 604-757. On Sept. 11, 1769, the Commission dispatched David Rittenhouse, the Philadelphia astronomer, to fix the latitude on the Delaware River, *ibid.*, 678.

[39]*Ibid.*, III, 765.

[40]*Ibid..* III, 782-785.

[41]*Ibidem.*

Although Commissioners and attorneys were delinquent in their duties, John Jay made the trip to Hartford in December of 1769. From the evidence that survives, it would appear that it was a journey filled with frustration. The fruitless trip took a total of sixteen days; while at Hartford Jay spent two shillings six pence for stationery to be used by the Court, which never convened. A trunk purchased in New York for thirteen shillings to carry the Commission's records to Hartford, broke on the way, and he was compelled to spend £ 1 10s. to replace it.[42] In addition, the failure of the colonies to either file appeals or accept the Commission's findings left matters at a standstill, including Jay's salary. At the age of twenty-four Jay was being introduced to the uncomfortable situation of being a forgotten creditor of government.[43]

Since appeals were anticipated, Jay was preparing to send the minutes of the Commission to England for review by the Privy Council. Conformed copies of the minutes and interrogatories were being prepared by six writers employed by the Commission and supervised by John Jay.[44] Their salaries are not reflected, but Jay recorded in his accounts that he spent £ 20 to provide them with heat and candle light during the two months they required to complete the two transcripts.[45] When July 4, 1770 arrived, Jay was ready for the Commissioner's meeting at New York City, but only one Commissioner arrived and no agents were present. The Commission adjourned until the first Tuesday in May 1771, and this was

---

[42]Accounts of John Jay with Agents of New York and Jersey, Jan. 1770, John Jay Papers, Box 6, Boundary Papers, 1, New York Historical Society, N.Y.C.

[43]Presumably Jay had received his fees for copying papers, which were computed at the rate of 9 d. per folio page and billed to the Agents requesting copies, see Accounts dated July 28, 1769-Sept. 19, 1769, and Aug. 14, 1769-Sept. 19, 1769, *ibidem*.

[44]Boundary Papers, III, 781; Accounts, *ibid.*

[45]Accounts, *ibid.*

destined to be the last meeting of that august body.[46] It was probably at this time that Jay hit upon the happy expedient of charging one-half of his salary and expenses to the agents for New Jersey, and presumably the other half to the agents for New York.[47]

When the New York council debated the advisability of auditing the accounts of the New York agents, it became clear that certain elements in the Governor's council exerting this form of financial pressure to compel New York's consent to the settlement proposed by the Boundary Commission. That settlement, when ratified by the King, would result in a large tract of land being awarded to New Jersey. According to William Smith, a member of the council who opposed the auditing of accounts, certain councillors were under the impression that they, rather than the Province of New York, would be compelled to pay the costs of the Commission because they individually held lands in the disputed tract.[48] Only upon the approval of a warrant directing payment to the surveyors, were members of the council found to be in accord.[49]

After the unsuccessful attempts to assemble a quorum of Commissioners in December of 1769 and May of 1770, the Privy Council issued an order in council permitting less than a quorum of the Commission to take action, and also authorizing the return of the Commission with its decision and proceedings.[50] Thereafter only one Commissioner appeared at the meeting scheduled for May of 1771, and the question naturally arose whether the arrival of one man could in any sense of' the term, be considered a "meeting". When two Comissioners were finally available the New York governor, William Tryon, requested the advice of his council concerning the question of whether the two commissioners might authorize the dispatch of the Commission's papers. By this time both provinces

---

[46]Boundary Papers, III, 784-85.

[47]Accounts, Jan. 1770, John Jay Papers, Box 6, Boundary Papers, 1.

[48]*Smith Memoirs*, pp.77, 79.

[49]0n May 10, 1770, *ibid.*. 81.

[50]*Ibid.*. p. 82.

had abandoned any desire to appeal the Commission's decision to the Privy Council, and the only thing remaining to be done to fix the boundary was to transmit the decision to the Privy Council for confirmation by the King. Nevertheless the New York council divided sharply upon the question of the authority of the two Commissioners to authorize the return of the commission and decision to London. Noting that the order in council, authorizing less than a quorum to act, had expired, the Governor wrote to the Board of Trade for instruction.[51] At the meeting, Tryon had expressed the opinion that the true boundary line of New York was below the New York City to Easton, Pennsylvania, line, and Oliver Delancy replied, ". . . if I thought your Excellency was right I would hang myself in the first crooked Tree." the Governor replied with warmth, "That you may do, but I communicate my Sentiments to Government. They may make what use of it they please. "52

While these unpleasantries were being exchanged in the New York council, the Board of Trade noted in its report on a New York act fixing the boundary, that since the boundary commission had not been properly returned in accordance with the King's order in council, no action should be taken concerning the New York legislation.[53] Later in 1772 the Governor of New Jersey, William Franklin, met with Tryon to determine how the return of the Commission could be expedited and the boundary dispute settled.[54] Not until January 6, 1773 was Tryon successful in obtaining an act of the New York assembly directing

---

[51]*Ibid.*, p. 116.

[52]*Ibidem.*

[53]*Journals of the Commissioners for Trade and Plantations, from January 1768 to December 1775, Preserved in the Public Record Office* (London: His Majesty's Stationery Office, 1937), p.299 (hereafter *Journal Comm. Trade 1768-75.*)

[54]Tryon to Hillsborough, Oct. 3, 1770, Colonial Office Papers, Series 5, Volume 1076, page 151 (hereafter C.O. 5/1076/151). Public Record Office, London. See also William Franklin to Tryon, copy at C.O. 5/1004/105, P.R.O., London.

John Jay to release a copy of the proceedings, which was delivered to Andrew Elliot, one of the Commissioners, who turned it over to Tryon for shipment to London.[55] The papers were received by Tryon on February 6, 1773, and arrived in Whitehall on April 10, 1773. This impediment to the consideration of the New York and New Jersey boundary acts having been removed, the Board of Trade prepared its representation concerning the two acts and forwarded them for approval to the Privy Council.[56] Concerning Jay's delaying the return of the proceedings in 1773, the Earl of Hillsborough commented to Governor Tryon,

> I do not well see upon what ground it was, that Mr. Jay had his doubts as to the delivery of the Commission and the proceedings thereupon for running the boundary line between New York and New Jersey; I am to presume, however, from the step taken by the Legislature, that there was some foundation in law for those Doubts;. . .[57]

While Jay may have been unnecessarily concerned with the formal requirements of law, it is clear that he was in a difficult position concerning the return of the commission without having the direction of a quorum of the members. Having been appointed by the Commissioners, he could exercise only the powers they conferred upon him; in their absence, he could act upon the instructions of the Governor, the Board of Trade, or the provincial council, but none of these bodies

---

[55]See C.O. 5/1077, C.O. 5/1104/99, 111, P.R.O., London, and *Journal of the Legislative Council of the Colony of New York* (2 vols., Albany: Weed, Parsons & Co., 1861), II, 1855.

[56]*Journal Comm. Trade 1768/75*, p.358. The matter was never acted upon by the Privy Council, hence the acts stood confirmed, W. L. Grant and James Monro, eds., *Acts of The Privy Council of England, Colonial Series* (6 vols., Hereford: His Majesty's Stationery Office, 1908-1912) V, *passim.*

[57]*Doc. Rel. Col. Hist*, VIII, 349; the original is at C.O. 5/1104/225-226, P.R.O. London.

were the source of his authority. On the other the enabling acts passed by the general assemblies of the provinces of New York and New Jersey, and the action of the Privy Council in issuing the Commission to fix the boundary, were basic to the function of the Commission and its clerk. Since Jay's salary remained unpaid, he would have jeopardized his claim if he acted precipitately in returning the commission without proper authorization. Therefore his insistence upon either an order in council or an act of the New York assembly as the basis for his action, does not seem unreasonable. At the same time his stand in the face of political pressure from the Governor and possible disapproval from London, indicates a certain tenacity in regard to following established procedures and forms. This trait was to reassert itself even more forcefully when, as a peace commissioner in 1782, he refused to treat with British diplomats accredited to deal with representatives from the "United Colonies".

Once royal approval of the boundary settlement had been secured, the two provincial governments dispatched a surveying team to fix the line. The difficulties encountered in this regard, and the resultant bowed line caused by the magnetic deflection due to iron deposits in the area of Greenwood Lake, did not concern John Jay as clerk of the Commission.[58] They remained of interest to landowners in the area until 1884, when the earlier boundary was resurveyed, and necessary legislative action taken to validate the mistakes made in 1774. As a result New York got back a small part of the land awarded to New Jersey in 1774. Jay's experience with the Commission gave him good grounding in the operations of a mixed commission. As Joseph H. Smith indicates, the colonial familiarity with this institution laid a basis, not only for the settlement of interstate boundaries under the Articles of Confederation, but also for the use of the device

---

[58]*See Report of the Commissioners on the Boundary Lines Between the State of New York and the States of Pennsylvania and New Jersey, for the Year Ending December 31, 1882.* New York State Assembly Document No. 161, Assembly Documents, VII (1883), pp.4,5,51; *Report of the Commissioners on the Boundary Line Between the State of New York and the State of New Jersey*, New York Senate Document 46, Senate Documents, III (1884) p.36.

in the adjustment of complex issues in international disputes.[59] We cannot dismiss as circumstantial the fact that the United States first utilized the mixed commission in international affairs when in 1794, John Jay negotiated the treaty with Great Britain which bears his name.

While the boundary commission recessed in October 1769, Jay returned to his private practice with Livingston. He soon found his attention occupied with the cases of Benjamin Kissam who had become lame and could not follow the Supreme Court judges on circuit. To his former clerk Kissam issued, ". . .a call to go forth unto my vineyard; and this you must do, too, upon an evangelical principle-- that the master may receive the fruits of it."[60] Jay was soon in the up river counties, where according to the observation of another lawyer, one had ample opportunity for "... exercising [his] lungs and tallents in the Supreme Court . . .".[61] Relying upon Jay to familiarize himself with the background of the cases, Kissam wrote that is doubtless one of the shortest briefs ever given to trial counsel:

> All I can tell you about the causes is little more than to give you a list of their titles; but this is quite enough for you. One is about a horse-race, in which I suppose there is some cheat; another is about an eloped wife; another of them also appertains unto horseflesh. These are short hints; they may serve you for briefs. If you admire conciseness, here you have it.[62]

---

[59]*Appeals to the Privy Council*, p. 462. Smith's, discussion of the empire-wide use of the boundary commission device is most valuable.

[60]Nov. 6, 1769, Wm. Jay, *Life*, I, 22.

[61]Quotation from a letter of Henry Cruger to Peter Van Schaack, June 20, 1770, Van Schaack Papers, Columbia University Libraries, Special Collections.

[62]Wm. Jay *Life*, I, 22.

Armed with Kissam's confidence in him, and the assurance that he could request Richard Morris' assistance whenever it was needed, Jay set forth to do his duty as Kissam's "apostolic lawyer". Despite the levity of Kissam's request, he took considerable risk in entrusting the affairs of his clients to his former clerk. Before the Juries Jay would strive for judgments in favor of Kissam's clients, or equally important, obtain a special verdict assessing their damages. He could easily have lost the case or decreased the judgment, and the return of the postea or endorsed writ of inquiry to New York might have brought with it a rude shock for both Kissam and his clients.[63] Jay's knowledge of the faith Kissam had placed in his abilities doubtless served to lighten his spirits as he rode northward in the chill November air.

Selection by a fellow lawyer to assist in the prosecution or defense of a case is the clearest indication of an attorney's ability; occuring so early in Jay's career, it marked him as a young lawyer who was known to be capable despite the short time he had been in active practice.

As 1769 drew to a close Jay could boast of a meager income from his partnership practice with Robert R. Livingston, Jr. His claim for salary from the Boundary Commission was still held up by the political debates in the New York council. In terms of financial reward, 1769 was not a good year. Yet John Jay had in this one year obtained invaluable training in the procedures of negotiation and settlement before a boundary commission; he had begun to apply his knowledge of the practice of New York courts for the benefits of his own clients, gained a singular mark of approval by being retained as trial counsel on the behalf of a leading attorney of New York City. The approval and continued support of Benjamin Kissam not only sustained John Jay at this early point in his career; it also opened to him opportunities not otherwise obtainable. Without any doubt, Kissam was firmly

---

[63]A wager on a horse race could only be litigated by assumpsit, for the conviviality of the track makes a formal writing obligatory improbable. In such a case a jury would be required to fix damages, even if the defendant did not contest the case. An elopement (the second "horse flesh" case) would be ground for the tort claim of alienation of affections; again a jury had to assess damages. Once fixed the amount of damages was certified by the circuit clerk, in the form of a postea.

convinced of the ability of his former clerk and was ever ready to assist Jay on the path to sucess.

VI. CIVIL PRACTICE IN THE PROVINCE OF NEW YORK

As a practicing lawyer John Jay was vitally concerned with the procedures followed in the litigation of civil causes in the provincial courts. By far the largest part of his practice centered in the Supreme Court of Judicature, the Court of Chancery, the Mayor's Court of New York City and the Common Pleas court of Westchester County. We must briefly divert our attention to the day-to-day work in those courts to obtain a clear picture of Jay's law practice in colonial New York.

The Supreme Court of Judicature, created in 1691, possessed all of these pages vested in the English courts of King's Bench, Common Pleas and Exchequer.[1] Since procedures in the English prototypes were not uniform, the Supreme Court of Judicature had a variety of alternatives from which to choose its practice. Consequently the colonials could adapt to their peculiar situation those English procedures that were most useful, and reject those practices at Westminster that were not appropriate or desirable.

Although the Supreme Court possessed broad civil and criminal jurisdiction, an act of 1728 limited civil litigation before the Court to causes in which the amount in controversy exceeded to £ 20.[2] Shortly after John Jay's admission to practice, the New York General Assembly raised the minimum amount to £ 50, and provided that a party beginning suit in the Supreme Court who recovered less than that amount, would be assessed to pay the defendant's costs.[3] These prohibitions and penalties against instituting certain cases in the Supreme Court also applied to the transfer of actions by means of habeas corpus or certiorari from the lower courts over which the Supreme Court of Judicature exercised appellate jurisdiction.

Preliminary process was necessary to bring an individual within the jurisdiction of the Supreme Court, thereby conferring upon the Court the power to render judgment against him. In the case of a resident of New York county, or a defendant found within the territorial limits of that county, the plaintiff's attorney

---

[1]Hamlin & Baker, *Supreme Court of Judicature*, I, 68.

[2]*N.Y. Colonial Laws*, III, 462, 464 (Sept. 20, 1728).

[3]*Ibid.*, IV, 1088 et seq. (May 20, 1769).

drew up a Bill of New York, and issued the document to the sheriff for service. When the potential defendant resided in any other county, the attorney for the plaintiff drew up a *capias ad respondendum* and forwarded this writ to the sheriff.[4] In either case the sheriff had to return the defendant in his custody at the next term of the Court, at which time the necessary *pro forma* rule would be made to retain the defendant in the Court's custody until the matter had been determined. Usually the defendant endorsed his appearance on the writ, and the plaintiff moved that his appearance be entered; this procedure conferred jurisdiction upon the Court through consent of the defendant. Should the defendant refuse to so endorse his appearance, he would be arrested and held in custody until judgment was rendered. In this situation the sheriff, upon returning the writ or bill, would be ordered by the Court to have the defendant in Court at the next term or the sheriff would be amerced forty shillings for contempt. Once the defendant was brought before the Court, he would be committed to prison to await the decision of his case. These preliminary steps, and the so-called "common rules" mentioned above, involved a minimum of work for the attorney, and it is likely the lawyer did not haye to appear in Court to request that the "common rule" be entered.[5]

---

[4]Cf. Law Reg. Jay, N.Y. State Library, p. 180, where a Bill of New York was used with *ibid.*, p. 147, where a *capias* was utilized. The matter is fully discussed at Julius Goebel, Jr., ed., *The Law Practice of Alexander Hamilton*, 5 vols., (New York: Columbia, University Press, 1964-81), I, 63, nt.l.

[5]The usual common rule required the defendant to plead in 20 days after receipt of the rule with the declaration of the plaintiff, Min.S.Ct.Jud., 1766-Jan. 21, 1769, p.624 (Beekman v. Noxon). If the defendant were in custody of the sheriff, upon the sheriff's certificate that he had received the papers on behalf of defendant, the plaintiff might move for judgment for lack of a plea, Min.S.Ct.Jud., July 25, 1775-Apr. 28, 1781, p.94 (Jay v. Lawrence). In early New York State practice a personal appearance by the attorney was not required, Goebel, *ibid.*, I, 57.

Doubtless some abuses arose through the commencement of vexatious actions, and the foregoing rules of preliminary process were to some degree ameliorated by several acts of New York General Assembly. For example the defendant in a replevin action was guaranteed interim possession of the property to which the action pertained.[6] A plaintiff bringing action in trespass, assault, false imprisonment or ejectment was deterred from acting precipitately by the rule that the defendant's costs would be assessed against the plaintiff should the defendant be held not guilty.[7] Furthermore, special bail in Supreme Court matters could be obtained by the defendant and his bondsmen appearing before local officials in the county of his residence, rather than travelling to New York to appear before a justice of the Supreme Court.[8]

In instances where the plaintiff failed to post a bond as security for costs, or to file his declaration within twenty days after entry of the common rule, the defendant might move to "non-pross" him.[9] This remedy was also available if the plaintiff delayed in taking steps to bring the case to an early trial. The motion to non-pross a plaintiff was usually made twice, and judgment was entered on the second motion for failure to heed the first order Court.[10]

Once jurisdiction over the person of the defendant had been secured, the parties then proceeded to make whatever pre-trial motions they deemed necessary. Demurrers on formal grounds were discouraged, and an attorney

---

[6]*N. Y. Colonial Laws*, V, 76, 77 (Jan. 27, 1770). Replevin is an action to recover possession of certain personal property which plaintiff claims defendant unlawfully from him.

[7]*Ibid.*, V, 287, 288 (Feb. 26, 1772).

[8]*Ibid.*, II, 464, 465 (Sept. 20, 1728).

[9]Law Reg. Jay, N.Y. State Library, p. 170. (Ross v. Costigan).

[10]Min. S.Ct. Jud?, Apr. 18, 1769-May 2, 1772, pp.164, 268 (Axtell v. Remsen); see also *N. Y. Colonial Laws*, V, 207, 208 (Feb. 16, 1771).

asserting a formal defect in his adversary's pleading had to specify the formal defect; it was statutory policy that a large number of such flaws would not defeat judgment upon the merits, and that demurrers based upon formal grounds would be denied.[11] In addition to demurring to the declaration or answer, a party might move for a change of venue so that the trial might take place in a county other than the one in which the defendant was served with process. Jay utilized this motion to good effect in several of his cases, one of which shall be examined in greater detail in the next chapter.[12]

With preliminaries completed the case was ready for trial, either before the Supreme Court *en banc* at New York, or, in cases arising outside the county of New York, before a circuit sitting of the Supreme Court at the county court-house in the appropriate county. Circuits were held in Richmond county during the last week in May, in Orange, Dutchess. Ulster and Albany, in that order in June. The September circuit was constantly rearranged during the period of Jay's practice. In 1769 it was held first in Kings county, then in Suffolk, Queens and Westchester. With 1770 and 1771 the order was changed to Kings, Queens, Suffolk and Westchester. In 1772 the sequence was again altered to Westchester, Queens, Kings and Suffolk, and this routine was retained in 1773, only to be changed in 1774 to Westchester, Queens, Suffolk and Kings.[13] Since Jay's practice would have been limited to appearances in the first circuit named and in Westchester county, the confused pattern of sittings in Long Island would not have greatly inconvenienced him.

---

[11]*Ibid.*, V, 537 (Mar. 8, 1773).

[12]Venue motion papers, consisting of notice affidavit, were served three days before the return date, see Law Reg. Jay, N.Y. State Library, p.87, and Law Reg, Jay & L., N.Y. Hist. Soc., p.22.

[13]Min.S.Ct.Jud., Apr.18, 1769-May 2, 1772, pp.17, 18, 62, 189, 235, 352, 359, 396, 522; *ibid.*, Apr. 21, 1772-Jan. 17, 1776, pp.27, 92, 110, 152, 162, 191; *ibid.*, July 25, 1775-Apr. 28, 1781, p.84.

The circuit sittings of the Supreme Court were held before one Justice of the Court and two or more judges of the county Court of Common Pleas. The issue roll, prepared by the plaintiff's attorney, was delivered to the Clerk of the Circuit Court; during John Jay's term of practice this office was held by Richard Morris, who in addition served as Judge of the Court of Vice Admiralty, the latter being an unsalaried office. Should the plaintiff's attorney neglect to file the issue roll, the defendant could move to compel plaintiff to do so upon pain of suffering a non-suit for failure to comply.[14] Once the issue roll, containing the declaration and answer, was on file with the Clerk of the Circuit, the case could be noticed for trial in the usual manner.

Cases were placed on the calendar for trial by means of a notice for trial. After May 1, 1771 the moving party was required to give fourteen days notice of trial if the other party resided more than forty miles from the place the trial would take place. When the other party resided at a lesser distance, eight days notice would be sufficient; however, the customary procedure was to give approximately three weeks notice of trial, and the notice could be countermanded upon the opposing party's motion within six days of trial.[15]

Since 1699 the assembling and selection of a jury had been regulated by acts of the General Assembly. The attorney bringing his case to issue was therefore required to comply with the statutory procedures, which were to

---

[14]*N. Y. Colonial Laws*, V, 207, 208. The importance of having an attorney available at New York City for service would seem to be readily apparent, however it was not the Supreme Court order of Oct. 13, 1772 that attorneys who did not maintain city offices were required to file with the Court Clerk a designation of an agent who would receive process on their behalf. If no agent was designed, the Clerk was authorized to accept process in the name of a non-resident attorney. Rule became effective Apr. 1, 1773, Min. St.Ct.Jud., Apr. 21, 1772-Jan. 17, 1776, p.61.

[15]*N. Y. Colonial Laws*, V, 207, 208 (Feb. 16, 1771). Cf. Hamilton's Practice Manual, Goebel, ed., *Law Practice Hamilton*, I, 59, with Law Reg. Jay, N.Y. State Library, p.137, showing a 25 day notice of trial in 1773.

suspension only when a foreign jury had to be selected.[16] After the case had been noted for trial, the attorney who had noticed the matter obtained a writ of venire which directed the sheriff of the county to assemble qualified jurors to serve in the case. All male inhabitants between the age of 21 and 70 listed on the county assessment lists, and possessing a freehold in land to the value of £ 60, were eligible to serve on juries.[17] In the event a freeholder summoned had served within the previous year, he would be excused from service.[18] The normal procedure was that the jurors, not less than forty-eight nor more than seventy-two in number, would be returned by the sheriff at least six days before the first day of the term at which they were to serve. Attorneys for the litigants would receive at least five days notice of the jurors returned.[19] Should either party desire a special jury, he might request the sheriff to bring before a justice of the Court a list of jurors, and upon three days notice to his adversary, move to strike a jury. This process permitted the attorneys to select from the sheriff's list a panel of twenty-four, the jurors so selected being certified to the Clerk of the Court as having been

---

[16]Act of May 16, 1699, *N.Y. Colonial Laws*, I, 387-388, renewed and amended Nov. 11, 1726, *ibid.*, II, 345; act regulating practice in Jay's time was that of Dec. 6, 1726, *ibid.* II, 185-192, made perpetual on Nov. 27, 1741, *ibid.*, III, 599. Foreign juries were used in causes involving the law merchant.

[17]*N.Y. Colonial Laws*, II, 185-187 (Nov. 27, 1741).

[18]*Ibid.*, II, 187.

[19]*Ibid.*, II, 188, 189. The names would be picked for each petty jury at random from a box, and counsel would be extended the opportunity to challenged any juror so selected to try the case.

specially selected to serve in the particular case.[20]

Precisely what occurred at a jury trial in the Supreme Court of Judicature is left to the reader's conjecture, for no written transcript of those hearings was made.[21] The minute books of the Court reflect only the names of witnesses and upon whose behalf they were called to testify. In Jay's case of Leadbetter v. Harison, Jay called ten witnesses for the plaintiff who was suing his former partner for slander. In opposition, Jay's college classmate, Richard Harison, called three witnesses to testify for the defendant, and then took the stand himself in support of his kinman's case.[22] One may surmise that the trial was conducted by direct, cross and re-direct examination of the witnesses, and the testimony adduced should have entertained the throngs who customarily assembled in the colonial court rooms. From contemporary proceedings in the Court of Chancery, we know that the two litigants in the Supreme Court action had been involved in a lengthy and bitter dispute over their respective shares in a brewery business, and that Jay's client had been subjected to considerable embarrassment and ridicule by the principal partner, George Harison.[23] Unfortunately, the testimony in the slander case did not inspire any of the onlookers to reduce it to writing; since the judgment roll is not in existence, the harsh words exchanged between the partners are no longer available to us.

---

[20]Law Reg. Jay, N.Y. State Library, p. 137. Cf. Goebel, ed., *Law Practice Hamilton*, I, 61. The three day notice would seem subject to waiver by the parties, Leadbetter v. Harison, Min. S.Ct. Jud., Apr. 18, 1769-May 2, 1772, pp. 349-450.

[21]From Chief Justice Horsmanden's comments concerning jury trials in *Report of an Action of Assault and Battery . . . Between Thomas Forsey and Waddel Cunningham*, p.12, it is clear that no written transcript of trial proceedings was taken taken.

[22]Min. S.Ct.Jud., Apr. 18, 1769-May 2, 1772, pp.358-359.

[23]See Chapter V, *infra*.

A month after Jay's admission to practice there was enacted a statutory method for resolving issues without trial by jury in the Supreme Court; this involved a reference of the matter to three referees when the controversy would require the examination of lengthy accounts.[24] The referees were authorized to make a decision upon the case, and their report in favor of the plaintiff would be confirmed as a judgment upon motion to the Court. If their determination was in favor of the defendant, judgment of non-pross would be entered and the action dismissed. One case where Jay represented the successful plaintiff was handled in this manner, and consumed a total of two days in hearings.[25] After decision was given by Jay's client, judgment was entered upon the filing of the referee's report and motion to the Court.

When trial was held before the Supreme Court *en banc* at New York City the judgment roll prepared by the successful party was presented to the Chief Justice for signature, and then filed with the Clerk of the Court. Thereafter execution could issue on the judgment. However, when trial was held at a circuit sitting of the Court, the issue roll duly endorsed by the Clerk of the Circuit with the jury verdict, was approved by the Court at its next sitting *en banc*, and then filed with the Clerk of Court, thereby reducing the matter to judgment.[26] Appeals by writ of error were possible, initially to the Governor and Council; final appeals to the King and Council, were possible in certain cases.

After judgment had been entered and docketed, forms of execution were available to the judgment creditor. Execution by *fieri facias* directed that the judgment debtor's goods be seized in satisfaction of the judgment; should the

---

[24]*N. Y. Colonial Laws*, IV, 1040-1042 (Dec. 31, 1768).

[25]*Halstead v. Lyon*, Law Reg. Jay, N.Y. State Library, p.65; the referee's report is filed under "Attachments vs. Vessels 1752-1835", N.Y. Co. Clerk's Office Hall of Records, N.Y.C.

[26]See Jay's case of Downing of Oakley, Parchment 1 K-2, N.Y. Co. Clerk, Hall of Records, N.Y.C. Recording of judgments, see *N. Y. Colonial Laws*, V, 636-638 (1774).

sheriff return that he had seized the property of the defendant and it remained in his hands for lack of buyers, a *venditione exponas* would issue on the motion of plaintiff, instructing that the goods be sold at public auction.[27] Far more likely to succeed was the second form of execution by *capias ad satisfaciendum*, requiring that the defendant be arrested and held in confinement until the judgment was satisfied.[28] In transmitting either writ to the sheriff the attorney for the plaintiff was required to endorse on the reverse the amount of the debt with interest and costs. Should the case involve a penal bill obligatory, the attorney issuing the execution was charged with endorsing only the amount of the debt, without regard to the penalty in the bond.[29]

In the county Courts of Common Pleas and the Mayor's Courts of Albany, New York and Westchester Borough, the foregoing outline of procedures seems to have been followed. However the Common Pleas Courts were to some degree hampered by the absence of province-wide jurisdiction. The Westchester Common Pleas Court, for example, issued an order that all parties defendant appearing without attorneys would be subject to service by posting notices in the Common Room of the county court house. Service of papers upon the official in charge of the room was to be due and sufficient service of the papers.[30]

Appeals from the lower courts by writ of error were not uncommon and John Jay had his share of this type of practice. Once the writ of error was returned to the Supreme Court with the record attached, the appellant filed his assignment of errors and the appellee joined issue with a rejoinder. The matter

---

[27]Smith v. Hickman, Law Reg. Jay & L., N.Y. Hist. Soc., N.Y.C., p.15.

[28]White v. Abeel, Law Reg. Jay, N.Y. State Library, p.205. Even in colonial times the harsh results of this type of execution were ameliorated, see *N.Y. Colonial Laws*, III, 753-756 (Act of Oct. 4, 1732).

[29]*N.Y. Colonial Laws*, II, 676 (Act of Oct. 29, 1730).

[30]See Minutes of the Court of Common Pleas, Wastchester County, I, under date Nov. 8, 1771.

then set down for a hearing in the Supreme Court by means of a motion made in the term preceding the term in which the hearing was to take place. The Supreme Court, after argument of the points of law at the hearing entered its order either reversing the Court below or confirming its judgment.[31] The procedures in regard to a writ of certiorari, directed to Justices of the Peace and Courts of General Sessions, were approximately the same as those outlined for writs of error.[32]

Quite distinct from the procedures followed in the common law courts were the steps necessary to prosecute a suit in the New York Court of Chancery. This tribunal exercised broad equitable jurisdiction, being concerned in the appointment of guardians for infants and incompetents, the foreclosure of equities of redemption in real property, the prevention of breaches of trust and confidence, and the granting of injunctive relief. Unfortunately the Governors who occupied the office of Chancellor were usually laymen, and the Chancery court was hampered by its presiding officer being inexpert in the law and limited in the amount of time he could devote to proceedings before the Court. With the appointment of a Master of the Rolls in 1773 the proceedings became more formal and hearings were held at more frequent interval.

Proceedings in Chancery were commenced by filing a bill with one of the Clerks in Chancery.[33] The bill in chancery was drawn upon a large piece of parchment that was approximately three feet square. After being signed by the

---

[31]See Bemus v. Fellows, Law Reg. Jay, N.Y. State Library, p.138, Hunt v. Leggett, *ibid.*, p.155. The practice was regulated by the act of Dec. 23, 1765, *N.Y. Colonial Laws*, IV, 801, 802. If the appellee failed to appear he was compelled to do so by a *scire facias ad audiendum errores*, see Vrooman v. Zeele, *ibid.*, p.143.

[32]*Ibid.*, pp.128, 197.

[33]This discussion is based upon my examination of papers filed in the Chancery Room, Court of Appeals Hall, Albany, N.Y., and the N.Y. Co. Clerk's Office, Hall of Records, N.Y.C.

solicitor and counsel for the complainant, the bill was ready for filing. This was done before an official termed a Clerk in Chancery; precisely how one was appointed to this office is difficult to determine. It is obvious, however, that the leading attorneys of the Province of New York functioned as Clerks in Chancery; among their number are included James Duane and John McKesson. The Clerk in Chancery was not counsel or solicitor for either party to the suit, but all papers in the suit were filed with the same Clerk, who would provide certified copies at a fixed fee per folio page. One is compelled to conclude that the Clerk in Chancery was a member of the Bar who made his office available as a repository for papers in Chancery litigation. When the Chancellor called a term of the Court, the various Clerks were alerted to attend the session at which time they were to make available the bills, answer, interrogatories, and other papers deposited with them. In this way the Chancery Court could sit wherever the Chancellor happened to be, and the attorney as Clerk in Chancery provided all of the papers deemed necessary for the Chancellor's consideration of the cause. Also, the presence of an independent lawyer serving as Clerk in Chancery would make available to the Governor a disinterested expert to whom he could turn for advice.

Testimony in Chancery matters was usually taken by means of interrogatories of witnesses. Questions and answers would be reduced to writing, much in the same manner as testimony was taken in the Vice Admiralty Court as discussed previously.[34] The witness would then swear to the authenticity of the transcript, and it would be filed with the Clerk of Chancery. In this manner testimcny could be obtained at the convenience of each party, and the affidavits and documents could be preserved until some later date when the case would be presented to the Chancellor for decision and decree. Once the decree was signed, a party wishing to appeal to the King and Council began appellate to the King and Council

[34]See Jager v. Van Benthuysen, Chancery Decrees Before 1800,V-33, Chancery Room, Court of Appeals Hall, Albany, N.Y.; cf. procedures in Vice Admiralty described in Chapter IV, *supra*.

began this appellate procedure by filing a notice of appeal.[35]

In these courts Jay spent a significant part of his time while he was engaged in the active practice of the law. Supplementing his work in the courts was doubtless a considerable amount of office business, all of which has disappeared with the bulk of his office files. Nevertheless we can be certain that he drew up a substantial number of deeds, mortgages and wills, as well as a large number of legal opinions. As we shall see, John Jay did fairly well in his legal career, and must have become a master of the system of civil practice outlined above.

---

[35]Decree and notice of appeal in Bloomer v. Hinchman, at BM-1425-B, N.Y. Co. Clerk, Hall of Records, N.Y.C.

VII. IN HIS MAJESTY'S SUPREME COURT OF JUDICATURE

Admission to practice in all of the courts of record in the province of New York carried with it the right to practice in the Supreme Court of Judicature and the High Court of Chancery. Also included within the license, was permission to practice in any or all of the inferior courts of justice in the province.[1] These included the Major's Courts of New York City and Albany, the Common Pleas courts in each county, and, in the rare event an attorney wished to appear in a criminal case, in the Courts of General Sessions or Oyer and Terminer. However in the subordinate courts of justice, the Supreme Court practitioner was in competition with a much larger group of lawyers, for each court was authorized to admit individuals to practice at its own Bar. For this reason the focal point of the attorney admitted to all of the courts of record, was his practice in the Supreme Court of Judicature. It was in this court of law that the newly admitted attorney was put to his severest test, just as the Court of Chancery was the proving ground for his ability in equity jurisprudence. Since most litigation can be resolved at law, the Supreme of Judicature far surpassed the Court of Chancery in the number of cases it offered to the Bar. For these reasons it is not surprising that the Supreme Court of Judicature cases formed the nucleus around which John Jay's law practice revolved.[2]

When Jay and Livingston decided to terminate their partnership practice, the former was confronted with the need to establish himself in a separate location

[1]Although these attorneys were licensed to practice in all of the courts of record, it was nevertheless necessary that an attorney so licensed appear before the lower courts and request formal admission.

[2]Since nearly all of the litigation before the Supreme of Judicature took place at New York City, most of the attorneys maintained their offices in that city.

in New York City.[3] While the Jay family owned some parcels of realty in New York City, none of the buildings or lots could have been suitable or available for John's use, for in January of 1771, Jay had made arrangements to use a house and store in the city. His brother Frederick, serving a term as merchant's factor in Willemstad, Curacao, commended him upon the "easy terms" for which he had secured.[4] The precise location of the law office and house, or whether Jay had arranged a rental or a purchase, is impossible to determine.

Assisting Jay at various times during his period of law practice were three young men who had engaged as clerks, Thomas H. Barclay, John Strang and Robert Troup. The exact dates of their apprenticeships are not available; however, since Barclay was admitted to practice in 1775 he must have been the first to serve with Jay. If Barclay served his full term with John Jay, he would have commenced clerkship sometime in 1772. From the law register of Robert R. Livingston, Jr., it is clear that both Barclay and Strang were clerks in July of 1774.[5] In the case of Strang, who was a clerk in 1772 at the age of 21 and was not admitted to practice until October of 1778, it seems that a five year clerkship was required because he did not have a college degree.[6] Barclay was probably replaced in Jay's office by Robert Troup, a young graduate of King's College (1774), who served with Jay until the outbreak of the war, and was finally admitted to

---

[3]I have found no reference to the location of the Jay-Livingston law office, although it may possibly have been at the home of Judge Robert R. Livingston, in New York City.

[4]Letter dated Jan. 23, 1770, [1771] Colutbia University Libraries, Special Collections.

[5]Law Reg. Jay & L, p.113 [Hake v. Wikoff]. For Barclay's admission, see Roll of Attorneys, Oct. 26, 1754-June 27, 1847, Ledgar B, Parchment Roll #1, N.Y.Co. Clerk, Hall of Records, N.Y.C.,

[6]Josephine C. Frost, *The Strang Genealogy*, (Brooklyn: Bowles, 1915), 33, 34: *New York Genealogical and Biographical Record*, II (1871), 184.

practice in April of 1782.[7]

In his first years of practice Jay exhibited a somewhat slavish devotion to business; while dedication to work is not a criticism of any man, in the case of John Jay it proved to be an unhealthy obsession. Even before the Livingston partnership had begun its dissolution, Jay's letter to one of his correspondents indicates that he was a highly excitable young man who placed duty above everything else in his life. Jay explained he had interrupted his writing to answer a call at Rye, New York; from there he went on legal business to Fairfield, Connecticut, and returned to New York shortly thereafter. All this in the wintry month of March![8]

As a sole practitioner no longer held back by Robert R. Livingston, Jr., Jay threw all of his energy into the task of building up his volume of cases pending. In November of 1770 he opened eighteen cases in the Supreme Court of Judicature; in June of 1771, another eighteen cases were commenced.[9] Separation, from the Livingston partnership shifted the geographical basis of Jay's practice from Dutchess to Westchester county; as a result Jay began forty-three cases in the Common Pleas court of Westchester during the November 1771 term.[10] Such an increase in practice soon took its toll of John's health. From the fall of 1770 until the summer of 1771, he was attended by three doctors for a swelling of muscles in his neck and a lingering fever.[11] Writing to his friend, Samuel Kissam, of his illness he concluded, perhaps in some sense for justification,

---

[7]Charles B. Salmon, "Colonel Robert Troup, Federalist; The Revolutionary Experience", Unpublished M.A. Essay, Columbia University, 1960, pp. 4, 7, 8; Roll of Attorneys, *ibid.*

[8]Johnston, *Corres.*, I, 11.

[9]See Appendix C, Table I.

[10]See Appendix C., Tables II and III.

[11]To Samuel Kissam, Aug. 1771, Frank Monaghan, "Samuel Kissam and John Jay", *Columbia University Quarterly*, XXV 127-133, at 131.

> With Respect to Business I am as well circumstanced as I have a Right to expect. My old friends contribute much to my Happiness, and upon the Whole I have Reason to be satisfied with my share of the attention of the Province.[12]

Despite these expressions of satisfaction with the status quo, Jay continued to expand his practice, which did not reach its peak volume until the latter part of 1773.[13] In regard to his health, the family tradition its that John cured himself by taking rooms six miles from the center of the city, and riding to and from the city on horseback everyday.[14] Thus he become one of the first commuting lawyers in the history of the city Bar. As an additional expense attributable to his commutation schedule, Jay required an extensive amount of repairs to his saddle and riding in

---

[12]*Ibidem*. Kissam, a medical doctor, took a diagnostic approach in his reply:

> In the name of the Gods my Dear Jay! what can have made you the subject of a Disease? I thought your Temperance might almost have baffled the unwholesome Blasta of Spring or Autumn, the glowing heat of Aug[us]t or the nipping frosts of January . . . ".

The letter, suggesting possible overindulgence in food or wine, is at *ibid*., p. 131. Temperate Jay certainly was; he was also ambitious, and from this trait came his susceptability to disease due to overwork and physical exhaustion.

[13]See charts of cases pending in Appendix C.

[14]The tradition, presumably an oral statement by Jay in later life, is reported at Wm. Jay, *Life*. I, 23. According to William Jay's account the period of commuting was only one season; it was suggested by his physicians and was completely successful. In later life, John Jay on several occasions suggested riding as a means to regain, or retain, health.

the autumn of 1771.[15]

Subsequent to this initial period of rapidly expanding practice, Jay seems to have been content to open relatively few cases in the years 1773 and 1774. Thereafter a lack of law registers, and a lost minute book of the Supreme Court of Judicature, make it difficult to generalize concerning the volume of cases carried by Jay in the two years before May of 1776 when the courts of the province formally suspended their proceedings. However it can be seen from the data that is available that Jay continued to carry a fairly constant number of cases during the entire period from 1773 to 1776, and it is quite possible that he had reached the limit on his capacity in late 1773. Thereafter he was content to gain a smaller number of new cases since his time was occupied with the litigation that remained in a pending status.[16]

Because of the location of his family's home at Rye, it is not surprising that John Jay drew an inordinately large number of cases in the Supreme Court from litigants who resided in Westchester county, or conducted business there. During the years 1769 to 1776, the firm of Jay and and Livingston, and John Jay individually, drew the bulk of their cases from Westchester. Sixty-five cases in the Supreme Court pertain to New York County. The next county in number of causes is Dutchess with twenty-six, followed Ulster with eight, Queens with the same number and Orange with seven. The relatively heavily populated county of Albany accounts for only six causes.[17] From this we must conclude that Jay's clients were drawn from among the aristocrats and yeoman of the lower Hudson

[15]Account of John Johnson, Sept. 2, 1771, paid in full Mar. 10, 1772, Columbia University Libraries, Special Collections.

[16]See Table I, Appendix C, and note particularly the fairly regular number of cases pending during the last two of years practice.

[17]The figures are of course not statistically perfect, since these details are not available for every case. It has been assumed that if a writ issues to a sheriff of a particular county, the case arose there.

River Valley. He had relatively few cases from Long Island or the Old Dutch settlements in the upper Hudson River Valley, and drew less than half of his Supreme Court business from New York City.

The titles of the causes tried by Jay indicates that his family connections were also useful in building his Supreme Court practice. For example, his Aunt Anne Chambers requested him to represent her in six cases; Jay also tried eight cases on behalf of her estate, and eleven cases for the executors of her husband's estate. The estate of Peter Delancey, a cousin, contributed eight cases to Jay's docket, and other Delancey matters accounted for an additional seven causes. From the DePeyster family, to which he was related through his mother, John obtained six cases. Although these cases represent but a small part of the 257 cases in the Supreme Court identified as those of John Jay and the Jay & Livingston partnership, they provided the young lawyer with a certain assurance that his family wished him well, and that he could depend upon receiving their patronage when the need for an attorney'services arose.[18]

We have noted before that within a year after he was admitted to practice, Jay was retained to be of counsel for Benjamin Kissam on certain causes to be

[18]At this point it is necessary to indicate the technique utilized to obtain a list of Jay's cases in the Supreme Court of Judicature. Each case in the law register of Jay & Livingston was listed, since it is impossible to distinguish which were Jay's cases and which were Livingston's; every Supreme Court case in the Jay register from 1770 to 1774 was listed. In addition, the minutes of the Supreme Court of Judicature were read in their entirety from October 1768 to May of 1776. When Jay's name was attached to a case, either on the motion days, or at the trial of the cause, the name of the case was listed. This list of cases was then used for the purpose of obtaining judgment rolls pertaining to the cases. No file papers are available, since all pre-Revolutionary documents other than final judgments and executions were destroyed by the county clerk pursuant to statutory authorization in 1799. Jay's own papers contain only a minute fragment of the files that must have been maintained in his law office.

tried on circuit.[19] Other examples of such retainers are the appearance of Jay in 1771 for Philip J. Livingston in two ejectment cases, and his being retained by Robert Yates of Albany when a cause Yates was trying in the Mayor's Court was removed to the Supreme Court by a writ of habeas corpus.[20] Throughout his years at the Bar, Jay could depend upon a certain number of cases being referred to him by other attorneys, thereby increasing his practice, and building his reputation in the community at large.

The cases which came into Jay's office covered nearly every phase of civil litigation. Of the cases identifiable as to subject matter, fifty-one pertain to actions of debt on writings obligatory; the bulk of these suits involve amounts in the range of £ 51 to £ 200. Next in order of occurrence are assumpsit causes, in which the amounts in controversy average between £ 51 and £ 100. These commercial actions are followed by twenty-five actions for assault and battery. Ejectment actions are next in frequency, numberings eleven cases; they are followed by nine certiorari proceedings. Slander cases, appeals on writs of error, customs causes, and actions for trover and conversion occupy a small, but interesting phase of Jay's practice.[21]

Despite the dearth of materials available concerning Jay's practice, the documents which survived from his pre-Revolutionary office files provides a good, albeit incorplete, picture of his practice. When supplemented by the file papers remaining from the office of John Tabor Kempe,[22] these papers provide a good example of the variety and nature of Jay's practice. The search for Jay materials

---

[19]See pages 87 and 88, above.

[20]For examples see Hogstrosser v. deCline et al., Law Register of John Jay, New York State Library, Albany, New York p.1965 (hereafter Law Reg. Jay); Min. S.Ct.Jud., Apr. 18, 1769-May 2, 1772, p.399 N.Y. Co. Clerk, N.Y.C.

[21]Most details on types of cases are from Law Reg. Jay, *passim*.

[22]John Tabor Kempe papers, Lawsuits, A-B, New York Historical Society, New York City.

in the papers of other New York attorneys has been generally unsuccessful.[23] Needless to say, it is the unusual case file which has survived, and the average commercial matter which formed the bulk of Jay's practice, is evidenced only by minute book entries and colorless judgment rolls. Although Jay's legal career is far from uninteresting, the cases which follow should not mislead the reader into the assumption that John Jay was a specialist in the trial of spectacular causes in New York. Rather he was a hard working attorney, dealing mainly with collection cases who upon occasion was called upon to prosecute or defend an unusually interesting case.

One of the most interesting assault and battery cases in Jay's career at the Bar, was that of Budd v. Tompkins, in which John Jay was retained to defend a group of men accused of attacking and imprisoning a school master. As is true of most tort cases, Budd v. Tompkins casts an interesting light upon the society of the day and particularly upon the low status occupied by pedagogues. The facts of the case are found in the file papers of Jay's adversary, John Tabor Kempe.[24] By a bond dated September 1, 1769, Tompkins and three other residents of White Plains promised to pay Budd the sum of seven shillings per quarter per child, and also undertook to provide the teacher with meat, drink and lodging during the term of his service. Apparently the latter part of the obligation was left unperformed, and the unfortunate Budd was forced to obtain a bag of corn under suspicious circumstances. When he brought suit upon the obligation to collect his salary and the value of his subsistence, the defendants in the collection action had Budd arrested for theft. While so inprisoned, Budd had been compelled to sign a receipt to Tompkins and his associates for the full amount due under the obligation. After he released the defendants in his collection action, he was severely

---

[23]Papers of John McKesson, Samuel Jones, and the law registers of William Livingston, revealed no evidence of practice with or in opposition to John Jay, other than an isolated case in which Jay was opposing counsel.

[24]John Tabor Kempe Papers, Lawsuits A-B, *sub. nom.* Budd, New York Historical Society, N.Y.C.

beaten, and then released from custody. Apparently the local constable was in league with the individuals involved in the assault on Budd, for no action was taken to protect the prisoner.[25] Quite properly Budd brought his case to Kempe, who was also attorney general of the province; Kempe must have advised Budd to sue for civil damages, and a complaint was drawn up on March 15, 1770.[26] Jay was retained by Tompkins on August 21, 1770, and received a copy of the narrative on the 29th of August, at which time he sent a bail piece to the Chief Justice to release Tompkins and his associates from prison in New York County.[27] Thereafter Jay made a motion upon notice to Kempe, and succeeded in changing the venue of the case from New York to Westchester county, based upon the assertion that all of the material witnesses were at Westchester.[28] In addition to convenience, the change of venue asserted that the trial would be had before a Westchester county jury. Although this did not necessarily guarantee a verdict of acquittal, the likelihood of a conviction was considerably reduced. After the change of venue had been granted, the defendant's plea of not guilty was filed, and Tompkins and his associates put themselves "on the country".[29]

---

[25]A11 of the documents mentioned are at *ibidem.*

[26]Kempe could also have instituted a criminal case against Tompkins and his confederates. As Budd had escaped without permanent injuries and the possibility of conviction was remote, Kempe probably felt that it would serve no purpose to prosecute in the name of the Crown.

[27]Law Reg. Jay, p. 22.

[28]*Ibidem.*, notice of motion with supporting affidavit at Kempe Papers, Lawsuit, New-York Historical Society, N.Y.C., order changing venue in Min. S.Ct. Jud., 1769-72, p.306, Records Div., N.Y. County Clerk, Hall of Records, N.Y.C.

[29]On Nov. 1, 1770 the plea was filed. "Putting oneself on the country" is equivalent to the present day demand for a trial by jury.

Kempe noticed the case for trial at White Plains in the September term, at which time the Supreme Court held its circuit sitting. The Westchester county jury returned a verdict of not guilty. At the trial Jay had argued upon the facts of the case; he admitted the law as alleged by the plaintiff. First, the plaintiff's original suit on the obligation was vexatious, and the plaintiff had secured the defendant's signatures through deceit. Secondly, the plaintiff had been caught in the very act of stealing the bag of corn. Finally, the receipt given by the plaintiff in the course of his detention was not a complete one and did not discharge the entire obligation; the detention itself, being based upon the order of a justice of the peace, was not unlawful. To counter this argument, Kempe introduced evidence that Budd had never been returned before the magistrate, as required by the warrant of arrest, and that Budd did not demand to be arraigned because as one of Kempe's witnesses expressed it, he was "A scarish Man, apt to be frightened."[30] The jury, swayed by Jay's argument and influenced no doubt by their sympathy for their neighbors, held for Jay's clients. The postea being returned by the Clerk of the Circuit, it was read and filed before the Supreme Court *en banc* on October 21st, 1771 and judgment entered for the defendants.[31]

In his handling of the Budd v. Tompkins case, Jay indicated his awareness of the value of obtaining a favorable venue for purposes of trial. The order changing venue greatly strengthened his client's position, and made his work as trial counsel considerably easier than it would have been in New York County vhere he was at the disadvantage of being relatively unknown to the jurors, and his clients were at the mercy of a jury that might tend to look upon the inhabitants of Westchester as a rather rowdy group. John Jay's success in this case, in which he was opposed by the attorney general of the Province, seems to have resulted in an increased practice in this field of the law. In

---

[30]Kempe Papers, Lawsuits A-B, supra. Quote from testimony of William Anderson on September 27, 1771.

[31]Parchment 157 E-10, N.Y.Co., Clerk, Hall of Records, N.Y.C.

1771 and 1772 Jay was engaged as attorney in no less than five Supreme Court matters involving assault and battery.[32]

While assault and battery cases provide the legal historian with an interesting view of violence in colonial society, slander cases furnish an abundant source of information concerning the verbal attacks made upon men's character and professional reputations. Since the pleader was required to set forth the slanderous words *verbatim*, some of the colorful language of the eighteenth century is in this way preserved for posterity. If Jay's cases are a measure of the damages awarded for defamation, it would seem that reputation in the eighteenth century was worth considerably less than it is today.

John Jay in June of 1772 was retained by Nesbit Deane, a New York City master hatter, to institute a slander action against one Thomas Vernon. According to the judgment roll filed in the action, Deane had been subjected to a great loss of reputation by the statements of Vernon concerning his ability as a hatter.[33] To the customers of Deane, and perhaps even more significantly, to the journeymen employed by Deane, Vernon was alleged to have said that Deane was incapable of making a good hat, that Deane was no man and that no man who considered himself a man would work for Deane. Vernon was alleged to have continued that Deane was so unknowledgeable in his trade, that he could not even identify a good hat after it had been made. According to the plaintiff's complaint, he had suffered a decline in his business as a result of the statements of the defendant, and all of his journeymen left his employ. The latter situation, if true, would have been a basis for a relatively large award, for the Hat Act of 1732 had severely limited the number of skilled hatters available in the North American colonies, and Deane Deane would have been hard pressed to obtain other

---

[32]Getfield v. Moreland, Have v. Miller, Hubbs v. Hageman, Hubbs v. Miller, Warner v. Kendall, Law Reg. Jay, New York State Library, Albany, pp.105, 124, 134, 135, 187, Min. S.Ct. Jud., Apr. 18, 1769-May 2, 1772. p. 541, 72-76, pp.47, 48, N.Y.Co. Clerk, Hall of Records, N.Y.C.

[33]Parchment 178 A-7, N.Y. Co. Clerk, Hall of Records, N.Y.C.

employees.[34]

Since the defendant Vernon defaulted in answering the complaint, Jay took judgment for want of a plea, and the matter was referred to a jury to assess damages. The award was only £ 6, for damages; when costs were added the total award was only £ 23 18s 9d.[35] A year thereafter Jay was still issuing executions against the defendant in the hope of collecting the jury award.[36]

Another slander case in which Jay took part was that of Smith v. Mills, tried at the circuit sitting of the Supreme Court at Jamaica in September of 1772. In this instance Jay represented the plaintiff, and James Duane appeared for the defendant who was alleged to have referred to the plaintiff as ". . . a forsworn Wretch ... a perjured Man ..." and that in a trial between the defendant and another "... Smith [the plaintiff] swore falsely, as false as can be and I ... can prove

---

[34]The allegations are from the judgment roll, *ibidem*. For Hat Act restrictions see Richard B. Morris, *Government and Labor in Early America*, (New York: Columbia University Press, 1946), p.154-156, indicating that prosecutions in New York during the 1760s for violations were not unknown. Deane would thus be required to seek his journeymen from among those few individuals in the colony who had been able to serve an apprenticeship.

[35]It would seem that Dean's reputation may have had some effect upon the jury's conclusion. Trained in Ireland, Deane had a shop on Broad Street, near the Royal Exchange in 1765, New York *Gazette or Weekly Post Boy*, Dec. 5, 1765. In 1772 his business permitted him to purchase the old coffee house at Wall and Water Streets, W. Harrison Bayles, *Old Taverns of New York* (New York: Frank Allaben Genealogical Co., 1915), p. 255, 275. His mistreatment of apprentices is evidenced by a proceeding before the Court of General Sessions in 1775, see Minutes of the Court of General Sessions, May 21, 1772 to November 1790, New York County Supreme Court Library, General Sessions Branch, Criminal Courts Building, N.Y.C., pp.144, 148.

[36]Law Reg. Jay, p. 178.

it . . ,".[37] James Duane for the defendant put in a defense of truth of the statements; the jury returned a special verdict, finding that the words as alleged were actually uttered, but released the defendant nevertheless.[38] It would seem that John Jay was not conspicuously successful in the trial of slander causes, but it is necessary to bear in mind that juries tend to frustrate the efforts of even the most able of lawyers.[39]

The more predictable aspects of law practice involve points of law, and in this connection Jay was fortunate in having some cases on appeal in which his ability as a student of the law was put to the test. One such case was Bemus v. Fellows, which was appealed from the Mayor's Court of Albany by means of a writ of error.[40] Jay was retained by the attorney for the plaintiff who had recovered judgment below. The case involved the question whether a party who has recovered judgment in another province can sue on the judgment in the province of New York. It was the defendant's contention upon appeal, that such an action was not proper, and that the prior judgment recovered in the province of Massachusetts could not form the basis for a suit in New York. When advised of the facts by Peter W. Yates, his Albany correspondent in this matter, Jay was very pessimistic concerning the chances of the judgment being sustained on appeal, and wrote,

> I assure you this Cause is a very critical one. Many of our best lawyers doubt

---

[37]Parchment 223 C-l, N.Y. Co. Clerk, Hall of Records, N.Y.C.

[38]*Ibidem*. Presumably they held the statanent to be true.

[39]0ther slander cases are Bailey v. Van Beuren, Lewis v. Rosenkrans, Law Reg. Jay, pp.158, 203.

[40]The writ of error was presented to the Albany Mayor's Court on May 20, 1770, Mayor's Court Minutes, City and County of Albany, Albany County Clerk's Office, Albany, New York, Vol. dated 1768-1778, page 65, John Morin Scott was the New York City attorney who had obtained the writ. The writ of error removed the proceeding from the Mayor's Court to the Supreme Court where the judgment below was viewed.

> whether an action in one province on a Judgment obtained in another can be supported. It is a point that can apply only to the Colonies and therefore much law respecting it cannot be expected. I have inquired whether actions in England can be brought on Judgments obtained in Ireland and find many authorities against it. As to other Countrys the Practice in several Instances has been to bring the Suit for the original Cause of Action, and give the Proceedings of the Court in Evidence. It is however a very important Point, and the Country is much interested in its determination.[41]

The pessimism with which Jay approached this case was justified, for when the Supreme Court of Judicature finally gave its decision in the case, it held that Yates had followed an incorrect procedure below, that the judgment upon which he based his debt action was one rendered in Massachusetts, which had not been proven as a fact, and for these reasons the demurrer of the defendant below should have been granted.[42] Jay thus had the satisfaction of knowing he was right concerning the law, even though he was unsuccessful in preventing the reversal of the judgment given for his client in the Mayor's Court of Albany.

While Jay's professional colleagues would have awaited with interest the decision in Bemus v. Fellows, his efforts in the Westchester election case of King v. Underhill had a much wider audience.[43] According to Jared Sparks the case

---

[41]To Peter W. Yates, Mar. 23, 1772, Misc. Mss Peter W. Yates #13, New York Historical Society.

[42]Parchment, 136 G-l, N.Y.Co. Clerk, Hall of Records, N.Y.C.

[43]Even his biographer George Pellew, notes his participation in this case at *John Jay* (Boston: Houghton, Mifflin & Co., 1890), pp.18, 19. Considering the relatively brief discussion of Jay's law practice, it is apparent that the author considered this one of the significant cases of his early career.

gave the attorneys involved ample opportunity to display their legal knowledge and forensic skills.[44] Although the details concerning this litigation are far from complete, it is apparent from the brief of John Tabor Kempe as prosecutor, that the Crown was basing its case upon the strict interpretation of the suffrage requirements of the Borough of Westchester. An information had gone unanswered in January of 1773, and only Jay's prompt intervention upon behalf of Nathaniel Underhill saved the unfortunate Mayor of Westchester Borough from imprisonment. Jay convinced the Court that he should be permitted to enter a not guilty plea on behalf of Underhill, and despite the opposition of Kempe, succeeded in gaining this request.[45]

Upon Kempe's noticing the cause for trial in April of 1773, Jay filed an affidavit that a material witness, Samuel Webb, was absent from the Province but was expected to return by July of 1773, at which time he could be subpoenaed.[46] The motion was granted, and Underhill thereby served another three months of his term as Mayor.[47] Thereafter the case seems to have lost vitality, for no further motion seems to have been made concerning it. Kempe had thus been temporarily stopped in his attempt to sharply curtail the number of persons qualified to vote in Westchester borough elections. In 1773 and 1774 Jay again represented the officials of the town of Westchester in a similar matter but upon this occasion a mandamus was issued against the Mayor, Aldermen and Commonalty of the Town

---

[44]*The Life of Gouverneur Morris*, 3 vols., (Boston: Gray & Bowen, 1832), I, 20. Other than the Pellew reference and a citation to Sparks by Henry B. Dawson in *Westchester County, New York, During the American Revolution* (Morrisania, N.Y. Henry B. Dawson, 1886) p.4, I have found no other references to this case. No reference to this Westchester election case appears in New York City newspapers of the day.

[45]Kempe Papers, Lawsuits-S-U, New York Historical Society, N.Y.C.; Law Reg, Jay, p. 176.

[46]Kempe Papers, *ibid.*

[47]*Ibidem.*

and Borough of Westchester, ordering them to admit Gilial Honeywell and Isaac Legget to the Office of Alderman. By procedural motions Jay had succeeded in excluding them from office from July of 1773 to April of 1774.[48] Nevertheless, he was powerless to prevent the Crown from directing the installation of those officials. Both cases taken together must have vastly increased Jay's popularity in the province of New York and brought his name to the attention of many who had never before known of the young lawyer from Rye who was quietly building his law practice in the city of New York.

All of the above cases have been discussed from sources other than the office files of John Jay. It not without significance that the two sets of papers saved by Jay, and which relate to his Supreme Court practice, are briefs and notes for oral arguments in ejectment cases. These particular documents were undoubtedly saved because they relate to the title to lands in Bedford township of Westchester county, where the Jay family had extensive holdings. Since Jay had a personal interest in the subject matter of the litigation, and unquestionably had spent a large amount of time in historical research concerning these titles, these papers were treated with such care that they survived the American Revolution, and remained in the hands of the Jay family until the twentieth century. The causes involved are John Doe ex dem. Philip Verplanck v. Ezekiel Griffin and Peter Quiet ex dem. Susannah Warren v. Frances Van Cortlandt; in both cases Jay represented the defendants who traced their titles to patentees from the colony of Connecticut.[49] The plaintiffs based their claims upon the grant of Cortlandt Manor to Stephanus Van Cortlandt in 1697, pointing to the fact that the 1683 boundary agreement between New York and Connecticut fixed the Connecticut boundary to the east

---

[48]Min, S.Ct.Jud., April 21, 1772-Jan. 17, 1776, pp.101, 131, 153. Despite the success of Kempe in these suits, Underhill seems to have remained at his post of Mayor. He was Mayor at the time of the Declaration of Independence and continued to serve under the government of the State of New York thereafter.

[49]Jay Papers, Colurribia University Libraries, Special Collections.

of the tracts in question. Jay's argument in reply was an artfully drawn exposition.

Pointing to the fact that the 1683 settlement was conditional and would not became effective until approval by the Duke of York and the King, Jay contended that only 1700, when the boundary was confirmed by King William, could it be held that New York had any right to grant lands in the disputed tract. Furthermore, the settlement 1683 pertained only to sovereign jurisdiction, and did not operate as a grant; hence it could not divest landowners who held legal titles in the town of Bedford. Finally, predecessors of Jay's clients had held title more than the twenty years required under the statute of limitations, hence they could not be ousted; in this regard, Jay was also careful to invoke the provisions of a New York act of 1708 which provided that if possession had been over ten years duration in 1708, and no claim had been made within two years thereafter, the person then possessed of the land should be deemed the owner.[50] I

Proving the Indian deeds of his clients Jay submitted a detailed memorandum on the law to convince the court that Connecticut granted lands by vote of the General Assembly, and without a formal land grant.[51] Based upon a number of English precedents and texts, the memorandum is evidence of careful preparation for any eventuality that might occur at trial when evidence was introduced.

Since the ejectment cases discussed above do not appear in Jay's register, it is safe to conclude that they arose subsequent to 1773, and very likely were

---

[50]*Ibidem.* The argument indicates that Jay was well aware of the value of carefully studying seventeenth century land grants. Probably the habit arose from his training as clerk to the Boundary Commission in 1769.

[51]Headed "Memorandum on Proof of Deeds", *ibid.* The problem has been covered in detail by Chief Judge Benjamin N. Cardozo in Beers v. Hotchkiss. 256 N.Y. 41 (1931).

tried in 1774.[52] During this period the minute books of the Supreme Court of Judicature are incomplete, only rough minutes having survived. I have not located either of the cases in the minutes of the court, but presume that since Jay was so careful in preserving these briefs from destruction, that they must have formed the basis of a favorable settlement, or perhaps even a judgment in favor of the defendants.

Jay's interest in land grants and real property investments was not unusual for a well-do-do gentleman of his day. Indeed in June of 1771 he had petitioned for a grant of land in Albany county on behalf of himself and twenty-five others;[53] this petition was apparently tabled by the Council when the Governor received instructions to suspend all grants in the disputed tract between New York and New Hampshire. This order caused considerable distress among the speculators of the province,[54] and the Governor's reluctance to make any land grants whatsoever resulted in Jay's writing to England on behalf of some of his clients whose titles were jeopardized by the *quo warranto* proceeding against John Van Rensselaer.[55] Having petitioned Governor Tryon on behalf of his clients, who held their lands by virtue of grants from Van Rensselaer's ancestors, Jay found that no confirmation of the grants would be forthcoming. He therefore addressed a somewhat impassioned appeal to the Earl of Darmouth, explaining that principles of humanity had interested him in their pitiable plight.

---

[52]The register in the State Library (Law Reg. Jay) contains a few causes as late as 1774, but most of Jay's cases for that year were entered in another ledger, now missing.

[53]New York Colonial Manuscripts, Land Papers, XXV, 69, New York State Library, Albany, New York.

[54]See Earl of Darthmouth to Gov. William Tyron, Dec. 9, 1772, C.O. 5/1103/440, 442; John McKesson toMoses Little, July 10, 1772, John McKesson Papers, Box I-Letters A-Y and family letters; New York Historical Society, N.Y.C., McKesson to Stephen Little, Oct. 8, 1772, *ibid.*

[55]Judgment against Van Rensselaer is recorded in Parchment 187 B-6, N.Y.Co. Clerk, Hall of Records, N.Y.C.

> It gives me Pain my Lord! to observe that the prevailing monopoly of Lands in this Colony has become a Grievance to the lower Class of People in it; and confines the Bounty of our Gracious Sovereign to mercenary Land-jobbers, and Gentlemen who have already shared very largely in the royal munificense.56

Even Jay's plea does not seem to have convinced the ministry to depart from its cautious policy concerning New York land grants, and the inhabitants of New Britain had to wait until after the Revolution to clear the cloud upon land titles.[57]

In everyday practice concerning collection matters Jay's language was as terse as his language in the above petition was flowery. To Garret Rapalje he wrote a collection letter for £ 56. 2s. 0d, expressing the demand in one sentence and concluding, "As an amicable Settlement will prevent the Trouble and Expense of a Suit, I hope this Notice will induce you to avoid Delays."[58] It was perhaps as well that Jay did not waste words in this instance for payment was not forthcoming, and suit was instituted two months later.[59] So many of Jay's cases were concerned with these commercial matters, it was a requirement that he reduce these demands to a formal, terse model. It was good experience for a man who would soon have more than enoungh administrative work to accomplish during the course of his public life. As far as Jay's practice is concerned, it indicates

---

[56]Covering letter and petition appear at C.O. 5/1104/260-263.

57Of course, had Jay been in the good graces of Governor Tryon, he might have had better success at home. In January of 1773 William Smith succeeded in obtaining the grant of 19,000 acres, also of land involved in the Van Rensselaer case. Noted Smith slyly, "... the Governor was under the impression I was writing a book on his defeat of the N. Car. Regulators. . .", *Smith Manoirs*, p.137.

[58]Apr. 21, 1771, Jay Misc Mss, New York Public Library, N.Y.C.

[59]Law Reg. Jay, p.127.

that he rapidly acquired the capacity to dispose of routine matters in a minimum amount of time, and with the least expenditure of effort on the part of himself or his clerks.

On the eve of the Revolution, Judge Thomas Jones noted that John Jay, like James Duane, was a gentleman of eminence in the law who had a sufficiency of ambiticon with a proper share of pride, and who adored the British Constitution in Church as well as state.[60] Such a complimentary comparison with one of the most distinguished members of the Bar, coming as it does from a man who found himself opposed to Jay concerning the Revolution, indicates the place Jay had earned for himself. Another loyalist is witness to the fact that Jay's practice netted him about £ 1,000, per annum.[61] Since the best five year average of William Livingston had been £ 1287, and that of James Duane £ 1400, Jay had reason to remark to Samuel Kissam that he was well pleased with his share of the legal business of the province.[62]

---

[60]*History New York*, I, 35.

[61]Hamlin, *Legal Education*, p.94.

[62]KLein, *William & Mary Quarterly*. 3rd Ser., XV, 355.

VIII. CONTINUING LEGAL EDUCATION

After surviving the ordeal of commencing a practice, the young lawyer finds it necessary to keep himself in touch with the changes in the law and to deepen his understanding of underlying principles of jurisprudence. This process of continuing legal education is two-fold: a conscientious attempt to read the contemporary literature of the law, and an earnest endeavor to learn as much as possible from one's fellow attorneys. A lawyer who neglects either path to knowledge is likely to fall by the wayside, and to lose valuable clients to his more diligent associates. This was as true in John Jay's day, as it is at the present time; while the techniques of continuing legal education have changed through the years, the fundamental need for study of current developments in the law remains characteristics of the practicing bar.

John Jay and his contemporaries improved their knowledge of the law through two processes. First and foremost, they assembled in their offices large collections of law books to assist them in their everyday research and to provide a broad background in the foremost legal philosophies of the day. Secondly, they organized a formal organization for the sole purpose of attending meetings to debate points of law raised by the members. This organization, called the Moot, met from 1770 to 1774; John Jay was a charter member and rarely missed a meeting.

By the second half of the eighteenth century, the law of the province of New York was unquestionably based upon the common law of England as amended by Acts of Parliament and the New York General Assembly. Since the decisions of New York courts were not available in printed reports, it is not surprising that the bulk of the volumes in John Jay's law library were printed in England and pertained to English common law.[1] These cases were cited before the courts of the Province, they formed the basis of discussion at the Moot, and were the fundamental law of Province of New York. In addition to the case reports, English treatises provided invaluable guidance to the colonial lawyer approaching a new area of the law, and in a few instances were guides to practice in the lesser known subjects of English law, such as

[1] A list of Jay's books is in Appendix D. It contains but one volume originating in New York, the 1752 edition of the laws of New York.

such as crimnal procedure and ecclesiastical practice relating to wills and testaments.

To those unfamiliar with the intense desire of lawyers for complete law libraries, and the equally fervent wish of booksellers to sell law books, it may come as a surprise that English lawbooks and treatises were readily available in the city of New York. A brief glance through the newspaper advertisements appearing during Jay's clerkship is sufficient to confirm the amount of legal literature that was offered for sale by the leading stationers of the city. For example, Hugh Gaine advertised to the profession a profusion of reports ranging from "Cook's" [Sir Edward Coke's] *Reports to Saunder's and Winch's Reports*, and in addition, a formidable list of texts ranging from Giles Jacob's *Clerk's Remembrance* to Brydall on *Bastardy*. This one advertisement alone listed twenty-eight distinct titles relating to legal subjects.[2] A year previously Garret Noel advertised, among several other titles, Bacon's *Abridgment of the Law* in four volumes, and a parliamentary or constitutional history of England in twenty-four volumes.[3] Although those two stationers seem to have been the largest suppliers of law books, James Livingston's regular advertisements also contain books dealing with legal materials.[4] That three printers were actively engaged in the importation of a large variety of expensive books, is a clear indication that there was a ready market for these publications in the city and province of New York.

Fortunately for Jay, he was able to begin law practice without having recourse to the booksellers. His godfather and uncle, John Chambers, died on April 10, 1764; while young John Jay had not commenced his clerkship with Benjamin Kissam, all of the arrangements had been made for him to follow Chambers into the legal profession. Consequently the old man, who had been weak and palsied for nearly a year, made arrangements that half of his law library was to go to John Jay under the terms of his will. Upon Chambers' death, the estate went into a long period of administration, and it

---

[2]*New York Mercury*, July 27, 1767.

[3]*Ibid.*, June 9, 1766.

[4]*Ibid.*

was not until 1771 that the law books were available for distribution to John Jay.[5]

At the peak of his career Chambers possessed a library second to none in the province of New York. Throughout a long life at the Bar and on the Bench, he had assembled a gigantic collection. Even after his nephew, Augustus Van Cortlandt, had been established in practice with part of Chambers' books, the Chambers library still consisted of 588 volumes, of which 170 related to the law.[6] It does not seem that Jay received one-half of the 170 volumes remaining in Chambers' library, for only thirteen works in the Jay law library at Columbia University bear clear markings that indicate an origin in the Chambers collection. Rather, it seems likely that the collection of law books was divided between Jay and his cousin, Augustus Van Cortlandt, upon the basis of the value of the book. Furthermore Van Cortlandt's earlier admission to practice would have resulted in his already possessing most of the basic case reports and statutes. Consequently these larger, and more expensive book, went to John Jay, while Van Cortlandt received most of the treatises. In addition, it is possible that many Chambers volumes were lost when the Jay law library was removed from New York City in 1776. With due consideration to the potential loss of books, and the monetary basis of dividing the books, it nevertheless seems unlikely that there were 170 volumes available for distribution among Jay and Van Cortlandt.[7]

---

[5]See references to Chambers' health at Peter Jay Letterbook #3, Columbia University Libraries, Special Collections, Apr. 14, 1763, July 18, 1763. See also Hamlin, *Legal Education*, p. 92, and Abstracts of Wills on file in the Surrogate's Office, City of New York, Vol. VI: 1760-1766, *New York Historical Society Collections*, XXX, pp.315-317.

[6]Hamlin, *ibid.*, 83, 184.

[7]Since the estate of John Chambers was quite solvent, is no reason to suspect that the books were sold to debts of the deceased.

Although the Chambers legacy of law books was probably not as substantial as appearances would indicate, the books received by Jay formed a solid basis upon which to build a good library. Jay's share included all of Sir Edward Coke's *Reports*, Sir George Croke's *Reports*, Peere William's *Reports*, and the reports of Keilway and Kelyng. Among the treatises received were Hale's *Pleas of the Crown*, Giles Jacob's *Lex Mercatoria*, and William Nelon's *Lex Testamentaria*.[8] Young Jay was extremely fortunate in having these sources in his library at the very outset of his professional career.

Simultaneous with the distribution of Chambers' books to him, Jay was actively engaged in acquiring new titles for his professional use. Of the surviving volumes clearly marked as being purchased, ten sets of reports and four treatises were added to the Jay library in 1771. In 1770 only two sets of reports and one treatise had been purchased. After 1771 the number of new purchases steadily declined to one set of reports in 1774 and no acquisitions at all in 1775 and 1776. The year 1771 was of course the first year of substantial earnings from practice, and Jay very wisely diverted part of his income of that year into the expansion of his library. Thereafter he seems to have limited his purchases to newly published reports. For example, in 1773 he purchased Salkeld's *Reports*, the new edition of which was published in London earlier in the year. The third volume of Peere Williams' *Reports*, to supplement the first two volumes inherited from Chambers, was purchased in 1772. It had been published in London in 1768.

Interspersed with the materials on English common law, are books dealing with the civil law and international law. Domat's *Civil law* and an English translation of Justinian's *Institutes* fall into this category. Vattel's *Law of Nations* and Pufendorf's *Law of Nature* also graced Jay's library shelves as physical evidence of the young practitioner's interest in the more esoteric areas of jurisprudence. Lest it be concluded that the library lacked practical treatises, one must counterbalance the foregoing works with Stubbs' *Crown Circuit Companion* and jleat Sheriff and *The Compleat Sheriff*.

The books in Jay's library show the effects of diligent but careful use. On

---

[8]See Appendix D, for a list of works in the Jay Collection at the Columbia University Law Library.

the flyleaf of each volume Jay was accustomed to place his signature and the date of acquisition. This constituted the limit of his markings in the books, and there are no interlinear glosses to reveal Jay's personal viewpoints concerning the cases repoted or discussed. Despite the original owner's care, the library shows severe damage due to events beyond his personal control. First of all, the retreat from New York City in July of 1776 involved Jay's junior clerk in a desperate attempt to save the bulk of his master's law library. Apparently the books were widely scattered, and Jay received news from his father as late as July 1777, that the various boxes had not been reassembled. From the family's refuge at Fish Kill, Peter Jay wrote,

> Hitherto Fady [Jay's brother Frederick] has not been able to succeed in providing wagons to remove your Books to Kent.
>
> Johnny Strang [Jay's senior clerk] was here about a fortnight or three weeks ago. . .' he then proposed to send a box or two he has of yours at his Father's [probably at Peekskill] to Salem, and promised to remove them from there in case of need and said he would be very careful of them.[9]

Those books which survived the retreat and the subsequent transfers for purposes of safekeeping bear the evidence of harsh treatment they received. Nearly all of the folio volumes must have been immersed in water or stored in a damp place; to this day they bear a persistent mold that has resisted all efforts of librarians to remove it from the pages of Jay's books. At least one attempt has made, probably not by librarians, to dry out the pages by heating the books. The net result has been that the edges of the pages and the bindings, when intact, have been scorched.

---

[9]To John Jay, July 29, 1777, Johnston, *Corres.*, I, 156-157.

In addition to the damage caused by the wartime retreat from the British, the rapacity of autograph collectors has resulted in a large number of John Jay's signatures being cut from the flyleaves of the volumes. Since Jay's signature was always affixed in the same place on the page, at the upper right hand corner, the very fact that an upper right hand corner has been cut off the title page of a volume in the collection is persuasive evidence that the book once bore Jay's signature. Far more frustrating to scholarship is the large number of title pages which are missing, and along with them, the opportunity to determine with any degree of certainty, the fact that Jay owned the volume in question. In such cases, the presence of the mold and mildew is the only circumstantial evidence that the book belonged to Jay during the time he was engaged in active practice.

In addition to the acquisition and study of law books, Jay's legal education was enhanced by his membership in The Moot. For over four years prior to the Revolution, this select group of practitioners met together to debate controversial points of law; at the same time they agreed to refrain from arguing the controversial issues of politics which sharply divided them and were soon to destroy their club and the society they knew.[10] Jay's name is listed as a charter member of The Moot, from the year 1771 to 1772, he served as Secretary of the organization. Even when not an elected officer, he was most regular in his attendance at the meetings. The interesting topics presented for debate, as well as the Rule against unexcused absences doubtless served to keep every member active in the proceedings.[11]

---

[10]The most complete copy of the Rules of the Moot is a contemporary copy of the original, John J. DuBois Manuscripts, on deposit in Columbia University Libraries, Special Collections. The rule concerning political discussions is Rule V, which provided that one persisting despite the admonition of the President, would be expelled from the Moot.

[11]The Rule against unexcused absences was Rule IX, which provided for expulsion for three unexcused absences from meetings. It was not applied until March 4, 1774 when Whitehead Hicks, a charter member who had attended only two meetings in four years, was expelled, *ibidem*. Jay

After electing officers on November 23rd, 1770, the Moot proceeded to select a legal topic for debate at their next meeting on the seventh of December 1770. The issue chosen was whether an executor sued on a book debt of the decedent, could plead the existence of an outstanding bill obligatory of the deceased in defense against the action. Six of the members concurred that if the executor has notice of the existence of the bond, he may plead it, and upon proving that he lacks adequate resources in the estate to pay both, he would be permitted to defend upon this basis. John Jay and John Morin Scott agreed with the majority, but insisted that only the pendency of a suit upon the bond will permit the executor of the estate to avail himself of this fact as a bar to recovery on the book debt.[12]

John Jay was present at the following meeting of the Moot, when the members debated one of several interprovincial problems which arose in everyday practice. The particular issue chosen for debate was whether the estate of a New Jersey resident, who owned assets only in New Jersey and whose executor had been appointed in New Jersey, could be sued in New York for the testator's debt. The discussion revolved around English cases

---

Jay missed the May and October meetings in 1771; presumably his excuse was the extent of his practice, for he was chosen to be Secretary for the coming year at the November 1771 meeting, Minutes of the Moot, BV Sec-Moot, New York Historical Society, N.Y.C., pp.6, 8.

[12]DuBois MS copy on deposit, Columbia University Libraries, Special Collections (hereafter DuBois copy). The point raised by Jay and Scott is well taken. It is questionable whether any debt has priority at law until it is reduced to judgment. The issue raises the collateral question whether the formalities of executing the writing obligatory before a Notary Public are equivalent to the recognizance in legal consequences. By the end of the eighteenth century it seems extremely unlikely that the formalities of execution attending the writing obligatory served any purpose other than to facilitate proof at trial.

defining the status of an executor prior to the probate of the will.[13] Despite the agreement upon the general rule that an executor may be sued before the will is admitted to probate, the Moot held that the New Jersey executor would not be so liable to suit except in New Jersey.[14] In reaching the decision the Moot admittedly used English law as a guideline, but clearly recognized the fact that the jural relationship between New York and New Jersey was quite different from that existing between the various counties in England. Hence they were dealing with a problem that rarely arose in England, and for which English law offered but little assistance. As we have noted before the questions of jurisdiction and enforcement of foreign judgments were quite perplexing to these colonial lawyers.[15]

Other examples of this concern of the Moot with these unique legal problems of British North America mark the subject of conflicts of law as one of paramount interest to the New York practitioners of the day. On March 5th, 1772 Jay was in attendance at a session of the Moot when the members debated the effect of a New Jersey insolvency proceeding upon creditors residing in the province of New York. The issue posed was the case of a New Jersey debtor who, having availed himself of the New Jersey statute for the relief of insolvent debtors then moved to New York. In the province of New York, the unfortunate man found other creditors, some of whom contracted with him in New Jersey. Can the New York creditors sue the New Jersey expatriate in spite of his release under the laws of New Jersey? The Moot gave as its opinion that as to all debts contracted in New Jersey, there could be no recovery; apparantly the New Jersey

---

[13]See citations at Minutes of the Moot, BV Sec-Moot, New York Historical Society (hereafter Minutes, Moot), p.3, which refer to the following cases among others: Wolfe v. Heydon, Hutton 30, 123 Eng. Rep. 1078-1079, Dowdale's Case, 6 Coke Reports 46b, 77 Eng. Rep. 323-326, Wankford v. Wankford, 1 Salkeld 302, 303, 91 Eng. Rep. 165-272.

[14]Minutes, Moot, p.4. The problem of course involves issues of jurisdiction of the New York court, which cannot be in rem since no assets are in New York.

[15]See discussion at pp.103, 104, *supra*.

law was held to operate in a fashion that would be quasi in rem in regard to New Jersey debts.[16] Also precluded from asserting their rights against the New Jersey insolvent, were those who had appeared in the New Jersey proceeding; in other words, personal appearance before the New Jersey court is evidence of submission to the jurisdiction and consent to the discharge. By inference from the decision of The Moot, we must conclude that those New York creditors who have dealt with the insolvent in New York, and who had not participated in the New Jersey insolvency proceeding, could maintain actions in New York. While this solution was far from a satisfactory one, it seems to have been the most equitable solution available under the circumstances.

Another question concerning inter-provincial relationships was raised in The Moot on April 30th, 1772, when Jay and the other members discussed the situations of a corporation organized in one province attempting to hold lands and sue in another. The decision given by the Moot was that the corporation could maintain a personal action in another province, but was incapable of holding title to land situated elsewhere.[17]

In addition to these inter-provincial questions, the Moot engaged in debates concerning matters of New York law, and on at least one occasion was apparently so divided upon the point that they could not come to a conclusion, and failed to enter a decision in their minutes. The issue was whether

---

[16]Minutes, Moot, p. 10. A proceeding in rem adjudicates rights to a specific piece of property subject to the jurisdiction of the court because of its physical location. Since a debt is a mere chose in action, there is considerable doubt where the debt is situated, at the domicile of the creditor or the domicile of the debtor. As the New Jersey insolvency act is held to have an effect upon the debt owed to creditors outside of the province, its action must be quasi in rem. Such a proceeding commenced without actual notice to known creditors, seems rather arbitrary and unjust. The Act was disallowed by the Privy Council on June 7, 1771, *Acts of the Privy Council, Colonial Series*, V, 315, 316.

[17]Minutes, Moot, p.11.

the statute of frauds applied to the province of New York. Ostensibly the answer was a simple one; the statute of frauds, having been enacted prior to the first meeting of the New York General Assembly in 1683, was part of the law of the province. This was the rule which had been enunciated by Chief Justice Horsmanden in his argument against irregular appeals in the case of Forsey v. Cunningham. English case law was as yet uncertain, it having been held that a conquered land was not subject to the common law of England unless the King chose to extend English law to his new territory; it was not until Campbell v. Hall, decided in 1774, that the English courts decided the legal consequence of granting legislative powers to a conquered colony. Absent any guidance from English in this regard, the colonials had attempted to resolve the question by an act of the New York General Assembly in 1767.[18] This act listed a number of English statutes which, according to the act, had become part of the law of New York through usage. Among the English statutes listed was the statute of frauds. Since the Assembly's act was later vetoed by the King, was this to be interpreted as a royal denial of the applicability of the statute of frauds? Did the statute of frauds continue to apply by customary usage in spite of the royal disallowance?

The problem concerning the reception of English statutes into New York colonial law is one that has perplexed generations of lawyers.

In Beers v. Hotchkiss, 256 N.Y. 41, The New York State Court of Appeals was presented with a complex question of title involving the applicability of the English statute of frauds and a similar ordinance in the Duke's Law of 1665. After extensive consideration of the issue, the Court by Judge Benjamin N. Cardozo, declined to resolve the question and held that regardless which piece of legislation applied in New York, the colony had by

---

[18]Minutes, Moot, p. 12; *The Report of an Action of Assault and Battery . . . Between . . . Forsey and . . Cunningham* (New York: John Holt, 1764), p.9; Blankard v. Galdy, Holt, K.B. 341 (1693), Campbell v. Hall, 1 Cowp. 204 (1774); *Colonial Laws of New York from the Year 1664 to the Revolution* 5 vols., (Albany: James B. Lyons, 1894), IV. 953.

customary use recognized an exception when the conveyance was by means of an allotment by town proprietors. Hence the problem remains undetermined to the present day. While the English solicitor or barrister could look with certainty to his statute books, the colonial lawyer acted with due caution when he asserted that a particular English statute applied to his colony. This uncertainty demanded of the colonial bar a great ability to resolve the many constitutional questions that arose in regard to the reception of English law. It is little wonder that the Moot failed to come to a decision concerning the applicability of the statute of frauds in New York; yet it is surprising that they neglected the substance of their debate for future use. It would have been of great use to judges and of great interest to legal historians if they had recorded their various opinions.[19]

Although the primary purpose of the Moot was the organization of debates upon points of law, the very membership of the organization put it at the head of the profession of the province. Consequently it recognized certain obligations to the profession, and to the encouragement of legal studies in New York. In discharging its professional obligation, the Moot took a strong stand concerning sheriff's fees, maintaining that the client, and not his attorney, was the party to whom the sheriff should look for the collection of the prescribed fees.[20] This was entirely in line with what appears to have been Jay's usual practice-- all writs, executions, subpoenas and other process were forwarded to the client, who in turn was expected to conclude the necessary agreement with the sheriff or other process server. The action of the Moot and the usual practice of Jay tended to remove the legal profession from the commercial aspects of practice, and to place the New York attorney on the same social plane as the English barrister.

---

[19]See some materials gathered by Julius Goebel, *Cases and Materials on the Development of Legal Institutions* (Brattleboro, VT. The Vermont Printing Co., 1946), pp.248, 312, 317. See also Beers v. Hotchkiss, 256 N.Y. 41 (1931).

[20]Minutes, Moot, pp.17, 18.

More significantly for future generations of lawyers, the Moot in April of 1773 appointed John Jay, Samuel Jones, and James Duane to serve as a committee to attend the sittings of the Supreme Court on the first Fridays of January, April, July and October, to take notes on the questions of law to be argued before the court at the succeeding term.[21] Presumably the members of the Moot who had an interest in a particular topic would thus have the opportunity to listen to the arguments presented by counsel in support of their positions. The step from this type of an activity to the actual preparation of reports of cases was never taken in New York during the colonial period; had the American Revolution not occurred it is quite possible that the Moot may have led the way toward the publication of New York case reports.

Last, but far from least, the Moot evidenced a certain concern for the public relations of the Bar. When Richard Wenman, the cryer of the Supreme Court, found himself in financial distress because of non-payment of his fees, the members of the Moot voted to advance him 40 shillings per member to relieve his necessities until his fees should be paid. Their concern with clerkship regulations is shown by the entry in the minutes providing that the matter be debated at the next meeting; unfortunately no minutes were taken of the discussion, if any was had.[22] In regard to the members of the Bench, the Moot stood ready to give advice whenever it was consulted. Answering queries of Chief Justice Horsmanden concerning the taxing of bills of costs and procedures for obtaining views by juries,[23] the Moot provided a convenient forum in which the Bench could gather the opinions and preferences of the leading lawyers of the province of New York. In these ways the Moot, during the short period of its existence did an admirable job of discharging its duties to the Bench, the Bar and to the public at large.

The pressure of law practice bearing heavily upon the various members of the Moot, its meetings began to draw a steadily decreasing number

---

[21]Minutes, Moot., p.15.

[22]DuBois MS copy.

[23]Minutes, Moot, pp.17, 18.

of members until in 1774 some action was taken to enforce the rather strict attendance rules. As mentioned before, Whitehead Hicks, the future Chief Justice of the Province, was expelled in that year. Younger members of the Bar were regularly admitted to the Moot membership, but their enthusiasm could not quite out-balance the departure of the older veterans such as William Livingston and Benjamin Kissam. Only James Duane remained faithful in his attendance until 1775.[24]

At the meetings of the Moot, Jay became well acquainted with the individuals who composed this Bar of the Supreme Court; their distinctive personalities doubtless lent zest to the proceedings! Charter member Whitehead Hicks despite his expulsion from the Moot in 1774, was a lawyer of good habits and had a reputation for good sense. Thomas Jones describes him as being ". . . of a gay, open disposition, cheerful and steady in his friendship, . . . a bon vivant, loved company, and . . . a jovial fellow."[25] Perhaps it was Hicks' easy-going ways that caused him to ignore the rule of the Moot concerning attendance.

Among the members of the Moot given particular attention by Judge Thomas Jones were William Livingston, John Tabor Kempe and Daniel Mathews. To the first Jones grudgingly conceded outstanding ability in the law, to the second he attributed ". . . a most brilliant share of legal knowledge," while the third, although later a loyalist was denominated,

> . . . a mere ignoramus in matters of law, and [one who] knew as little of the laws of the land, the acts of the province, or the Constitution of England, as any common pack-horse in the country.[26]

Among the younger members of the Moot, Jones fixed upon Gouverneur Morris as one who had great promise in the law, which attribute was tempered by ". . . a witty, genteel, polite, sensible, and judicious . . ." nature. According to Jones, young Gouverneur had ". . . more knowledge (though

---

[24]Minutes, Moot, *passim*.

[25]Jones, *History of New York*, 1, 223.

[26]*Ibid*., I, 3, 31; II, 22.

still a youth) than all his three brothers put together."[27]

The Moot thus drew its membership from among attorneys of widely differing abilities. It provided a common meeting ground for men who might have had little opportunity to gather either socially or professionally. John Tabor Kempe, although quite competent as an attorney, had become the attorney-general of the province at such a young age that his rapid rise to prominence was resented, as was his lack of provincial heredity.[28] On the other hand William Livingston, Richard Morris, James Duane and Robert R. Livingston, Jr., were well established in the provincial aristocracy. When Stephen DeLancey joined the Moot, in which the Livingston party predominated, it became obvious that this was one of the few organizations in colonial New York that was above the prejudices of provincial politics. While the approach of the American Revolution gradually weakened the non-partisan ties that bound the Moot together, it is remarkable that the group persisted until January of 1775. Apparently the rule against political discussions was useful in sublimating animosity until restraint was no longer possible. Until the Moot dissolved, almost contemporaneously with British power in North America, John Jay and his fellow members enjoyed the opportunity to increase their knowledge in the law through the exciting and gratifying medium of discussion with their fellow attorneys.

In John Jay's willingness to seize every opportunity to increase his training in the law through meetings of the Moot, as well as in the ever expanding library present in his law office, we can see Jay continuing his legal education while engaged in active practice. Although a lawyer for only a brief period in his life, John Jay remained a student in the law from the day he entered Kissam's law office in 1764 until the day he died.

---

[27] *Ibid.*, I, 140.

[28] *Ibid.*, I, 31; *History of the Bench and Bar of New York*, David McAdam, et. al., eds., 2 vols., (New York: N.Y. History Co., 1897), I, 407-408.

IX. JOHN JAY AND THE CIVIL LAW

Despite the extensive grant of jurisdiction to the Supreme Court of Judicature of the province of New York, certain cases demanded equitable relief not available at common law. In these instances, Jay found himself resorting to New York courts erected to perform those functions unknown to the common law courts at Westminster. Since this equitable and ecclesiastical jurisdiction had, in centuries past, been strongly influenced by the doctrines of canon and civil law, it was in these colonial courts that John Jay received his practical acquaintances with civil law. While the substantial law in these courts merely complimented the English common law, it was in matters of pleading, procedure and proof, that the historical divergence from common law was most apparent.

Civil law found its forum in the province of New York in three colonial courts: the Court of Chancery, the Prerogative Court, and the Vice-Admiralty Court. As we have noted previously, Jay did not take part in any litigation before the Vice-Admiralty Court subsequent to his admission to practice; hence, it is not possible to evaluate his knowledge of the civil law or equity practice as applied that court.[1] In the High Court of Chancery he was involved, in one capacity or another, with ten suits;[2] in the Prerogative Court he was retained in at least three proceedings.[3]

Chancery jurisdiction in the province of New York was vested in the person of the Governor, whose numerous other duties interfered with the efficient operation of the Court. For this reason litigation tended to be unduly prolonged, and few of Jay's cases which reached the point of decree had been pending less than two years. One case, that of Leadbetter v. Harison, requesting an equitable accounting, was before the Chancery court from February

---

[1]See pages 50-53, above.

[2]Anderson v. Arden, Bloomer v. Hinchman, Dyckman v. Lott, Hadden v. Hadden, Leadbetter v. Harison, Livingston v. Rapalje, Roberjott v. Simson, Ten Eyck v. Brinckerhoff, Udall v. Udall, Van Horne v. Van Kleeck.

[3]Dean v. Dean Estate, Montross v. Hermsen Estate, Everit v. Everit Estate.

of 1771 until January 1774, at which time a decree was still held in abeyance.[4] Subsequent to the appointment of James Jauncey, as the first Master of the Rolls, matters proceeded in a more regular fashion since in the absence of the Chancellor, the Master of the Rolls was authorized to proceed.[5]

One of the most important Chancery cases of the day was that of Bloomer v. Hinchman, involving the right of an Anglican minister to collect a salary from his parish despite the fact that the vestry had refused to accept him as rector pursuant to the Governor's appointment.[6] Jay's particular role in regard to the case is difficult to determine from the evidence that survives. However there can be no doubt that he followed the case with great interest, and if he was not in some way involved in the proceedings, he definitely felt his exclusion to be a great personal slight. The parish at Jamaica, now Grace Church, was incorporated in the spring of 1761 with Samuel Seabury, Jr. as rector and a Thomas Hinchman, probably a relative of the defendant in the

---

[4]Chancery Minutes, IV, 21, 137, N.Y.Co. Clerk, Hall of Records, N.Y.C.

[5]Hamlin, *Legal Education*, p. 111; see minutes on days Jauncey presided, at Chancery Minutes, IV, 170, 171. An additional difficulty was that the Chancellor (Governor) frequently held sessions of the Court at places other than New York City. For example Lieutenant Governor Cadwallader Colden held sittings of the Court at his home in Flushing, and in Brooklyn, Chancery Minutes, IV, 9, 10. That such itinerancy was not unusual in the case of civil law courts in New York, see Herbert Alan Johnson, "The Admiralty Court Comes to Morrisania", *The Advocate*, IX, 15-21.

[6]The vestry desired the appointment of a Presbyterian minister, and refused to present an Anglican candidate to the Governor for installation as rector. Consequently the governor appointed one Rev. Joshua Bloomer, a graduate of King's College who had been ordained an Anglican minister.

The case was noted in the legal press, see *New York Gazette or Weekly Mercury* Apr. 16, 1774.

Chancery case, as a member of the vestry.[7] When Rev. Mr. Seabury received a call to take a parish in Westchester County, the young parish attempted to install a Presbyterian divine in his place, but were blocked by the Governor. For this reason they were not at all reluctant to withhold the salary of the Anglican minister appointed by the Governor and installed without their consent. The unfortunate rector caught between these two contending forces was Joshua Bloomer, who eventually was compelled to begin suit against the vestrymen for the purpose of collecting his salary.[8]

Just when John Jay was approached to act for Bloomer in the case is not clear. We do know that by December of 1771 Jay had come to the conclusion that he was being ignored by John Tabor Kempe, another attorney retained by Bloomer, while the case was being prepared for argument.[9] At this time counsel for both parties were engaged in arguing a demurrer on the part of the defendant vestrymen, and consultation of all attorneys retained by Bloomer would have been most desirable.[10] Jay's letter to Kempe, his co-counsel, was abrupt and peremptory. The matter was now ripe for a determination and he had not been consulted at any stage in the proceedings. Since

---

[7]MS Vestry Minutes, Grace Church, Jamaica, 1764-1862, and Register 1700-[?], Grace Church Parish Hall, Jamaica, N.Y., p.2.

[8]Alexander, *A Revolutionary Conservative*, p. 22, Henry Onderdonk, Jr., *Antiquities of the Parish Church*, (Jamaica, N.Y.: Charles Welling, 1880), p.68. Bloomer is considered to have begun his service as rector in May of 1769; he served until 1790, MS Vestry Minutes, ibid., p.13.

[9]The letters, remarkable for their bitterness, are in the Sedgwick Papers, II, Massachusetts Historical Society, Boston, Mass., and bear dates from Dec. 27, 1771 to Jan. 1772.

[10]The defendants had demurred to the bill of complaint; although the plaintiff's successful opposition to this argument on the law might not carry the case, as it would in a common law court.

Bloomer retained Jay and Kempe was aware of this fact, the secrecy of Kempe put Jay in an awkward position with their client, and the case was argued without Jay's knowledge. Kempe, the attorney general of the Province and many years Jay's senior at the Bar, was shocked, and wrote back that he had never been addressed in such a manner, and that he did not deserve to receive such indelicate expressions from his young co-counsel. To this Jay replied that he believed if a gentlemen's conduct was misunderstood, he would iinmediately explain it as a compliment to those who ask, and to protect his own reputation. The inference was that Kempe, as less than a gentleman, had taken a contrary attitude. John Jay concluded that he did not wish to break off relations with Kempe, but would "reject the world rather than purchase it at the expense of silence under such indignities."[11]

This clash of personalities reveals much concerning both of the individuals involved. First, it is noteworthy that Jay reacted so sharply against a man many years his senior who had earned an established place at the Bar. At the time John was a young practitioner just beginning to build a practice, and with only two years experience. Despite these distinctions, Jay apparently felt the equal of Kempe, and was willing to risk his enmity to protect his own professional standing. That Jay should presume to treat Kempe in this manner attests to an assurance that came from family and standing in the community. To John Jay, Kempe was a man-on-the make and a social climber. Governors came, and governors departed, but Kempe was a court favorite of all. He gained his fortune too recently to be a member of the hereditary landowners who ruled New York; while land ownership was a mark of social status, those who exerted themselves to obtain land grants, rather than adding to the realty acquisitions of ancestors, were marked as inferior beings.[12]

---

[11]JJ to Kempe, Dec. 27, 1171 and Jan. 2, 1772; Kempe to JJ, Dec. 27, 1771, all in Sedgwick Papers, II, Massachusetts Historical Society, Boston, Mass.

[12]An excellent- picture of Kempe's rise to wealth is in Catherine Snell Crary's article, "The American Dream: John Tabor Kempe's Rise from Pov-

Secondly, the exchange between Kempe and Jay gives a fairly clear picture of Jay's feeling toward his professional reputation. As a young attorney his practice could have been hampered by the situation in which he had been placed by Kempe, and he quite properly resented the attitude taken toward him. Even if his inexperience marked him as incompetent to bear the responsibility of representing Bloomer, and there is no reason to suppose that this was the case, Kempe's excluding him from consultation was particularly reprehensible. Since James Duane had also been retained by Bloomer, Jay could have been controlled by the two of them if he proved to be deficient in knowledge. Between the attorneys there would have been no question that the younger man had not contributed greatly to the cause, yet the general public from which Jay drew his clientele would be unaware of his precise role and his reputation would have been protected. Jay did not trouble himself concerning Kempe's evaluation of his legal abilities; what was particularly galling to John Jay was the fact that the case was one of the great prominence which could have catapulted him into the public eye. Kempe's secrecy and failure to appear to consult Jay also was within public knowledge. In this way a retainer that could have brought Jay to prominence was being used to hurt his practice.

The records of the case of Bloomer v. Hinchman do not reflect that Jay took part in the case subsequent to the above exchange of letters, but the biographer of James Duane, after a review of that attorney's law papers at Duanesburgh, claims that John Jay assisted Duane and Kempe in the case.[13] If this be the case Jay had some ground for satisfaction in the outcome, for after extensive argument based upon colonial history and English ecclesiastical practice, the Governor entered his decree that the vestry was required to pay the salary of Rev. Mr. Bloomer from the date of his collation by the Governor until the date of suit. At the same time, Tryon decreed that the Church of England for the purposes of the Ministry Acts of 1693 and 1705,

erty to Riches", *William and Mary Quarterly*, 3rd Ser., XIV, 176-195.

[13]Alexander, *A Revolutionary Conservative*, p. 22.

was the established church in the four southern counties of New York.[14] Because the matter was in the process of being appealed to the Privy Council when the Revolution broke out, Bloomer did not receive his salary until 1780.[15] Thus installed by the authority of the British, Bloomer retained his post through the popularity he had acquired with his parishioners, and continued to serve his people in the troubled times of the Revolution, and for seven years thereafter until his death in 1790.

Although Bloomer v. Hinchman was doubtless one of the most significant Chancery cases to which Jay's name was attached, more than a year before the commencement of the Bloomer case Jay made his first appearance before the Chancellor. In partnership with Robert R. Livingston, he had prepared a complaint on behalf of a Dutchess county yeoman who wished to have title to a disputed tract of land settled by the Chancellor. The complainant, out of possession, lacked a deed or grant by which to prove his prior, or present title; hence he could not bring an ejectment action, and was compelled to proceed in Chancery in an attempt to discover the whereabouts of the deed, as well as to determine the source of the title of the party, who was occupying the land.[16] After being permitted to amend their bill of complaint, Jay and Livingston failed to proceed with the matter. Presumably

---

[14]Ibid., pp.22, 24. Decree dated Apr. 5, 1774, at BM-1425 B, N.Y. Co. Clerk, Hall of Records, N.Y.C.

[15]Appeal noticed Apr. 14, 1774 by John Morin Scott for the vestry, BM-1425-B, ibid. Payment at order of British provost court, noted at Onderdonk, *Antiquities Jamaica Parish Church*, p.68.

[16]Chancery Minutes, May 13, 1740-Mar. 30, 1770, Chancery Room, Court of Appeals Hall, Albany, N.Y., p.392 [Jager v. Van Benthuysen]. The answer by James Duane for the defendant is filed in Decrees Before 1800, V-33, Chancery Room, Court of Appeals Hall, Albany, New York. See also Egbert Benson, Legal Journal & Account Book, Miscellaneous Manuscripts, Benson, Box 1, New York Historical Society, under date July 3, 1769.

they found it possible to make an amicable settlement on behalf of their client, and withdrew the suit.[17]

The Chancery case concerning James Leadbetter's accounts with his partners in the operation of "Harison's Brewery" was one of great complexity, and bears some evidence that Jay was of counsel for the defendants.[18] The complainant had been employed as a brewer in the city of New York for several years when the defendants convinced him to enter into partnership with them. Unfortunately for all of the parties involved the substance of their agreement was not reduced to writing, for it was a rather complicated arrangement. Leadbetter was to supervise the single workman at the brewery, who was his brother; in return Leadbetter was to receive a salary for management. Since the complainant, Leadbetter, did not have funds to contribute to the partnership, he was required to execute a note to defendant Harison, and this note was the basis a suit instituted against him by Harison. When Leadbetter's brother took to drink, he not only continued to manage the brewery but also performed the labor previously performed by his brother at the salary of £ 100 per year. In his complaint, Leadbetter requested that the court adjudge him to be a partner in the brewery enterprise, and to fix the amount of this participation in the assets. The Chancellor was also requested to decree recovery to the £ 100 that Leadbetter claimed to have earned because he performed his brother's duties.[19] The affairs of the partnership were further complicated by the fact that Harison had leased some land from Trinity Church with partnership funds, and then used the lease for his individual purposes.[20]

---

[17]Amendment of complaint at Chancery Minutes, ibid., p. 392.

[18]Jay is indicated as recipient of copies of documents, Chancery Minutes IV, 38, 49, 126. N.Y. Co. Clerk, Hall of Records, N.Y.C. The Brewery involved is most likely the same one noted on page 1, *supra*.

[19]Bill is preserved at Decrees Before 1800, Chancery Room, Court of Appeals Hall, Albany, N.Y. L-76.

[20]*Ibidem*.

The answer, which is missing, was determined insufficient after a hearing before John Van Cortlandt, a master of the court, and counsel for defendant had leave to amend their answer. Jay doubtless worked with his associates in making the amendment required by the master's report, for only eight days were granted from the time of the filing of the report until the date the amended answer was to be filed. Preparing an answer in Chancery was a tedious task, for each allegation in the complaint had to be made the subject of a specific reply. Any error in preparing the answer would subject the pleader to a motion to strike the answer for insufficiency or to a demurrer on the law.[21] For this reason, a gathering between Kissam, Jay and Richard Harison, to determine how to amend the answer, would probably have been the mode selected for complying with the master's report.

Once the pleadings were in order, the entire case was referred to a panel of arbitrators, who proceeded to consider the accounts of the firm. After a considerable study, they held that Leadbetter was indebted to the defendant on the notes, that he had a three-eighths interest in the partnership, and that subject to the claims of creditors, he could demand such a proportional share of the assets upon distribution.[22] Because of the death of George Harison during the pendency of the case, the partnership had been dissolved, and Leadbetter could look forward to receiving his share in cash as soon as the affairs of firm were in good order.

The technical issue presented by the death of Harison was whether the arbitrator's report would be effectual to bind his estate. For this reason, the complainant's attorneys brought a bill of revivor, which was acquiesced in by the defendant's lawyers. Consequently the report of the arbitrators was filed, and upon motion of Benjamin Kissam as solicitor for the defendants,

---

[21]Goebel, *Law Practice Hamilton*, I, 175.

[22]The report of arbitrators, accounts they examined, orders of reference, and supplementary orders of reference, are at BM-1637-L, N.Y.Co. Clerk, Hall of Records, N.Y.C.

the report was confirmed and incorporated into the form of a decree.[23]

Other cases in Chancery brought Jay into contact with the large variety of matters which required equitable remedies. For example he was retained by the defendant in a suit to foreclose the defendant's equity of redemption in mortgaged real estate.[24] As counsel with Richard Morris, he prepared and signed the defendant's answer to a bill of complaint which, among other things, accused the defendant of unduly influencing his aged father against complainant, his brother.[25] In Dyckman v. Lott, Jay was of counsel to the solicitor for the complainant, Thomas Jones. The Dyckman case involved a rather unique factual situation that raised interesting points of law. The complainant, Dyckman, had made an agreement with Lott for the purchase of a pipe of wine. Before delivery Dyckman notified Lott that the wine was to be sold to Dyckman's father, who would pay for it. Subsequently the delivery was made; Dyckman's parent went bankrupt and Lott was one of his many creditors. Lott publicly accused the younger Dyckman of failing to pay his debt, and finally instituted suit on the ground that Dyckman had been a surety for the payment of the purchase price. Jay and Jones were retained by Dyckman to request an injunction against the action of law, to restrain Lott from stating publicly that the complainant would not pay his just debts, and to examine the wine merchant under oath concerning the

---

[23]Chancery Minutes, IV, 126, 137 N.Y.Co. Clerk, Hall Records, N.Y.C.

[24]Arden v. Anderson, Law Reg. Jay, p.133, Chancery Minutes IV, 77, 93, 117, 118, 147, 172, 176, 177, *ibid.*, master's report and affidavit upon which arrest of defendant ordered, at BM A-530, N.Y. Co. Clerk, Hall of Records, N.Y.C.

[25]Hadden v. Hadden, Law Reg. Jay, N.Y. State Library, p.177; bill of complaint, in what appears to be Jay's hand is in Decrees Before 1800, Chancery Room, Court of Appeals Hall, Albany, N.Y., H-38; since the case does not appear in the Chancery court minutes, it must have been settled before reaching the stage of a hearing.

transaction.[26] Again the suit was compromised before it reached the stage of a hearing.[27] Nevertheless, it is an excellent example of the flexible nature of the remedies that were available in the court of Chancery. It is most unfortunate that the matter did not proceed further, for it would be of interest to know how the Chancellor, untrained in the law, would resolve the complex issues of agency, consideration and suretyship which are involved.

A Chancery suit of considerable interest is that of Roberjot v. Simson, brought by John Jay as solicitor for the complaint against the administrator of the estate of a merchant named LaFargue.[28] One LaFargue had issued a writing obligatory to the complaint, Roberjot, and then left on a voyage. When Joseph LaFargue died in New York City, Roberjot demanded his administrator, Simson, pay the amount of the debt to Roberjot's agent. Simson refused, asserting that it was not clear that the LaFargue who executed the bond was his interstate. John Tabor Kempe, appearing on behalf of Simson, drew his memoranda to indicate that there was good reason to suspect that the LaFargue who signed the bond was not the same man who died in New York City and whose estate was being administered by the defendant. This was clear, maintained Kempe, because Roberjot's letter indicated that an attachment, or arrest warrant, had been issued against LaFargue; since such process would not, under French law be available against a deceased's executor, it was apparent that at the time Roberjot wrote, LaFargue was a living person.

---

[26]Law Reg. Jay, p. 206; Decrees Before 1800, Chancery Room, Court of Appeals Hall, Albany, N.Y., D-37.

[27]In like manner the cases of TenEyck v. Brinckerhoff, Van Horne v. Van Kleeck, and Livingston v. Rapalje, were withdrawn before decree or hearing, Law Reg. Jay, pp. 23, 24, 120.

[28]The original bill, once at R-54, Decrees Before 1800, ibid., is missing. Kempe's copies of the papers are at John Tabor Kempe Papers, Lawsuits R, New York Historical Society, N.Y.C.; Jay's register entries at Law Reg. Jay, Albany, N.Y. p. 148.

Another interesting fact concerning the Roberjot case is the manner in which Jay was compelled to post security for the defendant's court costs. Kempe made a motion upon notice that the defendant receive a bond as a guarantee that the complainant would pay all costs assessed against him. The purpose of this procedure is to make available some source within the jurisdiction from which a resident party can collect costs, if the non-resident litigant refuses to pay them. It is still in use in the state of New York at the present day, although at the present time notice to the non-resident's attorney is not required.[29]

The Roberjot case did not proceed to decree, and very likely was settled or abandoned. With the delay in obtaining final adjudications in the Court of Chancery as with the delay in obtaining jury trials today, the pressure upon the Bar is toward the early settlement of matters which in the event decisions were more rapidly attainable, would never be compromised. At the same time the inconvenience of representing a non-resident plaintiff might in such case result in prejudicial delay and eventual abandonment.

From the cases discussed above, it is safe to conclude that Jay had a good share of the Chancery business of the province by 1772. In addition, the frequent retainers he received as counsel with other attorneys kept him knowledgeable in this branch of the law. Since fees in Chancery were slightly higher than those in Supreme Court practice, the added effort and care required to prepare a Chancery case was well compensated.[30] Had his practice continued, Jay might very well have achieved an outstanding position as a counsellor in the Chancery Court, for his meticulous work habits in regard to drafting pleadings would have made him a most valuable advisor.

While practice in Chancery required exhaustive :attention to detail, matters before the Prerogative Court of the Province of New York were mere

---

[29]Secs. 8501-8503, [New York] *Civil Practice Law and Rules.*

[30]Compare Chancery fees with Supreme Court fees in William Livingston, Cost Book in the Supreme Court of Judicature, 1759-1772, Manuscript Division, New York Public Library, N.Y.C., pp.438, 439, 485.

formalities. The function of the Court, represented by the Deputy Secretary to the Governor, was to admit wills to probate and to grant administration over the estates of persons dying intestate. Upon the decease of a party who had executed a will, affidavits of the subscribing witnesses were affixed to the original copy of the document, and the will was admitted to probate and recorded.[31] The primary activity of the Court was the recording of instruments, but occasionally it compelled executors to file inventories at the suit of legatees. The three cases noted in Jay's law register concerning the Prerogative Court are of this nature.[32] Since no minute books of the court are extant, and the file papers of original wills are in far too fragile condition to permit an overall survey of their contents, it is not possible to contend that Jay's Prerogative Court practice was as limited as this small number of cases would suggest. However, the extremely small authority of the court makes it unlikely that Jay did any extensive amount of practice there.[33]

In addition to representing parties in the Prerogative Court, Jay was involved in the administration of estates as executor. The largest of the estates in which he had such an interest was that of his aunt, Anne Chambers. Her will was probated on April 18, 1774, and named John to be co-executor with his cousin, Augustus Van Cortlandt."[34]

---

[31]See discussion at pages 58, 59, concerning the estate of Abraham DePeyster, to whose will Jay was a subscribing witness.

[32]See cases listed at note 3, page 125.

[33]Goebel, *Law Practice Hamilton*, I, 22-24. As Goebel notes, most of the litigation concerning decedent's estates was conducted in the Supreme Court or the Common Pleas courts, and Jay had a number of these cases. Orphan's guardians were appointed by the Chancery Court, as were committees of incompetent persons.

[34]Old Liber 29, pages 77-83, new liber 29, pages 94-103, Record of Wills, Surrogate's Court, N.Y. Co., Hall of Records, N.Y.C.

legacy of £ 500, a one-fourth undivided share of his aunt's holdings in the Chesekos patent in Orange County and New York, and an undivided one-quarter interest in her lands in Bedford township.[35] His mother, Mary Van Cortlandt Jay, was to receive one-third of Mrs. Chambers' silver plate, and his sister another one-third.[36]

Although the Chambers estate silver had been distributed prior to the outbreak of the Revolution,[37] the final termination of administration was held up until after peace had returned to New York. By that time Jay had retired from active practice, and was interested in the estate only as an executor. Had he wished to reopen his law office the collection of the bonds payable to Anne Chambers would have occupied most of his time.

In addition to the Chambers estate, Jay was appointed executor of the estate of Arent Schuyler, a resident of New Jersey. A letter written to Jay in the winter of 1773 contains expressions of the trust which Schuyler's family had in John Jay's advice, and urges Jay to make the trip to New Barbadoes Neck, New Jersey, as soon as possible.[38]

As in the case of Jay's chancery practice, his appearances before the Prerogative Court as attorney and executor indicate that he was coming of age in his professional life. A young attorney who had proven himself competent in practice, he was being given opportunities to represent clients in the more complicated matters in Chancery, and in addition, was being entrusted with the financial affairs of his clients. The cases in Chancery and the office practice involved in estate administration would eventually have made it possible for Jay to stop riding the circuit with the Supreme Court, and cease his appearances in the Common Pleas courts of each county. With

---

[35]*Ibid.*, clauses 5, 9, 10.

[36]*Ibid.*, clause 6.

[37]Schedule of distribution, n.d. [1774], Columbia University Libraries, Special Collections.

[38]From Peter duBois, Jan. 30, 1773, *ibid.*

the growth of his active practice in these fields, he was building a basis for a professional career in his later years that would involve far less physical exertion than that which was demanded of him in 1773 and 1774.

X. THE INFERIOR COURTS OF JUSTICE

Supplementing the activities of the central courts of justice in New York City, was the justice available locally in County Courts of Common Pleas and Mayor's Courts of the cities of Albany and New York. These inferior tribunals rounded out the structure of justice in the Province of New York through the exercise of limited civil jurisdiction, while the Courts of General Sessions of the Peace enforced the criminal law and performed certain administrative functions. John Jay's practice in the inferior courts centered around the Common Pleas courts of Westchester and Dutchess Counties and the Mayor's Court of New York City. His appearances in other Courts of Common Pleas were infrequent; there is no evidence of Jay appearing in the Mayor's Court of Albany or in the Courts of General Sessions of the Peace.

Records of the Common Pleas court for Ulster County reflect that Jay had but one case before that tribunal, and in that matter he was represented by local counsel, John DuMont.[1] During the period of the Jay & Livingston partnership fifteen cases were noticed in the court by Robert R. Livingston, Jr., several of them confessions of judgment when George Clinton was opposing counsel.[2] It seems that young Livingston had been befriended by Clinton, the most active attorney in Ulster county, and the partnership drew most of its Ulster county litigation from the source. Jay, it would seem, never practiced in Ulster county and after the partnership was dissolved, his practice centered on the counties to the east of the Hudson River.

In the case of Albany county, the minutes of the Common Pleas court cannot presently be located in the office of the County Clerk, but the minutes of the Albany Mayor's Court are available. They show that Jay did not

---

[1]Bogardus Estate v. Hardenbergh, Minute Book Common Pleas, Ulster County, Sep. 15, 1759-Sep. 21, 1774, Room 101, Queens College Library, N.Y.C., under dates May 2, Sep. 20, Sep. 21, 1774.

[2]Confessions of judgment, see ibid., under dates 10 May 1771, Sep. 19, 1771.

practice in this court either.[3] From these facts, and from the counties from which Jay drew his Supreme Court cases,[4] it is clear that Jay's practice centered in Westchester, New York and to a lesser degree in Dutchess, counties.

Practice in the courts administering the criminal law was so rare in Jay's day that had he participated in any number of such cases, he would have been unique among the attorneys of his time. The minutes of the General Sessions courts of Dutchess, New York and Queens counties record no criminal causes in which Jay represented the defendant.[5]

While Westchester County cases in the Court of Common Pleas comprise the bulk of Jay's inferior court practice, the records remaining in the County Clerk's office after several fires are limited to the minute books of the Common Pleas court, from which only a limited amount of information can be obtained. For example, the return of writs is contained within the minute book itself, and we can be reasonably certain that during the course of his practice Jay began 227 cases in the Westchester Court of Common Pleas. The approximate number of cases pending gradually increased until May of 1774, at which time the rate of increase was considerably slowed by Jay's attendance to public affairs rather than his practice.[6] Unfortunately the minutes of the court provide little information concerning the nature of the

---

[3]Mayor's Court Minutes, City and County of Albany, Vol. 1768-1778, Albany County Clerk's Office, Albany N.Y., *passim*.

[4]See pages 95, 96 above.

[5]Common Pleas and General Sessions Minutes, Dutchess County, Libers D, E, F, Dutchess County Clerk's Office, Poughkeepsie, N.Y., *passim*., General Sessions Minutes, New York County, Nov. 4, 1760 - Feb. 6, 1772; May 21, 1772-November 1790, N.Y. Co. Supreme Court Library, Gene Sessions Branch, Criminal Courts Building, N.Y.C., passim., Queens General Sessions and Common Pleas Minutes, Queens County, 1722-1787, Queens Co. Clerk, County Courthouse, N.Y.C., passim.

[6]See Table II, Appendix C.

cases, or the procedures followed by Jay in the course of litigation. To obtain this information it is necessary to turn to the more voluminous files left by the Dutchess County Court of Cornmon Pleas, in which court Jay instituted seventy-seven cases.

The matters tried by Jay in Dutchess county are predominantly cases in debt based upon penal bills obligatory; a large portion of these matters came to Jay from Augustus Van Horne, a cousin, and Joseph Strang, the father of Jay's law clerk.[7] Only a small fraction of Jay's practice in Dutchess Common Pleas was composed of cases in assumpsit, ejectment and assault and battery.[8] A fairly large number of the cases were begun in 1769 while Jay was in partnership with Lavingston, and with the dissolution of the partnership there was a slight decrease in Jay's Dutchess county business.[9] Nevertheless his family connections guaranteed a fairly regular flow of cases from Dutchess county, and Jay found himself at nearly all of the January, May and October sittings of the Common Pleas court at Poughkeepsie. The May and October terms occurred before the May and November sittings of the Westchester Common Pleas Court, so that during those months it was possible for him to go up river to Poughkeepsie, and return to New York City by of way White Plains. Doubtless he made a slight detour to visit with his parents at Rye on the return from White Plains.

While fees in the Common Pleas court were considerably less than

---

[7]For examples of pleadings in these cases, see Ancient Documents, Dutchess County, Dutchess Co. Clerk's Office, Poughkeepsie, N.Y., #3961, 6764, 4971, 6769, 7966, 7965/7967, 7968/2120, 4959, 6481, 4968, 4965, 6703, all Jay & Livingston and Jay cases.

[8]Assumpsit, six cases, with pleadings at *ibid.*, #7712, 9228, 8511, 8791, 7172, 6744, 7945, 8900; ejectment, two cases, at *ibid.*, #6741, 6653; one case in assault and battery at ibid., #7948.

[9]See Table III, Appendix C.

those applicable to Supreme Court matters,[10] the large number of actions of debt, where no hearing concerning damages was required, made a large number of the Common Pleas cases merely matters of draftsmanship. All the attorney need to do was to issue the writ, have it recorded and sent to the sheriff. Upon the return date, the common rule, that the defendant appear and answer or judgment would be had against him, was ordered by the court. When the defendant defaulted, the cause was reduced to judgment by filing the narrative or complaint with a copy of the bond. On the back of the narrative was endorsed proof that the defendant, or someone representing him, had been served with the rule to plead and a copy of the narrative.[11]

This relatively prompt procedure for reducing actions of debt to judgment, was shortened and simplified if the defendant had signed a confession of judgment at the same time he executed the writing obligatory. If this were the case, the attorney for the plaintiff would issue the usual preliminary writ, and then have the common rule entered. On the same court day, or the next court day, another attorney would appear for the defendant pursuant to the authorization given when the debt was contracted. This attorney would confess judgment, which would be endorsed upon the back of the narrative. Once the endorsed narrative was filed in court, the plaintiff's attorney would move for judgment which would be entered as a matter of course.[12]

As noted previously nearly all of Jay's cases in Dutchess county were based upon writings obligatory, and hence the above procedures were applicable unless the defendant elected to appear and challenge the validity of the debt or the formalities of executing the bond. However there occasionally

---

[10]Retaining fee in Common Pleas as £ 1 Os. Od. in the Supreme Court the usual retainer taken by Jay was £ 1 9d, Od. For bill of costs in Dutchess Common Pleas see Bailey v. Brett, Ancient Documents, Dutchess Co. Clerk, #8791.

[11]Van Horne v. Mead., Common Pleas Minutes, Dutchess Co., Liber D, Jan. 5, 1770, May 17, 1770, Jan. 4, 1771, Ancient Documents, Dutchess Co. Clerk #4968, 8030.

[12]Strang v. Hitt Estate, Ancient Documents #8969, *ibid.*

arose a situation in which the more involved procedure of assumpsit was required. In such a case the plaintiff's attorney would plead at length the particular facts which entitled his client to recover, usually at far greater length than would be required in a debt action. Subsequently the plaintiff's attorney would enter a default if no appearance were made in compliance with the common rule. Judgment by default could be entered, but the damages in this instance would be fixed by the determination of a jury, summoned into session by a writ of inquiry. Once the jury's determination was returned by the sheriff, a final judgment was entered.[13] Unlike the Supreme Court which required judgments to be filed in parchment rolls, the Common Pleas court of Dutchess county permitted judgments to be filed in the form of flat folded papers. The resultant savings to clients must have been a welcome by-product of this altered procedure.

Attendance at the various courts of Common Pleas involved John Jay in some extended periods of time on circuit, away from the comforts of New York City and the business pending before the central courts of justice. For this reason, his acquisition of cases in Dutchess County, and also the number of new cases in Westchester county, begins to decrease as he found his Supreme Court practice on the increase. Of course, there were also a certain number of Supreme Court matters to be tried at nisi prius, or circuit, sessions of the Supreme Court. This made it desirable to maintain some Common Pleas cases in each county, so that a call to try a Supreme Court case there would not result in an unproductive expenditure of time.

The inferior court of justice most readily accessible to Jay's New York City office was the Mayor's Court of New City. In the absence of any of the Mayor's Court registers of Jay as well as the lack of any court minutes, it is impossible to determine how many cases of Jay were pending in the New York Mayor's Court. A writ book from 1769 to 1773, provides infor-

---

[13]Strang v. Hitt, Common Pleas Minutes, Dutchess Co., Liber E., May 21, 1772, Jan. 6, 1774, May 20, 1774; Ancient Documnets, #7712, 9228, *ibid.*

mation concerning case openings, and from this source,[14] it appears that Jay's practice in the Mayor's Court steadily increased. Out of the 145 cases noted in this writ book, 110 were actions upon the case, most likely in assumpsit, where the amount demanded was about £ 15. Fourteen actions in debt occur and thirteen assault and battery matters. While all of the actions upon the case need not have been assumpsit matters the likelihood is that they were; if this be true the majority of Jay's cases in the Mayor's Court, as in the Supreme Court, were concerned with commercial collections.

Due to the extraordinarily large dockets in the Mayor's Court, Jay's cases tended to move forward to trial at a leisurely pace. In 1770 only two writs of inquiry were issued on behalf of Jay's clients, the number increasing to five in 1771 and five in 1772. A similar increase is to be noted in writs of venire[15] from one in 1770 to twelve in 1771 and nine in 1772. Perhaps indicative of the low financial status of the defendants, Jay registered only one execution by fieri facias[16] but eight executions by capias ad satisfaciendum.[17]

Certain cases offer more details by their appearance in the writ book. In an action on the case commenced in May of 1771 Jay's clients sued for £ 15. By October of that year Jay had obtained the necessary writ of venire and subpoenas to go to trial; however it would appear that the matter was not reached at that term and new subpoenas and writ were issued for the May 1772 term. At trial Thomas Smith, the opposing counsel, moved success-

[14][Mayor's Court of New York City] Writ Book, Sep. 5, 1769-Jan. 5, 1773, N.Y.Co. Clerk, Hall of Records, N.Y.C. See Table IV, Appendix C.

[15]Unlike the writ of inquiry which issued after judgment to fix damages, the writ of venire was issued to assemble a jury to determine the case.

[16]This writ orders the sheriff to seize the litigant's goods; if sale of the goods is not possible an exponas issues, instructing public auction of the goods.

[17]Authorizing arrest of the defendant to secure payment of the judgment.

fully for a non-suit and a capias was issued against Jay's client for the cost of £ 5 14 s 3 d. After a year's delay, jay's client was required to pay £ 5 14 s. 3 d. for his pains; it was not the most successful case that John Jay tried.[18]

More frustrating, but less embarrassing, was the unique case of Udall v. Carpenter, in which Jay as the plaintiff's attorney issued no less than ten capias ad respondendum writs.[19] The lack of any subsequent mention of the case leads to the conclusion that the matter was dropped, and Jay's client suffered the loss of £ 21 in sullen contemplation of the inefficiency of the sheriff's office.

In addition to the writ book, some other evidence survives from Jay's Mayor's Court practice. Two pleas of not guilty in assault and battery cases remain,[20] along with a Jay confession of judgment on behalf of a defendant, indicate the variety of his practice in this court.[21] A defendant's plea that he was an infant at the time the debt arose, and also at the time of suit, was also filed by Jay;[22] presumably the defense was allowed to be a valid bar to recovery. Jay's Supreme Court register contains five cases noticed in the Mayor's Court, but it is apparent from certain related entries that all litigation in the

---

[18]Stinebrunner v. Lamb, Writ Book, Mayor's Court 1769-1773, May 2, 1771, Oct. 1, 1771, mar. 9, 1772, Apr. 28, 1772.

[19]*Ibid.*, Nov. 27, 1771, *et seq.*, to Aug. 8, 1772.

20Mayor's Court, Miscellaneous File Papers, Box 1766-1774, N.Y.Co. Clerk, Hall of Records, N.Y.C. [Lewis v. Miller]; Benjamin Salzer Collection, Columbia University Libraries, Special Collections [Smith v. Reid, 1770].

[21]Handlin v. Jones, June 24, 1771, Columbia University Libraries, Special Collections.

[22]Miller v. Patten, Mayor's Court, Misc. File Papers, ibidem.

Mayor’s Court was noted in a separate register after 1770.[23] The survival of these documents at such widely separated locations, including one confession of judgment at the Yale University Library,[24] is convincing proof that Jay had an extensive practice in the Mayor's Court of New York City, and that a fairly large body of his papers were once in the files of that court. From the evidence hand it may be inferred that Jay's Mayor's Court practice was very nearly equal to his work in. the Common Pleas court of Westchester County.

The Supreme Court attorney engaged in practice before the courts of Common Pleas was likely to draw unfavorable comparisons between the justice available in New York City and the more earthy ad hoc decisions that occasionally were handed down by the laymen who were appointed to the local offices of justice. In addition the local attorneys as a rule had served a shorter clerkship, and their knowledge of the English common law left much to be desired. Jay's actions would indicate that he concurred in the sentiments of his fellow attorney, William Smith, who remarked, "How dangerous it is to trust Life & Property to Judges who are not bred to the Profession they are called to execute."[25] He and Robert R. Livingston, Jr. at some time in 1772 came to the conclusion that they should suggest that legally trained men be appointed to advise the common pleas judges and if this plan were approved they would apply for appointments to serve as itinerant judges to sit with the Common Pleas courts. Jay was prepared to serve in Orange, Westchester and Richmond counties, while Livingston was ready to sit on the bench for Tryon, Albany, Ulster and Dutchess Counties.[26]

The proposal was made to the Governor, William Tryon, who seemed to be favorably inclined toward these appointments, and introduced the mat

---

[23]Law Reg. Jay, N.Y., pp.22, 47, 125, 183, 210.

[24]Holland v. Davenport, Jan. 11, 1774, Narrative endorsed by Jay's confession of judgment.

[25]Smith *Memoirs*, pp.50, 51.

[26]*Ibid.*, p.129.

ter to his Council in late November of 1772.[27] William Smith confided to his memoirs that the Governor would soon find himself involved in provincial politics, and commented that the suggestion was entitled to serious consideration, as the appointment might be an occasion of disgust to the county justices. John Watts, a merchant, countered with the observation that every judge lacking in legal training would welcome the skillful assistance so provided. The matter was adjourned to a future date, and Smith left the meeting commenting that delay was tantamount to defeating the proposal.[28] Apparently Smith expected the Governor's enthusiasm for the scheme would vanish when he became aware of the opposition to such a change in the judicial system.

When the judgeship question was again discussed in the Council, Oliver Delancey was strongly against it, and argued that it would be a repudiation of the county magistrates. In the intervening time, Watts had reconsidered, and was opposed to the measure. With Smith suggesting it might be best if the young men came upon the bench as a of matter of course, the Council took a vote and found itself generally opposed to the matter. A further discussion was provided for, and the question tabled. Shortly after this meeting letters were dispatched which, according to William Smith, stirred up the counties and guaranteed that when the Assembly convened they would oppose the proposed appointment.[29]

Opposition to the measure on the part of the Delancey party resulted in a coalescence of Livingston supporters behind the appointment, and William Smith who originally had strong reservations voted for it in the Council on December 16, 1772.[30] Earlier he had recorded, "I now warn that Jay's Friends as well as Livingston's are disgusted and that they consider Mr. Tryon

---

[27]*Ibid.*, p. 129.

[28]*Ibid.*, p.130.

[29]*Ibid.*, p.130.

[30]*Ibid.*, p.132.

as either terrified or led by the Delanceys."[31] By the 16th of December both Jay and Livingston, at the suggestion of William Smith, had volunteered to serve without compensation. Of this Oliver Delancey commented that he was certain such an offer was not due to generosity or any regard for the public interest.[32] Concerning the offer Smith opined, "At all events the Young Fellows free themselves from Public Censure."[33] The vote in the Council was three in the affirmative, and six against or for further delay; "[Chief Justice] Horsmanden like an old Fool, talked of Clamour & voted it to be inexpedient."[34]

The discussion must have been quite heated, for Smith pushed his colleagues on the Council to the end of their patience. Of Roger Morris he noted, "Poor Morris was driven to insist that a Man without Law, was a fitter Judge than a Lawyer -- I pushed him hard upon this ridiculous Assertion".[35] Despite the efforts of Smith, the situation of lay judges in the Common Pleas courts was destined to persist until the Revolution, and Jay in 1774 commented, "... Judges are taken from among the Farmers. . . ,"[36]

The question of itinerant judgeships was never brought up before the General Assembly, and was left relatively untouched until 1774 when John Jay corresponded with John Vardill concerning the question. Unfortunately we lack the text of Vardill's letters to Jay, but it seems that Vardill with the encouragement of his handlers in the royal Secret Service, offered such a

---

[31]Ibid., p.130.

[32]Ibid., p.132.

[33]Ibid., p.132.

[34]Ibid., p. 132; Smith never seems to have held Daniel Horsmanden in high esteem, and in this instance resented the old man's failure to take a stand for more uniform standards of justice in all provincial courts.

[35]Ibidem.

[36]To Rev. John Vardill, May 23, 1774, A.O. 13/105/283, Public Record Office, London.

post to Jay. In reply John Jay indicated that he could not accept such a post unless it was accompanied with a salary; if such were offered to him he "... would cheerfully resign the Toil of my Profession for Otium cum Dignitatae." While Governor Tyron had been civil to him, Jay had not taken any particular pains to cultivate his friendship, hence his principal hope for such an appointment was Vardill's influence with the British government.[37] This letter was turned over to the Commissioners on Loyalist Claims in 1784 as a basis for Vardill's assertion that he had assisted the British in the attempt to obtain information from the leaders of the revolutionary movement in America.[38] The letter written by Jay in September of 1774 contains no political intelligence, shows respect for that oath of secrecy he had taken as a member of the First Continental Congress.[39]

Despite the inference in Vardill's petition that he was instrumental in attempting to get political information from John Jay, there is no clear indication that any assistance was forthcoming from Jay. Because Jay had played such an active role in the determinations of the Continental Congress, he would have been in a position to release valuable information to Vardill, had he been so inclined. The very failure of Vardill to mention such collaboration by Jay is fairly strong evidence that political intelligence was not available to the British through Jay.

Judge Thomas Jones described Jay's adherence to the Revolutionary cause as a product of his frustrations in failing to marry into the Dalancey family. By retaliation, asserted Jones,

> Mr. Jay . . . took a wife in . . . the Livingston [family] a family ever opposed in politics to the DeLanceys, turned

---

[37]Ibidem.

[38]Ibidem.

[39]Sept. 24, 1774, ibid. All of these items were transmitted to the commission with the request they be returned, A.O. 13/105/321, Public Record Office, London.

Republican, espoused the Livingston interest,
and ever after opposed all legal government.[40]

The statement bears certain resemblance to the truth; Jay had been disappointed in affairs of the heart with two daughters of Peter Delancey, he had married Sarah Livingston, the daughter of William Livingston in April of 1774. Yet the adamant opposition of the Delancey party to his political advancement had two years before his marriage united him in interest with the Livingston party, as did his association in practice with Robert R. Livingston, Jr. This familial and political tie to the Livingston party reenforced by a long-standing opposition in the Jay family to British commercial regulation and taxation, resulted in Jay's adherence to the Patriot Party when the American Revolution arrived in the Province of New York.

With the approach of 1775 Jay was nearing his eleventh year in the legal profession. At the prime of his career at the Bar he yearned for the dignities and muniments of service upon the Bench. It was not his youth alone that militated against these ambitions, for in less than a year after the Jay and Livingston application for judicial position, young Robert R. Livingston, Jr. was appointed recorder of the City of New York to succeed David Jones.[41] His selection was upon the basis of a suggestion made to Governor Tryon by William Smith.[42] Had Jay enjoyed a stronger political position in the Province there would have undoubtedly have been a place for him in one of the public offices at the disposal of the Governor. This being the case, it was entirely reasonable for him to attempt to attain public office through his friend in London, John Vardill.

---

[40]*History New York*, II, 223; see editorial note at II, 474, 475. Jones himself had married into the Delancey family, and thus was doing some special pleading for the virtues of the Delancey party.

[41]General Sessions Minutes, N.Y. Co., May 21, 1772-Nov. 1790, pp.65, 89; "The Burghers of New Amsterdam and the Freemen of New York, 1675-1866", *New York Historical Society Collections* XVIII, 557.

[42]Smith *Memoirs*, pp.153-154.

Jay's desire for a position on the Bench quite likely was also attributable to his marriage to Sarah Van Brugh Livingston in April of 1774. Unlike many matches of the day, theirs was one based upon deep bonds of affection, and throughout his life John Jay spent as many hours as he could with his wife and their children. When his beloved Sally died in 1801, Jay became a changed man and aged far beyond his fifty-five years; twelve years his junior, Sarah Livingston had brought to John Jay's life a youthful exuberance that lightened the burden of a somber, business-like approach to life, that was so typical of Jay and his Huguenot ancestors. With her death Jay withdrew from involvement with politics, and retired from a world that held little joy except that which her children brought to him.

This dedication to his new bride and her happiness required that Jay make certain changes in his professional career. First of all, it is quite likely that Sarah Jay convinced her husband that he must reduce the number of cases pending lest he again ruin his health. We can see a clear decline in the number of cases opened after 1774. Secondly, Jay very probably became more reluctant to accept cases in the Common Pleas courts, as trials would take him away from the New York City residence he had established with Sarah. Thirdly, appointment as a Judge would guarantee him an income and professional activity, but limit his travels on the circuit. Marriage no doubt had a significant impact upon Jay's career, but the effect was quite different from that alluded to by Judge Thomas Jones. By 1774 Jay's political alignment was already fixed; his personal life was in a state of change, and those alterations could have had a significant impact upon the nature of his practice after 1775.

Ironically Jay's retirement from active practice in 1774 to 1775 was not to provide greater opportunity to be with his wife, but rather was to be accompanied by public responsibilities that would take him from her side for extended periods. When he attempted to obtain public office under the Crown in 1772 and 1774, it was with an eye to personal comfort and increased social and professional status. As the American Revolution approached, Jay was drawn into a position where acceptance of public office meant extraordinary personal sacrifice and treason against the Crown. The decision to enter public life was not an easy one under these circumstances, and Jay very naturally moved with causion and indecision toward the fatal choice.

Unlike the Massachusetts Bar, the lawyers of New York had not been sharply polarized into patriotic or loyalist groups by 1775. Of the attorneys practicing in 1765, twelve remained loyal to the Crown and thirteen joined the American cause. Among the loyalists was Jay's mentor and friend, Benjamin Kissam.[43] Among John Jay's contemporaries, Robert R. Livingston, Jr. and Gouverneur Morris joined the rebellion, while Peter Van Schaack and Lindley Murray remained loyal to Great Britain. In regard to Jay's Supreme Court clientele, I have identified thirty-two individuals who were loyalists, and only twenty-one who joined the patriots.[44] The conclusion seems inescapable that there was no pressure of professional expedience that made Jay a "reluctant rebel;" on the contrary there is evidence of strong professional reasons that would impel him to take the loyalist position. Decision itself meant painful alienation from close friends at the Bar. Is it strange that the choice was one to be postponed as long as possible?

Although Jay could delay his decision concerning the patriot cause, it was not possible for him to be totally disassociated with the political life of provincial New York. His extensive practice in Westchester, and his defense of the broadly based Westchester Borough franchise in the King v. Underhill case had brought his name before the public as an attorney opposed to the unbridled power of the royal governor. From the time he had refused to return the Boundary Commission papers without legislative authorization, Jay had demonstrated a stubborn independence; as his lack of influence with the Governor cost him political appointments under the Crown, it also rallied to his support the many factions in New York that were held together by their mutual exclusion from royal patronage. It was doubtless this reputation and support that cause Jay's selection to represent New York in the Continental Congress to be first assembled in September 1774.

---

[43]For polarization in The Massachusetts Bar see Richard B. Morris, "Legalism versus Revolutionary Doctrine in New England," *New England Quarterly*, IV, 195-215. Loyalists on the list in Appendix A, are Crannel, Whitehead Hicks, David and Thomas Jones, Kempe, Benjamin and Daniel Kissam, Ludlow, Mathews, Wickham, Woods and Smith, Jr.; patriots are Antill, Duane, Helme, Thomas Hicks, Samuel Jones, Philip Livingston, William Livingston, Cary Ludlow, Morris, Reade, and Scott.

At that meeting Jay labored faithfully to moderate the forces demanding an immediate break with Great Britain. In this he reflected the attitude of most New York residents who, like himself, wished to postpone an unpleasant decision to the last possible moment. The American Revolution came to New York against the wishes of its leading citizens; John Jay merely represented the majority of people in the Province who feared the consequences of rebellion. That their fears were well-founded can be seen in the large number of families divided by the revolt, the bitterness and inhumanity displayed by New York loyalists and patriots on the battlefield, and the friendships utterly destroyed over the issue of loyalty.

John Jay at last had received the public office he had so coveted in earlier, less terrifying times, yet now public office had as its accompaniment the destruction of family ties, the duty to harass old and dear friends, and the need to erect a new state and nation out of the ruins of a devastated colonial society.

XI. OUR LIVES, OUR FORTUNES, AND OUR SACRED HONOR

It was probably just as well that John Jay was not present in the Continental Congress when the Declaration of Independence was adopted and signed, for in at least one particular he might have voided the document for want of consideration. Each of the signers pledged to each other, in support of the Declaration, their lives, their fortunes, and their sacred honor; by July of 1776 a large part of Jay's fortune had been dissipated in the attempt to defend American liberties while retaining cherished ties with Great Britain. The story of this dedication is reflected in the rapid decline of the Jay law practice after 1774. In a very real sense, Jay's legal career was sacrificed to the demands made upon him for public service to his Province and nation.

Law practice makes varying demands upon the time of the sole practitioner; usually he is able to adapt himself to the situation by the expenditure of additional time devoted to his practice. However, when his presence is require at two places at the same time, he must make a difficult choice. Jay's attendanee at the meetings of the First Continental Congress in Philadelphia deprived his clients of counsel for a two month period. When George Clinton referred a matter to Jay to act as counsel for one of Clinton's clients, he noted that he would look forward to hearing from Jay, ". . .as soon as Convenient and you get a little diverted of Politicks,"[1] Fellow attorneys were, of course, sympathetic to Jay's predicament, clients seeking an attorney that would attend promptly to their private interests were little impressed with the public position of their legal counsel. I

Jay's ability permitted him to retain certain matters despite the diversion of politics, and he received from his friends heady commendations upon his success in the political arena.

> ... I have often foretold, that your integrity, your knowledge of the Law & the firmness with which you would maintain the Cause of your Client would with rapidity

---

[1]Letter to Jay Oct. 8, 1774, Columbia University Libraries, Special Collections.

> advance your Reputation as a Lawyer. But little did I think that in the Course of so few years you could have open'd your way to the first honors in the gift of a free People,...[2]

In spite of these felicitations, the business coming to the Jay law office began to decline, and by the end of 1775 Jay's clerks were at the point of despair. To his master at Philadelphia, Robert Troup wrote with concern,

> When I reflect upon the present Business of the office, I am filled with the deepest sorrow. Formerly it was extensive, and attended with much Profit: now it is confined within very narrow Bounds, and of Course, accompanied with little gain.[3]

The melancholy news, which could not have been unexpected, must have jarred Jay into the realization of how much he, as an individual, was sacrificing in the patriot cause.

By the time Troup wrote, Jay had already realized the difficulty of participating in the extended meetings of the Continental Congress while attempting to continue his New York law practice. In July of 1775 he and Gouvemeur Morris exchanged letters concerning the cases they had pending in the Common Pleas Court of Westchester county. Morris pointed out that he would have to bring at least one of these cases to trial at the next term of the Court since his client's interests required that he do so. Jay's reply indicates that he was fully aware of Morris' situation, and although he would have appreciated the opportunity to attend to the trial himself, he did not resent his opponents moving toward trial. Assuring Morris that if he delayed in moving for trial against Jay's clients, Morris need not fear non-suits being taken against him, Jay concluded that while he hoped Morris could

---

[2]Oct. 31, 1772, Samuel Kissam to John Jay, Columbia University Quaterly. XXV, 132.

[3]Oct. 30, 1775, Columbia University Libraries, Special Collections.

delay a little longer, he could not in good conscience request him to do so.[4] The situation was not an easy one, and both attorneys were placed in a difficult position by Jay's attendance at the Continental Congress. Only the forbearance of his fellow lawyers, such as that demonstrated by Gouverneur Morris, made it possible for Jay to continue in practice until 1776.

On October 24, 1775, Lewis Morris appeared on behalf of Jay in the Supreme Court of Judicature. In the July term, Jay had been represented by his cousin, Augustus Van Cortlandt.[5] These appearances by other attorneys acting in an "Of Counsel" basis for John Jay, were virtually the only manner in which Jay's court appearances could be handled. His clerks, Robert Troup and John Strang, did their best to collect the costs owed to Jay by his clients, and Troup wrote to Jay that he was acting as attorney while Strang was acting as counsel.[6] Precisely how much good this would do is debateable, but it is possible that the young men in Jay's office might have been admitted to practice in the inferior courts, and thus could be of assistance in that regard. I have not found any record of either clerk appearing on behalf of Jay. The records of admission clearly indicate that Strang was admitted to practice when the Supreme Court under the State of New York began to function in 1778; Troup was not admitted until 1782.[7]

During these trying times Jay's clerks also foundered for want of guidance and advice. To quote Troup,

> ... we feel the Want of [Jay's] Counsel,

---

[4]Morris to Jay, July 28, 1775, Jay to Morris, n.d. [c. July 28, 1775], Columbia University Libraries, Special Collections.

[5]Min. S.Ct. Jud., July 25, 1775-Apr. 28, 1781, N.Y.Co. Clerk, Hall of Records, N.Y.C. pp. 10, 11, Min. S.Ct. Jud., Apr. 21, 1772-Jan. 17, 1776 (rough), N.Y.Co. Clerk, Hall of Records, N.Y.C., p. 200.

[6]Oct. 30, 1775, Columbia University Libraries, Special Collections.

[7]See ledgers S and T, Roll of Attorneys, Oct. 26, 1754 June 27, 1847, Parchment Roll #1, N.Y.Co. Clerk, Hall of Records, N.Y.C.

> [and] cannot conveniently obtain a Solution to difficult Questions. Books are our only Informers, and these we peruse with as much Attention as the Disturbances in America, and this City in particular will allow.[8]

ln this manner, Jay's clients were being penalized by the iinexperience of his clerks, although Strang having reached the end of a lengthy clerkship could not have been as helpless as Troup in finding the law. To these two young men, Jay owed the continuance of his practice during 1775 and 1776. It is perhaps indicative of the personality of each that Troup was not all reluctant to rely upon Jay's sense of obligation for later political advancement, while Strang seems to have been largely independent of Jay in the years ahead.

Jay was in constant attendance at the Second Continental Congress from the date of his arrival on May 13, 1775 until the time he took leave to sit in the New York Provincial Congress in April of 1776.[9] He served on a large number of committees, and bore more than his share of the Congress' business. When he returned to New York from Philadelphia he was able to complete some matters for his clients, but even then the demands of public affairs pressed heavily upon John Jay.

A month after Jay's return from Philadelphia the older folder order began to change. Gradually the royal courts began to terminate their business, and a state of civil war began to replace the orderly processes of government. The last sitting of the Court of Chancery took place on January 9, 1776, General Sessions of the Peace for New York County ceased to function after May 10, 1776, to be followed by the inferior courts in Dutchess county on May 22nd, and the Westchester Common Pleas court on May 28,

---

[8]Oct. 30, 1775 to Jay, Columbia University Libraries, Special Collections.

[9]Worthington C. Ford, ed, Journals of the Continental Congress, 34 vols., (Washington: Government Printing Office, 1904-1937), II, 44, IV, 259.

1776.[10] Justice was coming to an abrupt halt as the province of New York drifted toward independence from the British Crown and Nation. Events were to so alter Jay's life that he never would return to private practice of his profession.

The coming of the British forces to New York City resulted in a loss of nearly all of Jay's office files; a portion of his law library seems to have been lost or destroyed, and the surviving books were badly damaged. The physical record of his practice remained only in the public records of the province, and his reputation as a lawyer was soon overshadowed as his renown in public life increased. The young lawyer who at twenty-six had temporarily undermined his health by his dedication to his law practice, in 1776 at the age of thirty, had sacrificed that practice for the sake of a public career that was to be strangely commingled with commendation and condemnation. Having made that choice, he could never turn back.

---

[10]Chancery Minutes, IV 221, 222, N.Y.Co. Clerk, Hall of Records, N.Y.C., Common Pleas Minutes, Dutchess Co., Liber E. Dutchess Co. Clerk, Poughkeepsie, N.Y.; General Sessions Minutes, N.Y.Co., May 21, 1772-November/?/,1790, N.Y.Co. Supreme Court Library, General Sessions Branch, Criminal Courts Bldg., N.Y.C., p.184; Common Pleas Minutes, Westchester Co., 1774-1793, Westchester Co. Clerk, White Plains, N.Y., p.58.

XII. THE LEGACY OF A LAWYER

During the course of the American Revolution, John Jay's career in public life was sufficiently demanding to require the application of all of his talents and time. A brief period of service as Chief Justice of the State of York in the years 1777-1778, was rapidly followed by legislative prominence at the Continental Congress, and election to the Presidency of that body. As minister to Spain Jay had endured much in the name of his country, and as a peace commissioner at Paris in 1782 and 1783, he had contributed greatly to her future greatness.

With the peace concluded, independence secure, and his personal affairs badly in need of attention, Jay prepared to return to private life. Included within his thoughts was the prospect of returning to law practice. To his friend Gouverneur Morris he confided "... the Education of my Son, the attention I owe to the unfortunate part of my Family, and the Happiness I expect from rejoining my Friends; . . ."[1] were the advantages to be gained from an early return to private life. In regard to his professional plans, Jay commented, ". . . my Pride is not of a Nature to be hurt by returning to the Business which I formerly followed."[2] Later letters written from Europe confirm Jay's intention to return to law practice,[3] and he still considered retirement from public life even after he arrived at New York City and learned of Congress' request that he assume the duties of Secretary for Foreign Affairs. When queried by his former partner, Robert R. Livingston, Jay wrote, "When I resigned my appointments in Europe, I purposed to return to the practice of the law, what Effect the unexpected offer of Congress . . . may

---

[1]Feb. 10, 1784, Columbia University Libraries, Special Collections.

[2]*Ibid.*

[3]A letter to Peter Van Schaack, a New York attorney who remained loyal to the Crown and left New York during the Revolution, shows that Jay contemplated return to practice and was willing to take Van Schaack's son as a clerk, Apr. 10, 1784, Columbia University Libraries, Special Collections.

have on that design as yet remains undecided."[4] Although John Jay eventually accepted the diplomatic post, it seems fairly clear that he did not do so to avoid practice. Rather he considered the public need to create a preference for his services, and sacrificed the opportunity of returning to private life and law practice in the interest of the national welfare.

The importance which Jay attached to the proper education of his son, Peter Augustus Jay, led him to take some time from his official duties to provide direction for the young man's endeavors. Personal letters of Jay provide a fairly accurate picture of the regimen he set for the boy. While Secretary for Foreign Affairs, Jay wrote from Trenton to his eight year old son, the following discussion of perseverance in the study of Latin:

> . . . I am persuaded you have too much Resolution, to be deterred by a few unpleasant Difficulties, from the Pursuit of important Objects. Nothing can be done without Perseverance; without that Quality, Talents avail but little . . . your Happiness is concerned in having both a sound Body, and a sound Mind; in Play Hours, play with spirit; and in Study Hours, study earnestly.[5]

When on circuit as Chief Justice of the United States, Jay admonished Peter Augustus, then nearly fifteen, concerning an omission in one of his letters.

> . . . when you answer a Letter, it is always advisable to read it over carefully and attentively, and to mark accurately what part it may be proper or necessary to answer, and what not.
>
> A Habit of this kind will always lead you to write what may be proper and prudent, and restrain you from writing what had

---

[4]Aug. 18, 1784, Wm. Jay, *Life*, I, 186.

[5]Dec. 13, 1784, John J. DuBois Manuscripts (Columbia University photocopy).

> better be omitted. Remember that what a man says or writes affords the strongest Evidence against him;. . .[6]

Throughout life, John Jay took a deep interest in the career of his eldest son, and when his second and youngest son, William Jay, came to the point of receiving his education, Jay displayed similar concern.

It is not without significance that both Peter Augustus and William were trained in the law; while the elder son went on to a highly successful career at the Bar, the younger man, because of weak eyes, retired from active practice at an early date and became a gentleman farmer. Legal training provided a living to Peter Augustus Jay; it gave wisdom and ability to William Jay who served for many years as a judge of the Common Pleas Court of Westchester County. In this manner, John Jay left a legacy in the law to both of his sons, and the Jay family played an important role in the formulation of law in nineteenth century New York. Since two of John Jay's sons followed their father's footsteps into the profession, it is clear that their father had never expressed serious doubts concerning his, or their, choice of a career. When Jay's son, Peter Augustus Jay, and his nephew Peter Jay Munro, represented Westchester County at the 1821 Convention to revise the 1777 constitution, drawn in part by the efforts of John Jay, the old man must have looked on proudly from his retirement to see that younger Jays continued the family tradition of law making in the State of New York.[7]

As an executor, Jay continued to be involved with the law throughout his public career. Appointed executor and trustee under his father's will, Jay was involved in administering this estate until the death of his sister Eve Jay Munro in 1815.[8] Even more significantly, Jay had been appointed an

---

[6]Dec. 4, 1790, John J. DuBois Manuscripts (Columbia University photocopy).

[7]Robert Bolton, *A History of the County of Westchester* (2 vols., New York: Alexanders. Gould, 1848), I, xxii.

[8]JJ to Peter Jay Munro, Sep. 16, 1785, Jay Papers, Museum of the City of New York, N.Y.C. Accounts Re: Trust for Eve Munro, Nov. 16,

executor of the will of his fellow peace commissioner,[9] Benjamin Franklin, and was concerned in the administration of that very substantial estate and its famous charitable requests for the support of needy apprentices and tradesmen.

In regard to his personal affairs John Jay also remained a sharp eye for legal matters. For example, he was careful to inquire of the New York City authorities concerning the zoning regulations, prior to commencing construction of his new home in New York City.[10] When the Common Pleas Court of Westchester County heard argument concerning lands in Bedford, he obtained a leave of absence from his work as Secretary for Foreign Affairs to enable him to assist counsel retained by him in that matter.[11] Even when burdened with the administrative duties of the Governor of New York, Jay was quick to discover a defective description in a deed, and suggest a method of remedying the mistake.[12]

Although retired from private practice at a relatively young age, John Jay remained a student of the law throughout his life, and retained the abilities and skills of a lawyer long after he needed to utilize them for the welfare of his clients. His attitude toward the profession is best exemplified by a bit of advice given to Peter Augustus Jay in 1800, fourteen years after John Jay had severed his

---

1785-July 1815, Jay Ledger, 1774, New York State Library, Albany, N.Y.

[9]Henry Hill to JJ, Apr. 24, 1780, Columbia University Libraries, Special Collections. The Jay papers contain no further reference to the Franklin estate; we must therefore assume that Jay's participation in its administration was limited to mere formalities.

[10]Letter to Mayor James Duane, Sep. 30, 1785, Duane Papers, III, #155, New York Historical Society, N.Y.C.

[11]To President of Congress, Nov. 2, 1785, Domestic Letters I, Office of Foreign Affairs, Papers of the Continental Congress, National Archives, Washington, D.C.

[12]To Peter Jay Munro, July 1, 1800, Jay Papers, Museum of the City of New York, N.Y.C.

connections with law practice. The young man desired advice whether he should apply for appointment as a notary public, and received the following reply from his father, the Governor:

> I have frequently and I believe maturely considered the Expediency of your holding any of the little offices which so many are solicitous to have. Such offices give their Possessors no additional consideration, but on the contrary tend to diminish Confidence in their Professional Merit and Qualifications. The Emoluments of them are not worth the Time they consume, and cannot ultimately compensate for the Neglect of professional Studies and Pursuits. An Eminent Counsellor will attract more Respect, and command more influence, as well as money, than almost any office can confer or produce. Your Time for office is not yet come; the wisdom of accepting them is frequently dubious.[13]

Noting that Peter Augustus Jay's Chancery practice was growing, Jay concluded with an eloquent compliment to the nation he had helped form, and the profession in which he was trained,

> Aim at this--stand independently on your own legs, and next to providence, trust to your Talents, your Industry and Prudence. They who deserve Success, are in this Country in no Danger of being disappointed. . . . Only continue to do Justice to your Business and your self, and your Business will reward you handsomely.[14]

---

[13]Dec. 18, 1800, Columbia University Libraries, Special Collections.

[14]*Ibid.*

In so advising his son, Jay revealed his own satisfaction at having achieved success in the practice of law, and his lasting affection for his chosen profession. This was the professional legacy he left to his two sons--contentment with the title of "attorney and counsellor at law", a continuing interest in exploring the intricacies of jurisprudence, and an abiding faith that devotion to self-improvement and the affairs of one's clients provides a sure path to success at the Bar. In his retirement from public life after 1801, John Jay watched with pride as his sons followed his example and began to achieve success in the legal profession.

APPENDIX A

ATTORNEYS PRACTICING BEFORE THE SUPREME COURT OF JUDICATURE IN THE YEAR 1765

The following list of attorneys admitted to practice in the Supreme Court of Judicature was obtained by a review of the minute books of the Court. Additional information concerning the age and family relationships of these lawyers was obtained from various genealogical tracts concerning their own, or the related families.

Attorney	Age in 1765	Education	Relations by blood or marriage
Edward Antill (1742-1789)	23	King's, 1762	
Barthlomew Crannel	?	?	Livingston
Henry Cuyler	?	King's 1762	Cruger
James Duane (1733-1797)	32	?	Livingston
James Emott	?	?	
James Graham, Jr.	?	King's	Morris
Benjamin Helme	?	?	
Thomas Hicks	?	?	
Whitehead Hicks (1728-1780)	37	?	

Attorney	Age in 1765	Education	Relations by blood or marriage
David Jones (1699-1775)	66	?	
Samuel Jones (1734-1819)	31	?	
Thomas Jones (1731-1792)	34	Yale, 1750	Delancey
John Tabor Kempe (c.1735-1795)	c.30	?	
Benjamin Kissam (1728-1782)	37	?	Rutgers
Daniel Kissam (1726-1782)	39	?	Rutgers
Philip Livingston	?	?	
Philip F. Livingston	?	?	
William Livingston (1723-1790)	43	Yale, 1741	French

Attorney	Age in 1765	Education	Relations by blood or marriage
Cary Ludlow (c. 1736-1815)	c.29	King's, M.A. 1758	
George Duncan Ludlow (? - 1808)	?	?	
David Mathews (1700-1784)	65	?	
John McKesson (C.1735-1798)	30	Princeton, 1753	
Robert Moore (? - 1784)	?	?	
Lewis Morris (1726-1798)	39	Yale	
Joseph Reade, Jr.	?	Kings, 1758, Pennsylvania, 1760	Livingston, French
James Riker	?	?	
John Morin Scott (1730-1784)	35	Yale, 1746	Rutgers

Attorney	Age in 1765	Education	Relations by blood or marriage
John W. Smith	?	?	
Thomas Smith (1734-C.1800)	31	Princeton, 1754	
William Smith (1699-1769)	68	Yale, 1719	Livingston
William Smith, Jr. (1728-1793)	37	Yale, 1746	Livingston, Schuyler
Richard Snedecker	?	?	
Peter Silvester	?	?	
Augustus Van Cortlandt (1728-1824)	37	?	DePeyster, Jay
William Wickham (c.1734-1813)	c.31	Yale, 1754	
John Woods (c.1732-1797)	33	Yale, 1755	

APPENDIX B

MAP PREPARED BY THE NEW YORK - NEW JERSEY BOUNDARY COMMISSION OF 1769

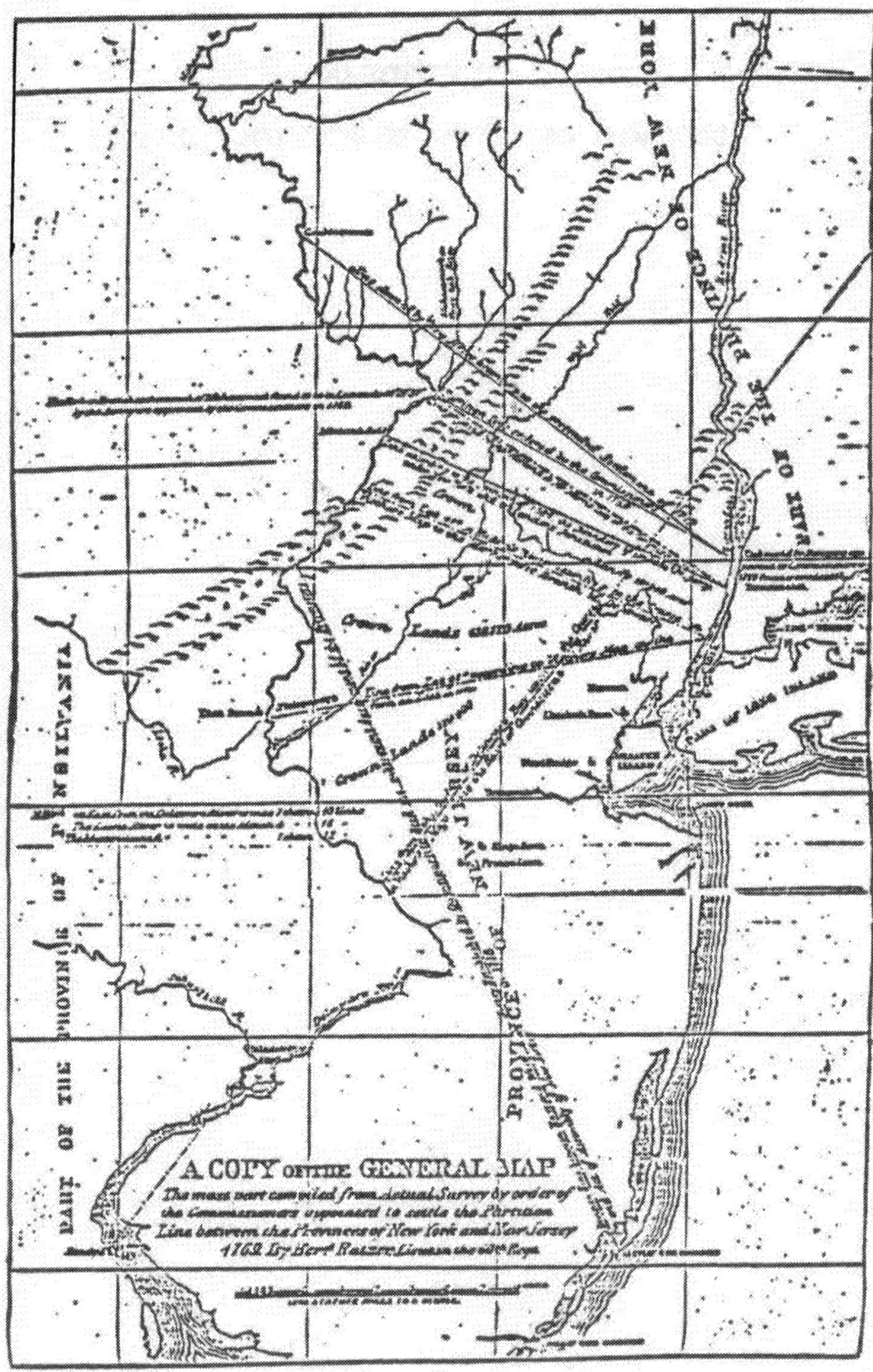
A COPY OF THE GENERAL MAP
Line between the Provinces of New York and New Jersey

APPENDIX C

GRAPHIC ANALYSIS OF JAY'S LAW PRACTICE

The graphs which follow represent Jay's cases in the Supreme Court of Judicature, the Mayor's Court of the City of New York, the Common Pleas Court of Dutchess county and the Common Pleas Court of Westchester county.

In each case, the figure of cases opened includes those cases where an original capias has been noted in court minute or writ books. Cases closed, when represented, is derived from the total of cases settled during the month added to the total of cases going to final judgment during the month added to the total of cases going to final judgment during the month. For example, a judgment by default on an assumpsit narrative would not be counted as being a final judgment until the writ of inquiry was returned by the sheriff, and judgment entered for the amount of damages found.

Cases pending categories represent an attempt to depict the backlog of cases which was built up during the active years of practice. It is merely the arithmetic difference between the cases opened and the cases closed, added to the number of cases on hand from the previous month.

TABLE I(A)

140
120
100
80
60
40
20
Supreme Court of
Judicature
Cases Pending
1769
1770
1771
1772
1773
1774
1775
1776

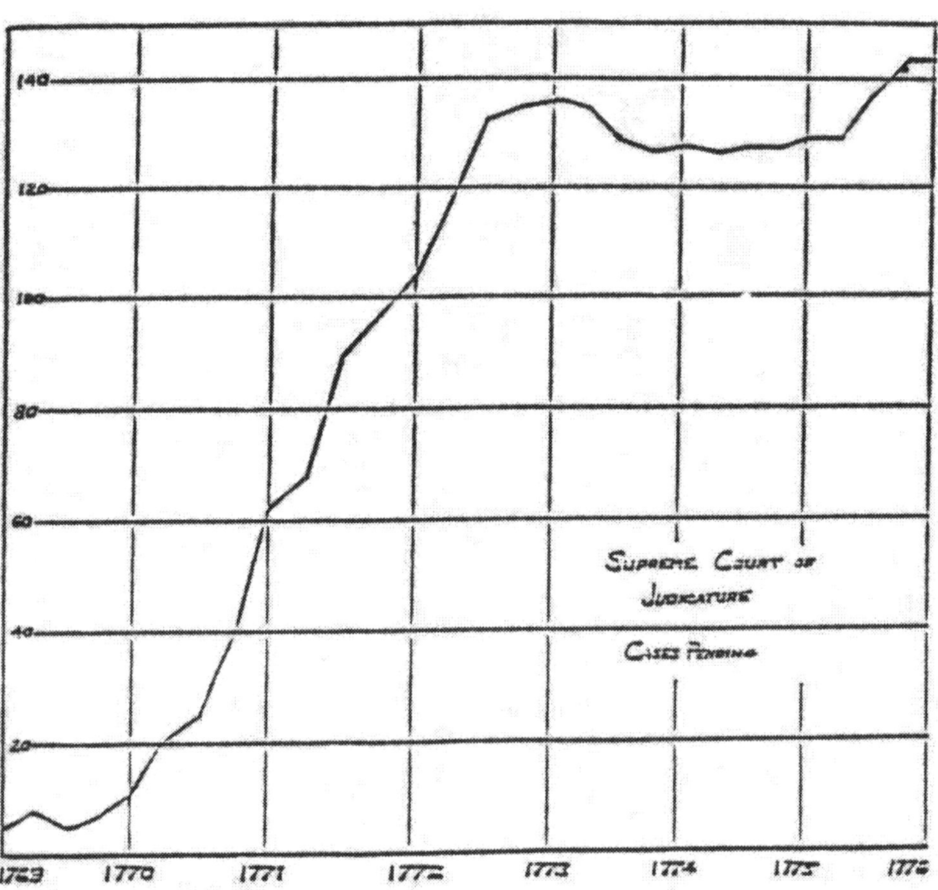

TABLE I(B)

Supreme Court of Judicature
Cases Opened
Cases Terminated
20
15
10
5
1769
1770
1771
1772
1773
1774
1775
1776

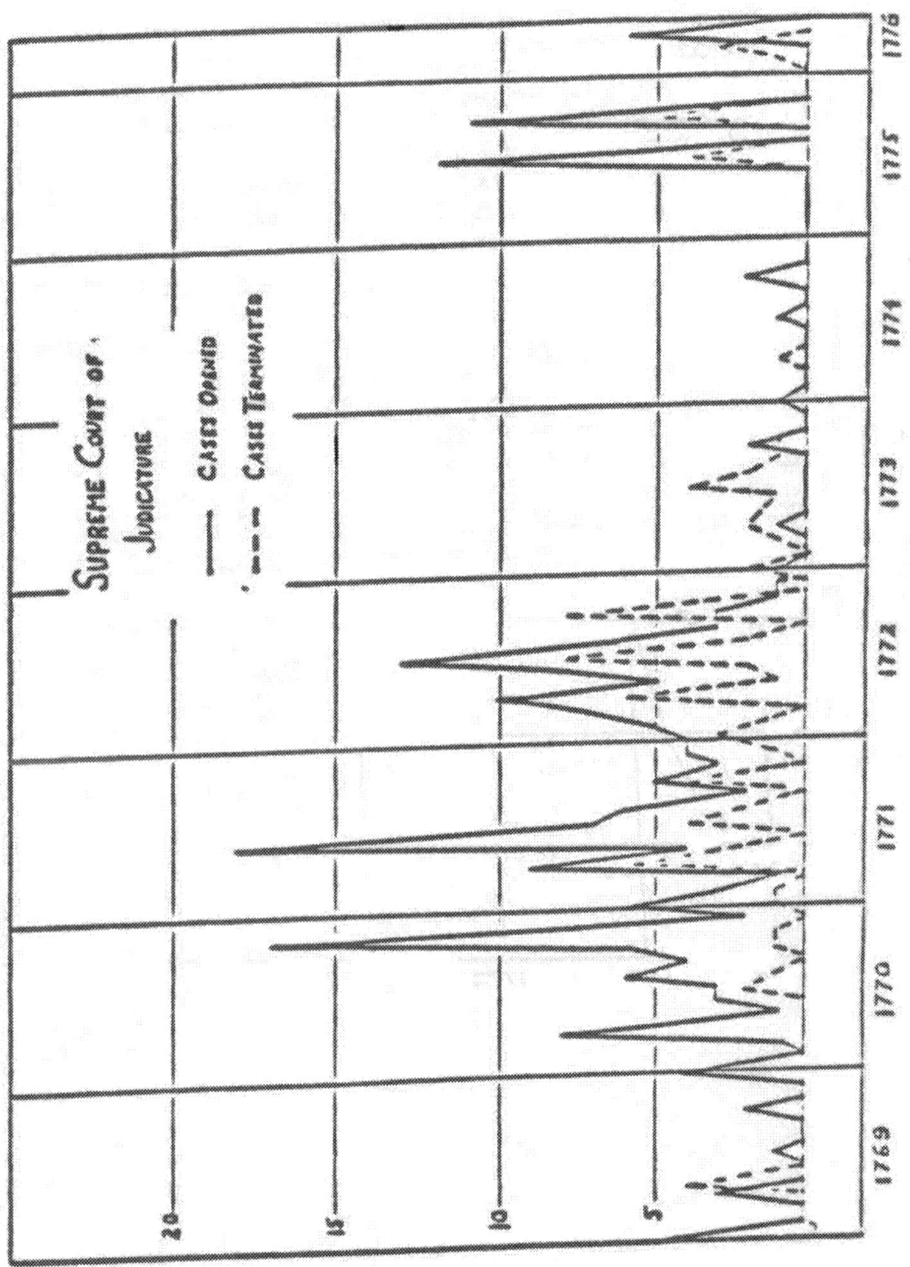

TABLE IIw

WESTCHESTER COUNTY
COMMON PLEAS
CASES PENDING
150
120
90
60
30
1769
1770
1771
1772
1773
1774
1775
1776

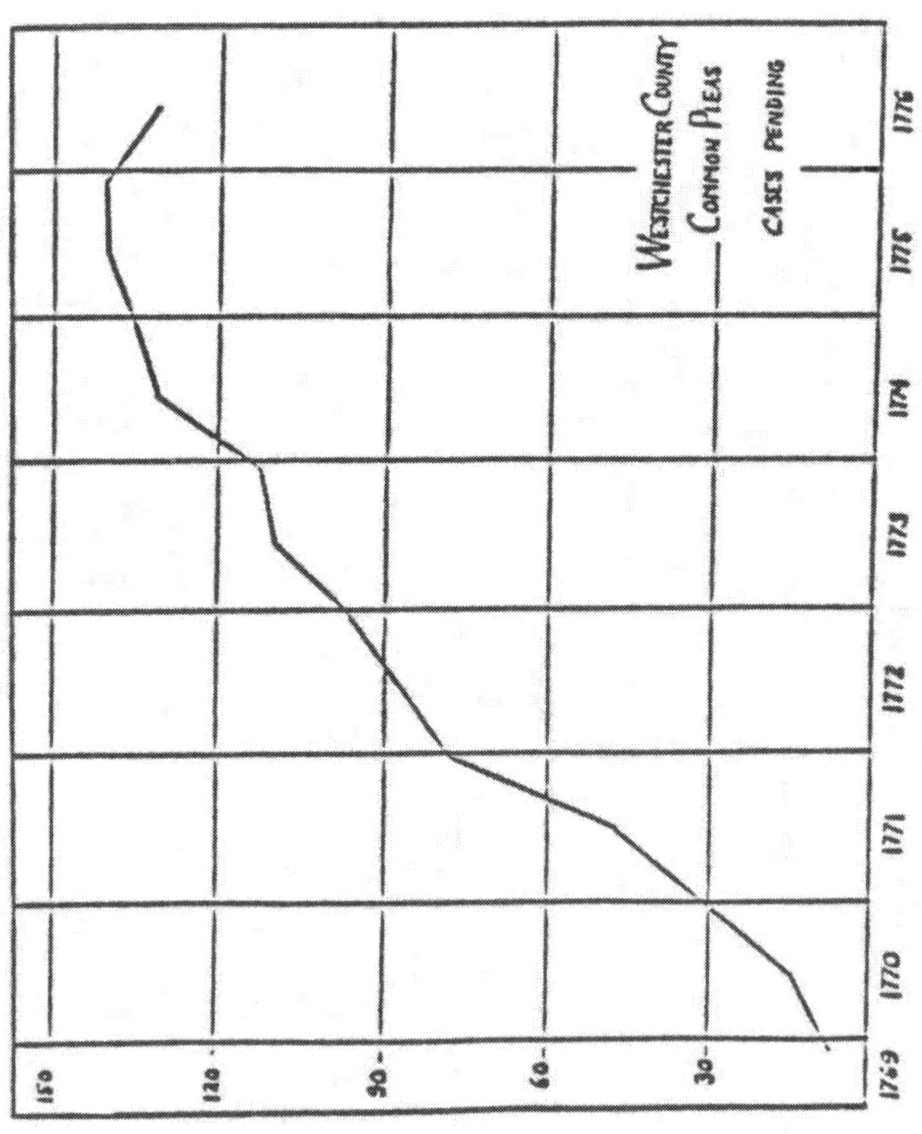

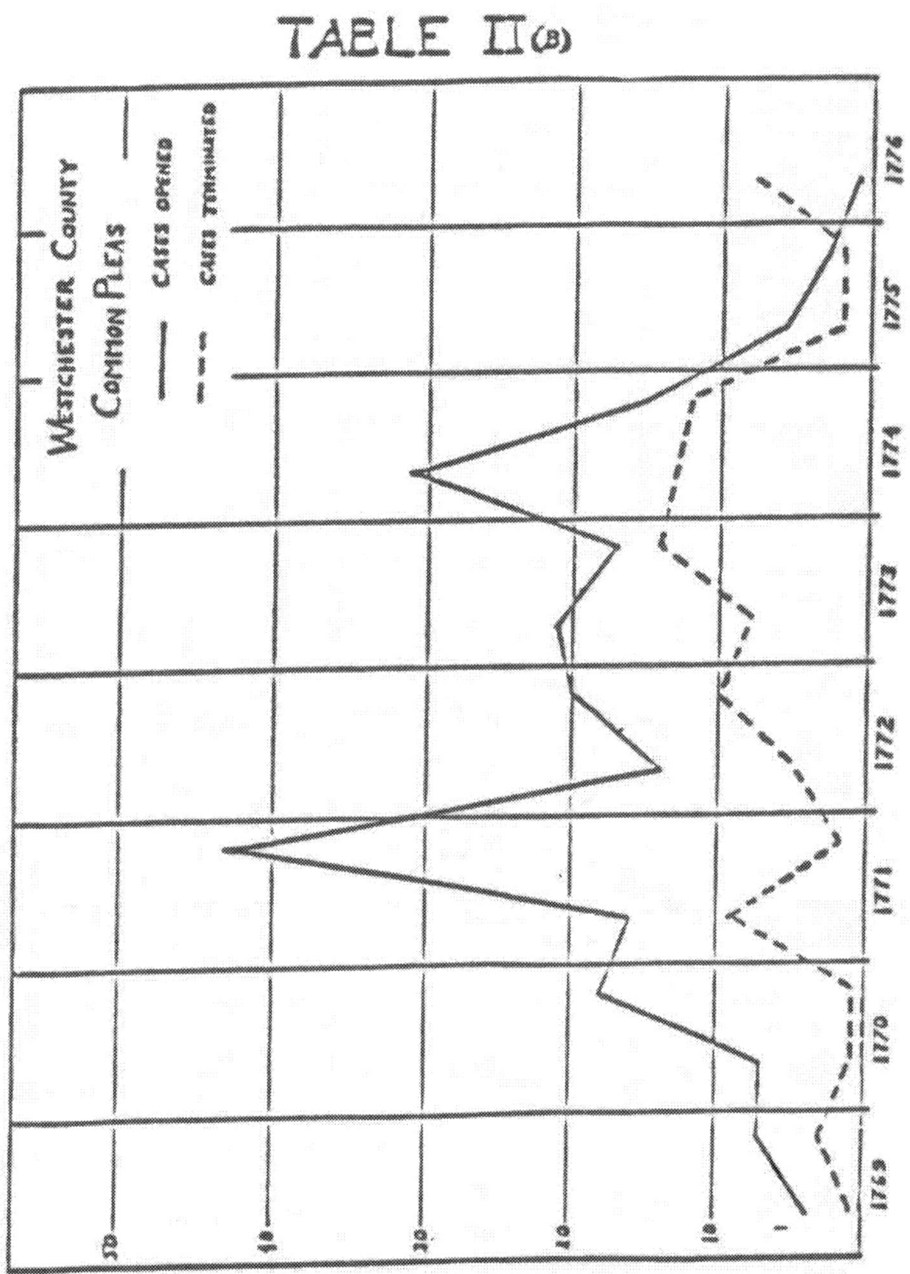
TABLE II (B)
WESTCHESTER COUNTY
COMMON PLEAS
CASES OPENED
CASES TERMINATED
50
40
30
20
10
1769
1770
1771
1772
1773
1774
1775
1776

TABLE III(a)

DUTCHESS COUNTY
COMMON PLEAS
CASES PENDING
1769
1770
1771
1772
1773
1774
1775
1776
0
10
20
30
40

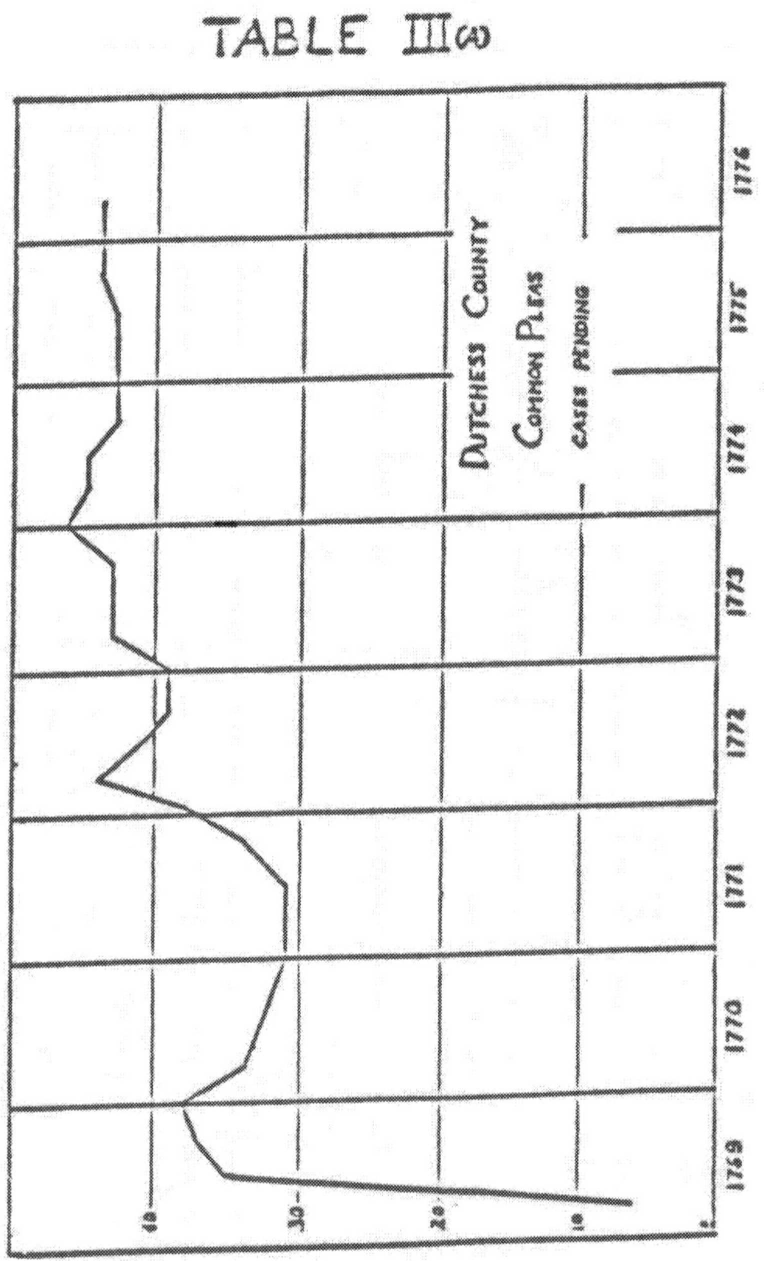

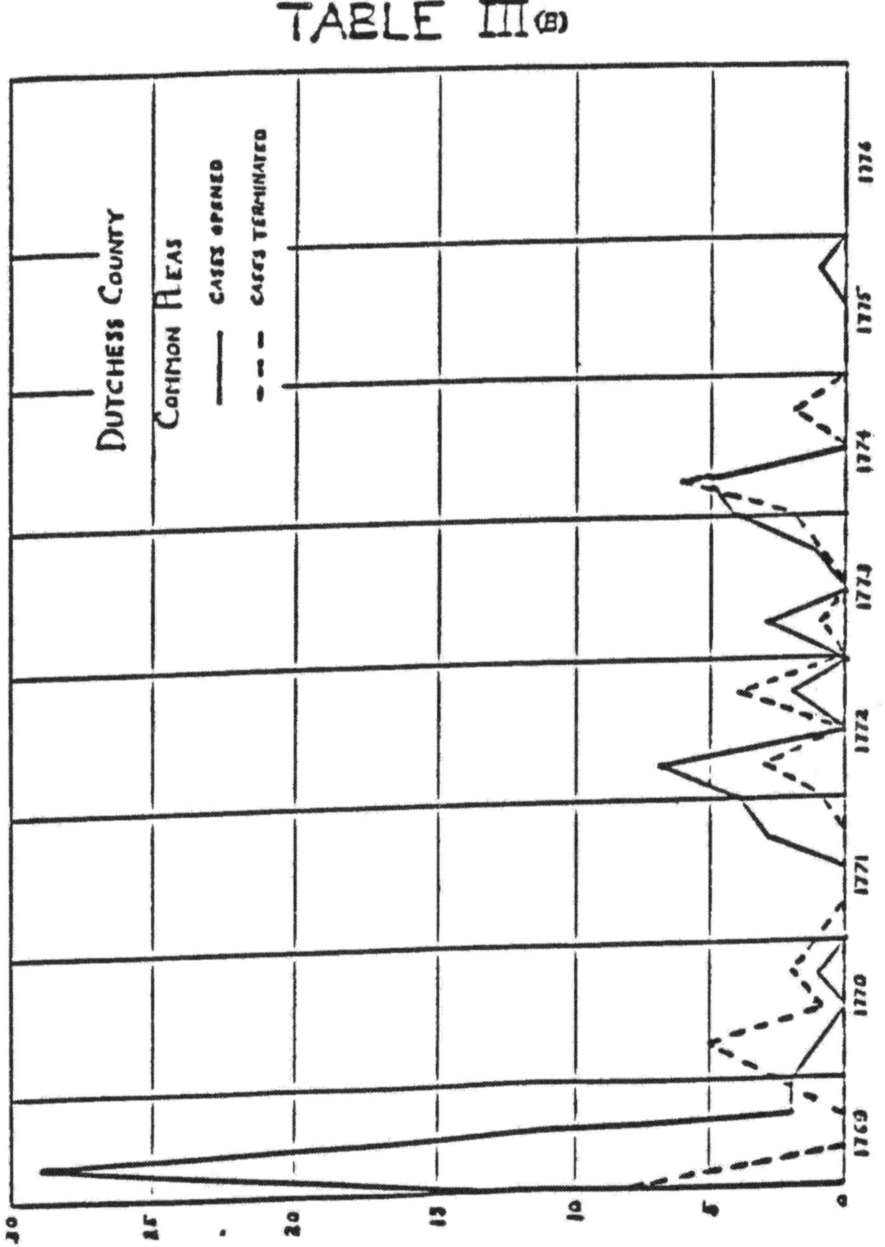
TABLE III (B)
DUTCHESS COUNTY
COMMON PLEAS
CASES OPENED
CASES TERMINATED
1769
1770
1771
1772
1773
1774
1775
1776
0
5
10
15
20
25
30

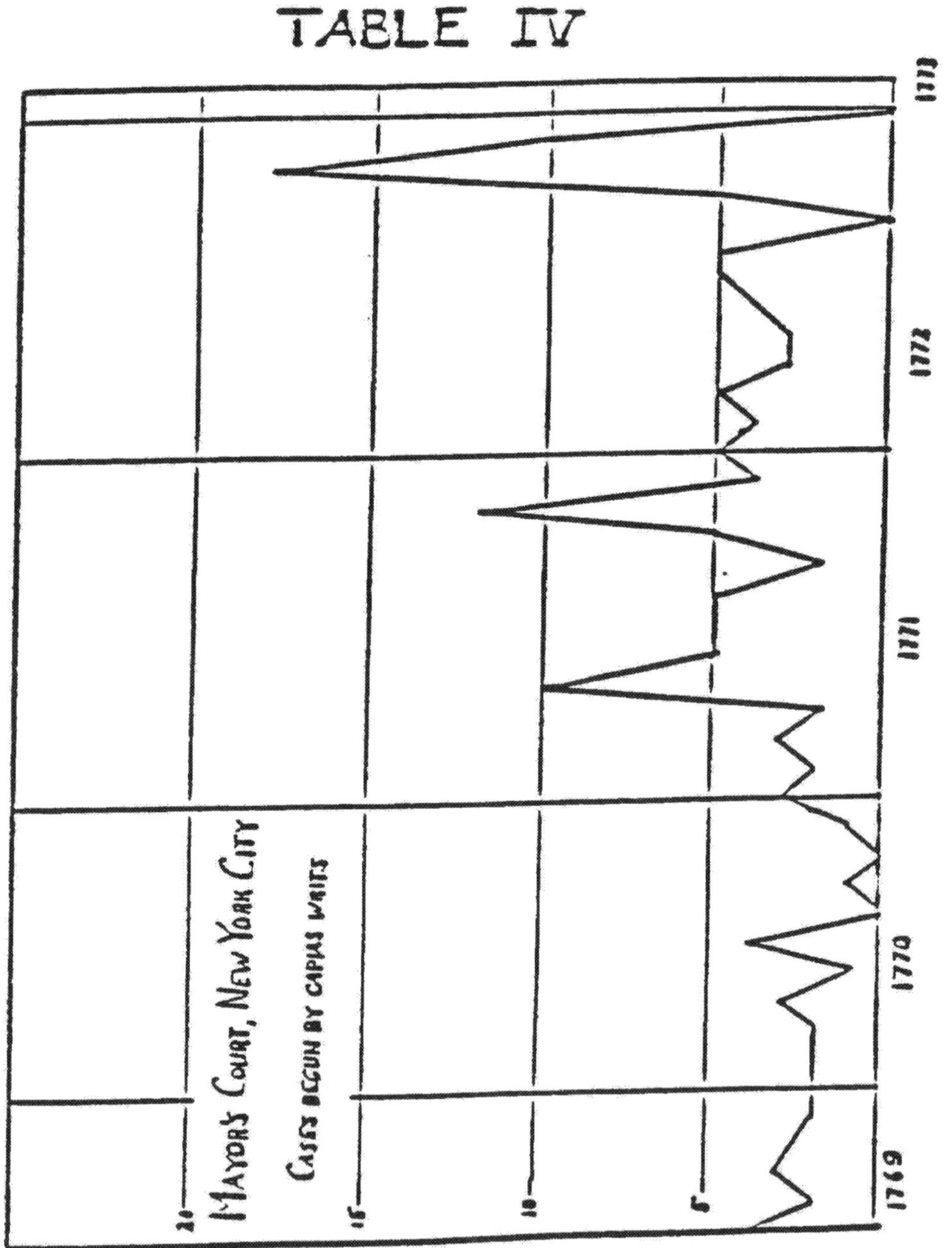
TABLE IV
MAYORS COURT, NEW YORK CITY
CASES BEGUN BY CAPIAS WRITS
20
15
10
5
1769
1770
1771
1772
1773

APPENDIX D

JOHN JAY'S LAW LIBRARY

The following list was obtained by a physical examination of the collection of law books deposited in the Treasure Room of the Columbia University Law Library. Although the collection as a unit is known as the "John Jay Collection", it is readily apparent that a large proportion of the volumes contained in the collection are books acquired subsequent to Jay's retirement from active practice in 1776. The list which follows contains only those volumes which are clearly marked as belonging to Jay prior to 1776, or those books that bear physical damage which makes it extremely likely that they were in Jay's library prior to the evacuation of New York City in the summer of 1776. Opposite the identifying data is listed whatever evidence is available concerning John Jay's acquisition of the book.

CASE REPORTS

Barnes, Henry. Notes of Cases in Points of Practice, 2 vols., London: Henry Lintot, 1754. Purchased in 1770 for 2s. 6d., the set.

Burrows, James. Reports of Cases Adjudged in the Court of Kings Bench, London: His Majesty's Law Printers, 1771. Purchased, date unknown, for £ 6 6 s. O d.

Coke, Sir Edward. The Reports of Sir Edward Coke. 13 parts in 6 vols., from John London: E. & R. Nutt & R. Gosling, 1727. Inherited from John Chambers in 1770.

Comberbach, Roger. Report of Several Cases argued and adjudged in the Court of King's Bench. . . . London: E. & R. Nutt & R. Gosling, 1724.

Comyns, John. Reports of Cases argued and adjudged in the Courts of King's Bench, Common Pleas and Exchequer. London: Henry Lintot, 1744.

Croke, Sir George. The Reports of . . . . Harebottle Grimeton, trans. and ed., 2 vols., London: Thomas Newcomb & John Field, 1657-1663. There are two copies of volume one, one acquired in 1774, the other presumably inherited from John Chambers earlier. The copy of volume two bears the acquisition date 1771.

Dyer, Sir James. Les Reports des Diverse sel matters & Resolutions. . . . London: W. Rawlins, S. Roycroft & M. Flesher, 1688.

Finch, Sir Henry. Reports of Cases . . . London: E. & R. Nutt & R. Gosling, 1725.

Fitz Gibbons, John. Reports of Several Cases . . ., London: E. & R. Nutt & R. Gosling, 1732.

Lord Fortescue, John. Reports of Select Cases . . ., London: Henry Lintot, 1748.

Holt, Sir John. Modern Cases . . . London: J. Nutt, 1716. Inherited from John Chambers. Dated 1771.

Jones, Thomas. The Report of Several Special Cases . . ., 2nd ed., London: E. & R. Nutt & R. price not Gosling, 1729. Purchased in 1773, shown.

Keilwey, Robert. Reports d'ascuns Caes . . . 3rd ed., London: Charles Harper, 1688. Inherited from John Chambers; no date.

Kelyng, Sir John. A Report of Diverse Cases in Pleas of the Crown. London: Isaac Cleve, 1708. Inherited from John Chambers; no date.

Latch, Jean. Plusiers tres-bons cases . . . London; H. Twyford, 1661.

Leonard, William. Reports of Cases of Law . . . 2nd ed., 4 vols. in 1772, London: William Hughes, 1687. Purchased in 1772, price not shown.

Levinz, Sir Crewell, Les Reports . . . 3 parts in 2 vols., London: Assigns of Richard and Edward Atkins, 1702. Purchased, no date. One vol. bears signature of May Bickley early 18th century N.Y. attorney.

Lord Littleton, Edward, Les Reports des Tres Honorables Edw. Seigneur Littleton. London: W. Rawlinson, S. Roycroft & H. Sawbridge, 1683.

Lutwyche, Edward. Un Livre des Entries: . . . 2 vols., dated 1771; London: Assigns of Richard and Edward Atkins, 1704. One volume dated 1771; then.

Noy, William. Reports and Cases Probably . . . London: Samuel purchased; Herrick, 1669. Probably purchased; no date.

Peere Williams, William. Reports of Cases . . ., 2nd ed., 2 vols., London: Hairy Lintot, 1746. Inherited from John Chambers in 1771.

Peere Williams, William. Reports of Cases . . . 3rd ed., 3 vols., London: H.

Woodfield & W. Strahan, 1768. [only vol.111 in Jay library]. Purchased in 1772.

Pickering, Danby. Modern Reports . . . 4th ed., 12 vols., London: Henry Lintot, 1757. [Jay Library has volumes II, III, V, VI, and XII.]

Pollexfen, Sir Henry. The Arguments and Reports . . ., London: R. Smith, 1702. Purchased, no date.

Lord Raymond, Robert. Reports of Cases . . . 2nd ed., 3 vols., in 1772. London: H. Woodfield & W. Strahan, 1765. [Jay library has first two volumes.] Purchased in 1772.

Rolle, Henry. Les Reports de . . . 2 vols., London: A. Roper, F. Titon, T. Barnes, 1665. Purchased, no date.

Salkeld, William. Reports of Cases. New ed., London: W. Strahan & M. Woodfall, 1773. Purchased, 1773.

Siderfine, Thomas. Les Reports des diverse Special Cases . . ., London: W. Rawlinson, S. Roycroft, & H. Sawbridge, 1683-89. Purchased, 1771.

Strange, Sir John. Report of Adjudged Cases, 2 vols., Dublin: O. Nelson, Purchased, 1772.

Vaughan, Sir John. The Reports and Arguments of . . ., London: 1770. Thomas Roycroft, 1677. Purchased, 1770.

Ventris, Sir Peyton. Reports ... 2 vols., London: Assigns of. Richard and Edward Atkins, 1696. Purchased, 1771.

Wilson, George. Reports of Cases . . . 2 vols., London: His Majesty's. Law Printers, 1770. [Jay Library contains only volume one.] Purchased, 1771.

Yelverton, Sir Henry. Reports . . . London: W. Goldbid, 1674.

EARLY YEAR BOOKS

Les Reports des Cases [Edward I, Edward II], Sir John Maynard, ed., London: George Sawbridge, Willian Rawlinson & Samuel Roycroft, 1678. Purchased, 1771.

Le Livre des Assises et Pleas del Corone [Edward III, 1-40] London: George Sawbridge, William Rawlins & Samuel Roycroft, 1679. Purchased, 1771.

Les Reports del Cases en Ley [Edward III, 40-50], 2 vols., London: George Sawbridge, William Rawlins, & Samuel Roycroft, 1679. Purchased, 1771.

Les Reports des Cases [Edward IV], 2 vols., London: Sawbridge, Rawlins & Roycroft, 1679.

Les Reports des Cases en Ley [Edward IV], London: George Sawbridge, William Rawlins & Samuel Roycroft, 1680. Purchased, 1771.

Les Reports des Cases [Henry VI], 2 vols., London: George Sawbridge, William. Rawlins & Samuel Roycroft, 1679. [Jay Library has only the second volume.] Purchased, 1771.

STATUTES

The Statutes at Large from Magna Carta . . . 10 vols., London: Mark Baskett & Assigns of Robert Baskett, Henry Woodfall & William Strahan, 1769-1771. [The Jay library contains volumes I, II, III of this edition, and volumes V, VI, and VII of an earlier edition. Volumes IV and VIII are missing.] Purchased, 1772.

Laws of New York from the Year 1691 to 1751, inclusive. New York: James Parker, 1752. Inherited from John Chambers, no date.

TREATISES

Comyns, Sir John. A Digest of the Laws of England. 5 vols., London: H. Woodfall & W. Strahan, 1762-1767. Purchased, 1771 for £ 2 16s. 0d.

Cowel, [John]. -------- or The Interpreter . . ., 2nd ed., Thomas Manley, ed. London: Assigns of Richard Atkins, 1684.

Domat, [Jean], Civil Law in its Natural Order. William Strahan, trans., 2 vols., London: J. Bettenham, 1722. [Jay library has only volume I.]

Fortescue, Sir John. De Laudibus Legum Angliae. 2nd ed., London: Henry Lintot, 1741. Purchased, no date.

Hale, Sir Matthew. The History of the Pleas of the Crown. 2 vols., London: E. & R. Nutt & R. Gosling, 1736. Inherited from John Chambers,[1771?]

Hale, Sir Matthew. The History of the Pleas of the Crown. 2 vols., London: J. N[utt], 1716. [A smaller copy of volume I, volume II is missing from Jay library.] Inherited Chambers, [1771?]

Jacobs, Giles, Lex Mercatoria; or the Merchant's Companion. 2nd ed., from John London: E. & R. Nutt & R. Nutt & R. Gosling, 1729. Inherited from John Chambers, [1771?]

Justice, Alexander. A General Treatise of the Dominion of the Sea . . ., 2nd ed., London; D. Leach. Inherited from John Chambers, [1771?]

Molloy, Charles. De Jure Maritimo et Navali; or a Treatise of Affairs Maritime and of Commerce. 2 vols., London: T. Walters, 1769. Purchased, 1772.

Nelson, William. Lex Testamentaria; or a Compendious System of all the Laws of England . . . concerning last. Wills and Testaments. London:

E. & R. Nutt & R. Gosling, 1724.

Pufendorf, Samuel, Baron von. Of the Law of Nature and Nations, Basil Kenneth, trans., London: J. Walthoe, R. Wilkins, J. & J. Brunswicke, S. Birt, T. Ward & T. Osborne, 1729.

Rutherforth, Thomas. Institutes of Natural Law. Cambridge, Eng., J. Bentham, 1754. Given to Jay by William Livingston, no date.

Swinburne, Henry. A Treatise of Testaments and Last Wills, 5th ed., London: E & R. Nutt & R. Gosling, 1728. Probably inherited from John Chambers, 1770.

Stubbs, William. The Crown Circuit Companion. 2nd ed., 2 vols., London: Henry Lintot, 1749. Purchased 1770.

De Vattel, Emerich. The Law of Nations; or Principles of The Law of Nature. 2 vols., London: J. Newberry, J. Richardson, T. Carton, J. Longmans, P. Law, J. Fuller, K. Coste, G. Kearsely, 1759-60. Purchased, 1772 for 30s.

Viner, Charles A. General Abridgment of Law and Equity. 23 vols., 1771. Aldershot in Hampshire: Charles Viner, 1741-1753. Purchased, 1771.

ANONYMOUS TREATISES

The Compleat Sheriff, 3rd ed., London: E. & R. Nutt & R. Gosling, 1727.

D[igesti] Justiniani Institutionum Librii Quatuor: The Four Books of Justinian's Institutions, With Notes. George Harris, trans., 2nd ed., London: J. Powers, 1761. Purchased 1772.

A General Abridgment of Cases in Equity Argued and Adjudged in the High Court of Chancery. London: E. & R. Nutt & R. Gosling, 1769.

The Law of Attorneys and Solicitors. London: H. Woodfall & W. Strahan, 1764. Purchased, 1773.

The Law of Corporations. London: Richard & Edward Atkins, 1702. Purchased, 1773.

The Law of Errors and Writs of Error. London Assigns of Richard and Edward Atkins, 1703. Purchased, 1771.

Officium Clerici Pacis; A Book of Indictments, Informations, Inquisitions and Appeals . . ., 3rd ed., London: E. & R. Nutt & R. Gosling, 1726. Purchased, 1771.

The Pleadings. Arguments and Other Proceedings in the Court of King's Bench upon the Quo Warranto touching the Charter of the City of London. London: T.D. and B.T., 1636. Purchased, no date.

BIBLIOGRAPHY

Manuscripts

COURT RECORDS

Albany. New York

Decrees Before 1800, New York Court of Chancery, Chancery Room, Court of Appeals Hall. [Aug. 1988. Series J0065. Decrees and Papers before 1800. 1684-1815. New York State Archives. Albany.]*

Mayor's Court Minutes, City and County of Albany, Albany County Clerk's Office, Volume 1768-1778. [Aug. 1988. Albany County Hall of Records, 250 South Pearl Street. Albany.]

Orders, Minutes & Proceedings, Court of Chancery, Province of New York, May 13, 1740 to March 30, 1770, Book 1130, Chancery Room, Court of Appeals Hall. [Aug. 1988. Series J0090. Orders in Chancery. 1701-1708. 1740-1770. New York State Archives. Albany.]

This volume, despite its title, is only a minute book, and is the missing volume of the set on deposit with the New York County Clerk.

Flushing, New York

Minutes of the Court of Common Pleas, Ulster County, September 18, 1759 to September 1774, Room 101, Queens College Library. [Aug. 1988. Ulster County Hall of Records. Kingston.]

Jamaica, New York

Minutes of the Court of General Sessions of the Peace and also of Common Pleas, 1722-1787, Queens County Clerk's Office.

---

*Italicized locations are those in effect on Aug. 1, 1988.

New York City. New York

File Papers, Court of Chancery, Records Division, New York County Clerk's Office, Hall of Records, New York City. [Aug. 1988. Series J0065, Chancery Decrees and Papers Before 1800. 1684-1815. New York State Archives, Albany.]

This set of papers consist of various documents connected with Chan cery cases, and occasionally contains original decrees. It is distinguished by the "BM" file designation.

Minutes of the Court of Chancery, Volume IV, April 5, 1770 to January 9, 1776, Records Division, New York County Clerk's Office, Hall of Records. [Aug. 1988. Series J0090, Orders in Chancery. 1701-1780. New York State Archives, Albany.]

Minutes of the Court of General Sessions, New York County, November 4, 1760 to February 6, 1772, May 21, 1772 to November 1790, New York Supreme Court Library, General Sessions Branch, Criminal Courts Building, 100 Centre Street.

Minutes of the Mayor's Court of New York City (Rough), January 25, 1765 to October 29, 1765, Records Division, New York County Clerk's Office, Hall of Records.

This is the last volume of Mayor's Court minutes prior to the American Revolution, the later volumes not having survived that War.

Minutes of the Supreme Court of Judicature:
October 19, 1762 to April 28, 1764
July 31, 1764 to August 8, 1766
October 21, 1766 to January 21, 1769
April 21, 1769 to May 2, 1772
April 21, 1772 to January 17, 1776 (Rough)
July 25, 1775 to April 28, 1781
Records Division, New York County Clerk's Office, Hall of Records.

Miscellaneous File Papers, Mayor's Court of New York City, 1766 to 1774, 1775 to 1784, Records Division, New York County Clerk's Office, Hall of Records.

Original Wills, 1767 to 1768, Surrogate's Court of New York County, Hall of Records. [Aug. 1988. Series J0038. Court of Probates. Probated Wills. 1671-1815, New York State, Archives, Albany.]

Parchments, Records Division, New York County Clerk's Office, Hall of Records.

These manuscripts include the surviving judgment rolls of the Supreme Court of Judicature, and a limited number of writs of execution from that Court.

Pleadings, 1754-1837, Records Division, New York County Clerk's Office, Hall of Records.

For the colonial period this collection of flat filed documents consists entirely of writs of execution.

Record of Wills, Surrogate's Court of New York County, Hall of Records.

Roll of Attorneys of the Supreme Court of the State of New York, 1754 to 1795, Records Division, New York County Clerk's Office, Hall of Records.

Writ Book, Mayor's Court of New York City, September 5, 1769 to January 5, 1773, Records Division, New York County Clerk's Office, Hall of Records.

Poughkeepsie, New York

Ancient Documents, Dutchess County Clerk's Office

This collection of litigation file papers ranges from pleadings in civil actions to judgments and writs of execution. It appears to be arranged by terms of the Common Pleas Court, but the County Clerk has indexed and serially numbered each paper.

Minutes of the Dutchess County Court of Common Pleas:

Liber D., 1766 to 1771
Liber E., 1771 to 1774
Liber F., 1775 to 1781
Microfilm Copy, Dutchess County Clerk's Office.

Washington. D.C.

File Papers, Customs Cases M-Z, Vice Admiralty Court of the Province of New York, National Archives. [Aug. 1988. National Archives. New York Branch. Military Ocean Terminal. Bldg. 22, Bayonne. N.J.]

File Papers, Salvage Cases A-Z, Vice Admiralty Court of the Province of New York, National Archives. [Aug. 1988. National Archives. New York Branch, Military Ocean Terminalf Bldg. 22. Bayonne. N.Y.]

Minutes of the Vice Admiralty Court of the Province of New York, Volume III, 1758 to 1774, National Archives. [Aug. 1988. National Archives. New York Branch, Military Ocean Terminal. Bldg. 22. Bayonne. N.J.]

White Plans, New York

Minutes of the Westchester County Court of Common Pleas:
Volume I, 1723 to 1773
Volume II, 1774 to 1793
Westchester County Clerk's Office.

OTHER MANUSCRIPTS

William Alexander Papers, New York Historical Society, New: York City.

Egbert Benson Papers, Box 1, New York Historical Society, New York City.

Colonial Office Papers, Series 5, Volumes 1076, 1103, 1104, 1105, Public Record Office, Chancery Lane, London, England. [Aug. 1988. Kew Depository, Public Record Office. London.]

James Duane Papers, New York Historical Society, New York City.

John J. DuBois Collection of John Jay Manuscripts, Columbia University photocopy, Columbia University Libraries, New York City.

Grace Church, Jamaica, New York, Vestry Minutes 1764 to 1862, Parish Office, Jamaica, New York.

Gratz Collection, Case 1, Box 7, Historical Society of Pennsylvania, Philadelphia, Pennsylvania. Colutrbia University photocopy, Columbia University Libraries, New York City.

Jay Miscellaneous Manuscripts, Manuscripts Division, New York Public Library, New York City.

Jay Papers, Museum of the City of New York, New York City.

John Jay Ledger 1774, Manuscripts and History Division, New York State Library, Albany, New York. Columbia University photocopy, Columbia University Libraries, New York City.

John Jay Papers, Special Collections Library, Columbia University, New York City.

John Jay Papers, New York Historical Society, New York City.

Peter Jay Letterbook, December 17, 1748 to October 30, 1772, Special Collections Library, Columbia University Libraries, New York City.

Peter Jay-Peloquin Correspondence, Collection of John Jay of Williamstown, Massachusetts. Microfilm copy at Columbia University Libraries, New York City.

Samuel Jones Papers, Correspondence 1721 to 1833, accounts, land papers, etc., Manuscript Division, New York Public Library, New York City.

John Tabor Kempe Papers, lawsuits, New York Historical Society, New York City.

King's College Papers, 1754 to 1775, Special Collections Library, Columbia University Libraries, New York City.

Klein, Frederic Shriver, "John Morin Scott", unpublished M.A. Essay, Columbia University, 1926.

Klein, Milton H., "The American Whig: William Livingston of New York", unpublished Ph.D. Dissertation, Columbia University, 1954.

Law Register of John Jay and Robert R. Livingston, Jr., BV Sec., New York Historical Society, New York City.

Robert R. Livingston Papers, Box 1, New York Historical Society, New York City.

William Livingston, Cost Book in the Supreme Court of Judicature, 1759-1772, Manuscript Division, New York Public Library, New York City.

William Livingston Papers 1695-1774, Massachusetts Historical Society, Boston, Massachusetts. Microfilm edition at Columbia University Libraries, New York City.

John McKesson Papers, New York Historical Society, New York City.

Minutes of the Moot, BV Sec., New York Historical Society, New York City.

Minutes of the Moot (Copy). Owned by Dr. John J. DuBois, on deposit with Special Collecticns Library, Columbia University Libraries, New York City.

Miscellaneous Manuscripts, Dutchess County, New York Historical Society, New York City.

Miscellaneous Manuscripts, Elizabeth Hamilton, New York Historical Society, New York City.

Miscellaneous Manuscripts, Jamas Parker. New York Historical Society, New York City.

Miscellaneous Manuscripts, Peter W. Yates, New York Historical Society, New York City.

New York City Miscellaneous Manuscripts, Box 9, #22, New York Historical Society, New York City.

New York and New Jersey Boundary Papers, Volume III-Commission of 1769, New York Historical Society, New York City.

Notes on the Assizes of July 1766, New York Historical Society, New York City.

Pocket Note Book Containing Minutes of the Moot, BV Sec. (Moot). New York Historical Society, New York City.

Salmon, Charles B., "Robert Troup, Federalist: The Revolutionary Experience", unpublished M.A. Essay, Columbia University, 1960.

Benjamin Salzer Collection of Mayor's Court Papers, 1720 to 1780, Special Collections Library, Columbia University Libraries, New York City.

Sedgwick Papers, Volume II, Massachusetts Historical Society, Boston, Massachusetts, Columbia University photocopy, Columbia University Libraries, New York City.

Trinity Church Vestry Minutes, Volume I, Trinity Parish Office Building, New York City.

Trinity Church Records, Draft of Deed to Pew 7 to James Emmott, Trinity Parish Office Building, New York City.

Peter Van Schaack Papers, Special Collections Library, Columbia University Libraries, New York City.

Published Materials

SOURCES

"Abstracts of Wills on file in the Surrogate's Office, City of New York", in New York Historical Society Collections. XXX-XXXIII.

Acts of the Privy Council of England. Colonial Series, W.L. Grant and James Munro, eds., 6 vols., Hareford, England: His Majesty's Stationary Office, 1908-1912.

Authentic Account of the Proceedings of the Congress Held at New York In MDCCLV On the Subject of the American Stamp Act. Annapolis, Md.: 1767. Copy in Special Collections Library, Columbia University, New York City.

"The Burghers of New Amsterdam and the Freemen of New York" in New York Historical Society Collections, XVIII.

Burnaby, Andrew, Travels Through North America. Reprinted from the Third Edition of 1798. New York: A. Wessels Co., 1904.

The Correspondence and Public Papers of John Jay, Henry P. Johnston, ed., 4 vols., New York: G.P Putnam's Sons, 1890-1894.

Despatches and Instructions of Conrad Alexandre Gerard, 1778-1780. John Joseph Meng, ed., Baltimore: The Johns Hopkins Press, 1939.

Documents Relative to the Colonial History of the State of New York. Edmund B. O'Callaghan, ed., 15 vols., Albany: Weed, Parsons & Co., 1853-1887.

Evening Post (Boston), 1765-1766.

Gazette and Weekly Mercury (New York City), 1764-1776.

Historical Memoirs from 16 March 1763 to 9 July 1776 of William Smith., William H. W. Sabine, ed., New York: Colburn & Tegg., 1956.

Journal of the Commissioners for Trade and Plantations From January 1768 to December 1775, Preserved in the Public Record Office. London: His Majesty's Stationery Office, 1937.

Journals of the Continental Congress. 1774-1789. Worthington C. Ford, ed., 34 vols., Washington: Government Printing Office, 1904-1937.

Journal of the Legislative Council of the Colony of New York. 2 vols., Albany: Weed, Parsons & Co., 1861.

Journal of the Votes and Proceedings of the General Assattoly of the Colony of New York. From 1766 to 1776. Albany: J. Buel, 1820.

"Letter Book of John Watts", in New York Historical Society Collections. LXI.

"Letters and Papers of Cadwallader Colden, Volume VI, 1761-1764", in New York Historical Society Collections, LV.

Memoirs of the Life and Writings of Lindley Murray, Elizabeth Frank, ed., New York: Samuel Wood & Sons, Richard Wood, Collins and Mannay, Collins & Co., Mahlon Day, G. and C. Carvill, W.B. Gilley, E. Bliss and E. White and A.T. Goodrich, 1827.

Minutes of the Governors of the College of the Province of New York in the City of New York in America 1755-1768 and of the Corporation of King's College in the City of New York 1768-1770, In Columbia University, Early Minutes of the Trustees, New York: 1932).

"The Montressor Journals", G.D. Scull, ed., New York Historical Society, Collections. XIV.

New York State Assembly. Report of the Commissioners on the Boundary Lines Between the State of New York and the State of Pennsylvania and New Jersey, for the Years Ending December 31. 1882. Assembly Document No. 161, Vol. VIII, Assembly Documents for 1883.

New York State Senate. Reports of the Commissioners on the Boundary Line Between the State of New York and the State of New Jersey. Senate Document 46, Vol. Ill, Senate Documents for 1884.

New York or Weekly Gazette; the Post Boy (1764-1768).

The New York Gazette and the Weekly Mercury (1768-1772).

The New York Mercury (1766-1768).

The Papers of Sir William Johnson, 13 vols. to date, Albany: The University of the State of New York, 1921- .

Reports of Cases in the Vice Admiralty of the Province of New York and in the Court of Admiralty in the State of New York. 1715-1788. Charles M. Hough, ed., New Haven: Yale University Press, 1925.

Smith Memoirs, see Historical Memoirs . . . William Smith.

SECONDARY

Alden, John R., General Gage in America. Baton Rouge: Louisiana State University Press, 1948.

Alexander, Edward P., A Revolutionary Conservative: James Duane of New York. New York: Columbia University Press, 1938.

Byles, W. Harrison, Old Taverns of New York. New York: Frank Allaben Genealogical Co., 1915.

Becker, Carl L., Every Man His Own Historian: Essays on History and Politics. New York: F.S. Crofts & Co., 1935.

________________, The History of Political Parties in the Province of New York 1760-1776. Madison, Wisc., University of Wisconsin Press, 1909.

Bolton, Robert Jr., A History of the County of Westchester. 2 vols., New York: Alexander S. Gould, 1848.

Chandler, Thomas Bradbury, The Life of Samuel Johnson. New York: T. & J. Swords, 1805.

Chroust, Anton-Hermann, "The Lawyers of New Jersey and the Stamp Act", American Journal of Legal History VI, 286-305. (1962).

Crary, Catherine Snell, "The American Dream: John Tabor Kempe's Rise from Poverty to Riches", William and Mary Quarterly. 3rd Series, XIV, 176-195 (1957).

Dangerfield, George, Chancellor Robert R. Livingston of New York. 1746-1813. New York: Harcourt, Brace & Co., 1960.

Dawson, Henry B., Westchester County New York During the American Revolution, Morrisania, N.Y.: Henry B. Dawson, 1886.

Dix, Morgan, ed., A History of the Parish of Trinity Church in the City of New York. New York: G.P. Putnam's Sons, 1898.

Frost, Josephine C., The Strang Genealogy. Brooklyn: Bowles-Printer, 1915.

Goebel, Julius, Cases and Materials on the Development of Legal Institutions. Brattleboro, Vt.: The Vermont Printing Co., 1946.

________________, The Law Practice of Alexander Hamilton. 1 vol. to date, New York: Columbia University Press, 1964.

Hamlin, Paul M., Legal Education in Colonial New York. New York: New York University Law Quarterly Review, 1939.

Handlin, Oscar, see Mark, Irving.

A History of Columbia University; 1754-1904. New York: Columbia University Press, 1904.

Jay, William, Life of John Jay. 2 vols., New York: J. & J. Harper, 1833.

Johnson, Herbert A., 'The Admiralty Court Comes to Morrisania", (Bronx County Bar Association) The Advocate. IX, 15-21 (1962).

Jones, Thomas, History of New York During the Revolutionary War. Edward Floyd DeLancey, ed., New York: The New York Historical So ciety, 1879.

Keys, Alice Mapelsden, Cadwallader Colden; A Representative Eighteenth Century Official. New York: The MacMillan Co., 1906.

Kissam, Edward, The Kissam Family in America From 1644 to 1825. New York: Dempsey & Carroll's Art Press, 1892.

Klein, Milton M., "Prelude to Revolution in New York: Jury Trials and Judicial Tenure," William and Mary Quarterly, 3rd Series, XVII, 439-462 (1960).

_______________, "The Rise of the New York Bar: The Legal Career of William Livingston." William and Mary Quarterly. 3rd Series, XV, 334-358 (1958).

Lynd, Staughton, Anti-Federalism in Dutchess County, New York. Chicago: Loyola University Press, 1962.

Mark, Irving, Agrarian Conflicts in Colonial New York. 1711-1775. New York: Columbia University Press, 1940.

Mark, Irving, and Oscar Handlin, "Land Cases in Colonial New York, 1765-1767: The King v. William Prendergast", New York University Law Quarterly Review, XIX, 164-194 (1942).

McAnear, Beverly, "The Albany Stamp Act Riots", William and Mary Quarterly. 3rd Series, IV, 486-498 (1947).

Monaghan, Prank, John Jay; Defender of Liberty against Kings and Peoples. New York: Bobbs-Merrill Co., 1935.

_______________, "Samuel Kissam and John Jay", Columbia University Quarterly. XXV, 127-133 (1933).

Morgan, Edmund S. and Helen M. Morgan, The Stamp Act Crisis; Prologue to Revolution. Chapel Hill, N.C.: University of North Carolina Press, 1953.

Morris, Richard B., Government and Labor in Early America. New York: Columbia University Press, 1946.

_______________, "Legalism versus Revolutionary Doctrine in New England", New England Quarterly, IV, 195-215 (1931).

Onderdonk, Henry Jr., Antiquities of the Parish Church, Jamaica. Jamaica, N.Y.: Charles Welling, 1880.

Pellew, George, John Jay. Boston: Houghton, Mifflin & Co., 1890.

Sedgwick, Theodore Jr., Memoir of the Life of William Livingston. New York: J. & J. Harper, 1832.

Smith, Joseph Henry, Appeals to the Privy Council from the American Plantations. New York: Columbia University Press, 1950.

Sparks, Jared, The Life of Gouverneur Morris. 3 vols., Boston: Gray & Bowen, 1832.

Thomas, Milton Halsey, "King's College Commencements in the Newspapers", Columbia University Quarterly, XXII, 226-247 (1930).

Van Schaack, Henry, The Life of Peter Van Schaack. New York: D. Appleton & Co., 1842.

Vance, Clarence Hayden, "Myles Cooper", Columbia University Quarterly, XXII, 261-286 (1930).

OTHER PUBLISHED MATERIALS

Foster, Sir Michael, A Report of Some Proceedings on the Commission of Oyer and Terminer and Gaol Delivery for the Trial of the Rebels in the Year 1746. Oxford: At the Clarendon Press, 1762.

Hawkins, William, A Treatise of the Pleas of the Crown, 2nd edition revised, 2 vols., London: E. & R. Nutt & R. Gosling, 1724-1726.

John Jay Collection of Law Books, Treasure Room, Columbia University Law Library, presented to the University by John Jay II. This collection contains the law library of John Jay, and his son, Peter Augustus Jay; its contents, so far as they pertain to John Jay, are set forth in detail in Appendix D.

Kelyng, Sir John A Report of Diverse Cases in Pleas of the Crown . . . London: Isaac Cleave, 1708.

Montressor, John, A Plan of the City of New York and Its Environs, 1766. Map Division, New York Public Library.

Popham, Sir John, Reports and Cases Collected By the Learned Sir John Popham. London: Thomas Roycroft, 1656.

A

B

C

D

E

F

G

H

I

J

M

N

O

P

Q

R

S

T

U

V

W

www.ingramcontent.com/pod-product-compliance
Ingram Content Group UK Ltd.
Pitfield, Milton Keynes, MK11 3LW, UK
UKHW041856190726
13854UKWH00002B/935